Asia's Water Crisis and New Security Risk

ASIA's WATER CRISIS AND NEW SECURITY RISK

Col. C. P. Shankar (Retd.)

NEHA PUBLISHERS & DISTRIBUTORS
DELHI

Publisher
NEHA PUBLISHERS & DISTRIBUTORS
4832/24,Prahlad Lane,S-207 Ansari
Road, Daryaganj, Delhi-110002
Ph.: 43570976, 23278261
Email: nehapubdistributors@gmail.com

Edition: 2015

ISBN: 978-93-80318-83-7

Laser Typesetting
JEE-VEE Graphics, Delhi

Price: 1295/-

Printed
Neeta Press, Delhi

Preface

"Water, water, everywhere, nor any drop to drink" aptly describes the problem of water in South Asia – a problem of scarcity amid abundance. Transboundary rivers such as the Ganges, Indus, and Brahmaputra have defined the geography, history, and culture of South Asia for centuries and are critical to economic growth, food and energy security, and sustainable development within the region. But over the last few decades, these rivers have come under considerable pressure from industrial development, urbanization, population growth, and environmental pollution. This situation has been compounded by poor domestic management of water resources and increasing variability in rainfall and climate patterns that have made South Asia highly susceptible to floods, droughts, and natural disasters.

In the face of rising populations, rapid growth of the middle class, expanding irrigation and water-intensive industries, and spiralling household consumption, per capita water availability in Asia is actually declining by 1.6% per year. The decline is greater across central, southern, southwestern and western Asia as well as in semi-arid northern China. In areas where water availability has traditionally been very low, such as the Near East and the Arabian Peninsula, even small declines or annual variation in precipitation can exacerbate the vulnerabilities of entire communities by creating drought-like conditions. The spreading water stress in Asia has direct consequences for economic and human development as well as environmental protection.

Water scarcity is set to become Asia's defining crisis by midcentury," he opens. Throughout, water serves as a common thread connecting economic growth and development, societal pressure and geopolitical posturing. Chellaney does an admirable job of weaving these components together, providing valuable insights for international relations (IR) aficionados and laypeople alike.

To underpin strategic stability, protect continued economic growth, promote environmental sustainability and prevent the struggle for water resources from tipping into overt conflict, Asian states must invest more in institutionalized cooperation on transboundary basin resources. Water has emerged as a test case of Asia's ability to build cooperation rather than competition over a critical resource.

Water security is sometimes sought by implementing water desalination, pipelines between sources and users, water licences with different security levels and war.

Water allocation between competing users is increasingly determined by application of market-based pricing for either water licenses or actual water.

This book would serve the students, as a semi-textbook and the teachers, as a guiding reference book.

—Author

Contents

1

Asia's Worsening Water Crisis

Of all the natural resources on which the modern world depends, water is the most critical. There are replacements for oil, but there is no substitute for water. It is essential to produce virtually all the goods in the marketplace, from food to industrial products, as well as to produce electricity, to refine oil and gas, and to mine coal and uranium. Put simply, water scarcity and rapid economic advance cannot go hand in hand. Yet water scarcity now affects more than two-fifths of the people on Earth, and by 2025 two-thirds of the global population is likely to be living in water-scarce or water-stressed conditions. Water-scarce nations face very tough choices and serious socioeconomic consequences. And the majority of the world's people living in water-related despair will be in Asia.

Water has emerged as a key issue that will determine if Asia heads toward greater cooperation or greater competition. Asia is the world's driest continent, with availability of freshwater less than half the global annual average of 6,380 m^3 per inhabitant. Asia's rivers, lakes and aquifers give it, per capita, less than one-tenth the water of South America or Australia and New Zealand, less than one-fourth of North America, almost one-third of Europe, and moderately less than Africa.

Yet the world's fastest-growing demand for water is in Asia, which now serves as the locomotive of the world economy. Today, the most dynamic Asian economies, including China, India, Indonesia, South Korea and Vietnam, are all in or close to being in conditions of water stress. The exceptions are few: Bhutan,

Brunei, Burma, Cambodia, Laos, Malaysia and Papua New Guinea. Yet Asia continues to draw on tomorrow's water to meet today's needs.

Worse still, Asia has one of the lowest levels of water efficiency and productivity in the world. Against this background, it is no exaggeration to say that the water crisis threatens Asia's economic and political rise and its environmental sustainability. For investors, it carries risks as potentially damaging as non-performing loans, real-estate bubbles, infrastructure overbuilding and political corruption. The water crisis means that the cost of doing business in Asia is set to rise. Water has also emerged as a source of increasing competition and discord within and between nations, spurring new tensions over shared basin resources and local resistance to governmental or corporate decisions to set up water-intensive industries.

ASIA'S WATER CHALLENGES

In the face of rising populations, rapid growth of the middle class, expanding irrigation and water-intensive industries, and spiralling household consumption, per capita water availability in Asia is actually declining by 1.6% per year. The decline is greater across central, southern, southwestern and western Asia as well as in semi-arid northern China. In areas where water availability has traditionally been very low, such as the Near East and the Arabian Peninsula, even small declines or annual variation in precipitation can exacerbate the vulnerabilities of entire communities by creating drought-like conditions. The spreading water stress in Asia has direct consequences for economic and human development as well as environmental protection.

With aquifers being drained to dangerously low levels, a number of cities in Asia that rely on groundwater, such as Yemen's capital Sana'a and Quetta in Pakistan, face the spectre of running out. Beijing increasingly depends on water brought in from elsewhere. In an ever-deeper search for water, millions of pump-operated wells threaten to suck Asia's subterranean reserves dry, even as the continent confronts river depletion. Asian economies can import fossils fuels, mineral ores and timber from distant lands, but they must make do with their own water resources.

Pressure on national water resources is said to be high when water withdrawal exceeds 25% of total renewable water resources. This ratio is 34% for India and 26% for South Korea. China's 18.57% may be relatively decent, but the country remains chronically unable to meet its water needs in the north, where almost half its population lives and where rivers are dying. In contrast, Japan, at 21.26% is doing a better job than China in managing its water resources by maintaining water quality.

The United Nations Economic and Social Commission for Asia and the Pacific (UNESCAP) captured the Asian crisis through its 2009 Index of Water Available for Development, a measure of per capita water availability for human, economic and ecological uses per year on the basis of each country's internal renewable water resources minus total water used. This index reveals that there have been steep declines in water availability for development since the baseline year of 1980 in a number of Asian nations, including the two giants, China and India, that make up nearly two-fifths of the global population. The water situation in India looks particularly ominous. The report warned that 'water shortfalls on this scale heighten competition for a precious resource and frequently lead to conflicts, which are emerging as new threats to social stability'.

Although Asia's overall population growth has slowed, an important factor driving the water crisis is growth in consumption due to rising prosperity. This is best illustrated by changes in diet, especially a greater intake of meat, whose production is notoriously water intensive. In China, for example, meat consumption rose fourfold between 1980 and 2010, with its beef sector growing from almost nothing to become the third largest in the world. By 2030, Chinese meat consumption is projected to double further. This shift from traditional rice and noodles to a meatier diet has already fuelled a doubling of China's water footprint for food production since 1985: it takes ten times more water to raise a kilo of beef than grow a kilo of rice or wheat.

Once plagued by serious food shortages and recurrent famines, Asia opened the door to its dramatic economic rise by emerging as a net food exporter on the back of an unparalleled expansion of irrigation: total irrigated cropland in Asia doubled between 1960 and 2000. It is notable that few advanced industrial countries depend on other countries to feed their populations; many of them, on the contrary, are important food exporters.

This may explain why Asian nations have attached great strategic importance to food security, often equating that goal, rather imprudently, with food sovereignty. Yet the extension of agriculture to semi-arid and arid areas in Asia has necessitated intensive irrigation, which, in turn, has created serious waterlogging and soil-salinity problems and undercut crop-yield growth. Even in Asia's fertile valleys drained by major river systems, irrigation is usually necessary in the dry season; much of the continent's rainfall is concentrated in a three- or four-month monsoon period. By contrast, Europe, with its temperate climate and long rainy periods, is able to produce most of its food through rain-fed crops. In fact, such is the widespread prevalence of rain-fed agriculture among rich nations that industry, not agriculture, is their leading water consumer, except in Australia and New Zealand.

Asia now boasts the lion's share, about 70%, of the world's irrigated land. Three sub-regions — South Asia, China and Southeast Asia — by themselves account for about 50% of the global total. It is thus hardly a surprise that Asia leads the world in the total volume of freshwater withdrawn for agriculture. Indeed, almost 74% of the total global freshwater withdrawals for agriculture by volume are made in Asia. As a proportion of its own renewable water resources, Asia's yearly agricultural water withdrawals aggregate to 81%, or at least 10 percentage points higher than the global average. By contrast, that figure is just 29% in Europe and 38% in North America. Water withdrawals for industrial purposes account for a mere 11.4% in Asia; and for household needs the figure is 7.3%.

Yet the growth of rice and wheat output in Asia, after the dramatic increases of the previous quarter century, has slowed since the late 1990s, raising concerns that Asian countries such as China and India that are largely self-sufficient in food will become major food importers, disturbing the international market, which is not large enough to meet such demands. With population, consumption and developmental pressures growing and increases in yield gains flattening, Asia needs a second green revolution, for which water will be the single biggest constraint.

The fastest increase in water demand in Asia, however, is coming not from agriculture but from the industrial sector and urban households. The United Nations projects that industrial water withdrawals in the world will double between 2000 and 2025, with much of the increase likely to occur in the Asia-Pacific region, 'given its rapidly rising status as a global industrial production centre and the fast growth in subsectors with high water consumption, such as the production of transportation equipment, beverages and textiles'.

The fastest rise is projected for India, whose economy is currently led by the services sector but where industrial water use is expected to almost quadruple by 2050 as manufacturing rapidly expands. But water shortages are already impeding this rapid industrial expansion in Asia; water scarcity is, for example, causing billions of dollars' worth of annual losses in industrial output in China.

A final factor underlying water stress in Asia is the long-term environmental impact of large-scale sequestration of water resources through dams, barrages, reservoirs and other structures. Dams do bring important benefits: if appropriately designed and scaled, they aid economic and social development by regulating water supply, controlling floods, facilitating irrigation, generating hydroelectricity and bringing drinking water to cities. But they can affect water quality and quantity downstream, alter fluvial ecosystems, damage biodiversity and promote coastal erosion and saltwater intrusion.

Large dams have caused sedimentation, inundation, habitat damage, destruction of fish species, and other environmental and public-health problems in Asia. Equally significant is the fact that heavy damming upsets a river's natural tropical flooding cycle, which is critical to fisheries and the re-fertilization of soil. The Aral Sea in Central Asia has shrunk by more than half owing to the over-damming of its sources, the Amu Darya and Syr Darya rivers, and the heavy extraction of their waters for irrigation.

The vast majority of dams in the world have been built since the 1950s. The construction of large dams has, by and large, petered out in the West but continues in full swing in Asia, where a host of countries from Japan to Turkey are involved in major dam-building activities. Over the next decade, the number of dams in developed countries is likely to remain about the same, while much of the dam building in the developing world (in terms of aggregate storage-capacity build-up) will be concentrated in China, which already has slightly more than half of the approximately 50,000 large dams on the planet. But most of the best dam sites in Asia are already in use.

New dam construction to boost water supply may no longer be a viable option other than in underdeveloped countries such as Laos, Myanmar and Nepal that have not adequately exploited their water resources or in autocracies that can effectively stifle grassroots opposition. Yet the numerous new projects in Asia show that the damming of rivers is still an important priority for national and provincial decision-makers.

This focus on dam building has intensified water disputes and tensions in Asia, with implications for regional security and stability. These disputes are bound to worsen, given China's new focus on erecting mega-dams on international rivers, exemplified by its latest addition on the Mekong River (the 4,200MW Xiaowan Dam, which dwarfs Paris's Eiffel Tower in height) and a 38,000MW dam planned on the Brahmaputra at Metog, close to the disputed border with India.

The Metog Dam will be twice as large as the 18,300MW Three Gorges Dam, currently the world's largest, construction of which officially uprooted at least 1.7 million Chinese. Turkey, too, is building big dams on the Tigris and Euphrates rivers.

The countries likely to bear the brunt of such massive diversion of waters are those located farthest downstream on rivers such as the Brahmaputra, Mekong and Tigris–Euphrates: Bangladesh, whose very future is threatened by climate and environmental change; Vietnam, a rice bowl of Asia; and Iraq, still internally torn. China's water appropriations from the Illy River threaten to turn Kazakhstan's Lake Balkhash into another Aral Sea.

Continued dam building in a number of Asian nations is also creating new intra-state tensions and challenges. Degraded watersheds constitute one of the most serious problems for sustainable development in Asia. Dams are also having other impacts, including changing river hydrology, sediment load, riparian vegetation, patterns of stream-bank erosion, migration of fish, and water temperature.

RISING SECURITY RISKS

With increasingly fierce intra- and inter-state water competition, the risk of water conflict is higher in Asia than elsewhere in the world.

Water is a new arena in the Asian Great Game. In fact, political, diplomatic or economic 'water wars' are already being waged between riparian neighbours in several parts of Asia, fuelling a cycle of bitter recrimination and fostering mistrust that impedes broader regional cooperation and integration. The resources of transnational rivers, aquifers and lakes have become targets of rival appropriation plans. Securing larger portions of shared resources has become a flashpoint in inter-country relationships; there is no incentive to conserve or protect supplies for users beyond national borders, unless there are specific water-sharing arrangements in place.

With a particular river or groundwater basin often tied into a country's identity and self-image, ownership and control over such resources can be perceived as crucial to national interest. This has helped give rise to grand but environmentally questionable ideas: China's Great Western Route to divert river waters from the Tibetan Plateau to its parched north; South Korea's politically divisive Four Rivers Project; India's proposal to link up its important rivers; and Jordan's plan to save the shrinking Dead Sea by bringing water from the Red Sea through a 178-kilometre-long canal (which is also to serve as a source for desalinated drinking water).

India's river-linking plan was conceived by a poet prime minister, which may explain why it never took off and was abandoned by the current government. In contrast, the Great Western Route plan was conceived by the engineers who dominate China's top political leadership.

Asia's water map fundamentally changed after the 1949 Communist victory in China. Most of the continent's important international rivers originate in territories that the People's Republic of China either forcibly annexed or reasserted Chinese control over. The annexed Tibetan Plateau, for example, is the world's largest freshwater repository and the source of Asia's greatest rivers, including those that are the lifeblood of mainland China and South and Southeast Asia. Other such Chinese territories contain the headwaters of rivers such as the Irtysh, Illy and Amur, which flow to Russia and Central Asia.

This makes China the source of cross-border water flows to more countries than any other upstream power in the world. Beijing now controls the headwaters of more than a dozen important international river basins. Yet China rejects the notion of water sharing or institutionalized cooperation with downstream countries. Whereas riparian neighbours in Southeast and South Asia are bound by water pacts that they have negotiated between themselves, China does not have a single water treaty with any coriparian country.

For example, it is a dialogue partner but not a member of the Mekong River Commission, suggesting a desire to listen to discussions among other basin states without agreeing to abide by the commission's rules or taking on legal obligations by becoming a party to the 1995 Mekong Treaty. Moreover, while promoting multilateralism on the world stage, China has given the cold shoulder to multilateral cooperation among river-basin states. The lower Mekong countries view China's strategy as an attempt to divide and conquer. It is hardly a surprise, then, that China is at the centre of much of the current water-related tension in Asia.

Although China publicly favours bilateral initiatives over multilateral institutions in addressing water issues, it has not shown any real enthusiasm for meaningful bilateral action. As a result, water has become a new political issue in the country's relations with neighbours such as India, Kazakhstan, Nepal and Russia. China deflects attention from its refusal to share water, or to enter into institutionalized cooperation to manage common rivers sustainably, by promoting the accords it has signed on sharing flow statistics with riparian neighbours. These are not agreements to cooperate on shared resources, but rather commercial accords to sell hydrological data that other upstream countries provide free to downriver states.

Beyond China, there are water tensions between India and Pakistan, among the Central Asian nations, between Turkey and its downriver neighbours, and between Israel and the Palestinians. But given China's unique riparian position and role, it will not be possible to transform Asian water competition into cooperation without its active participation.

Internal water disputes are also rife across the continent. The lopsided availability of water within some Asian nations (abundant in some areas but deficient in others) has given rise to plans for mega-dam projects or grand diversion structures, which have run into stiff grassroots opposition over issues of population displacement and submergence of land. To compound matters, governmental or commercial decisions on where to set up new manufacturing or energy plants are increasingly being influenced by local availability of adequate water resources.

Where availability is already low, a decision to establish a new plant often triggers local protests because it is likely to spur greater competition over scarce water resources. It has become virtually impossible to site nuclear power plants along freshwater bodies in water-scarce Asia, the centre of the so-called global nuclear renaissance. These water-guzzling plants must instead be built on coastlines where they can rely on seawater for their operations. Yet, Fukushima has served as a warning of the vulnerability of coastal nuclear facilities to extreme events, which are likely to become more common as the climate changes.

Water conflict within nations, especially those that are multi-ethnic and culturally diverse, often assumes ethnic or sectarian dimensions, accentuating internal security challenges. Such intrastate water disputes rarely get the kind of international attention that interstate discords do, but as the internal conflicts in Yemen and Afghanistan show, recurrent drought and water scarcity can poison inter-ethnic or inter-sectarian relations and trigger bloodletting. Endemic local conflicts over water in some drought-ridden areas in Asia have even led villagers to engage security guards to protect their sources of freshwater, such as wells or water trucks. Asia's experiences over the past quarter century show that internal water conflicts tend to be more damaging and violent than disputes between countries.

CONTAINING THE RISKS

To underpin strategic stability, protect continued economic growth, promote environmental sustainability and prevent the struggle for water resources from tipping into overt conflict, Asian states must invest more in institutionalized cooperation on transboundary basin resources. Water has emerged as a test case of Asia's ability to build cooperation rather than competition over a critical resource.

National dependency on waters from transnational rivers or aquifers is widespread across Asia. China is an exception: with less than 1% of its water resources dependent on cross-border inflow (one of the lowest rates in the world) it is happily placed. There are at least 57 transnational river basins in Asia, and most lack any kind of cooperative institution. The exact number of transnational groundwater basins is unknown as no scientific assessment has been undertaken.

Yet some of the shared aquifer systems have already become targets of rival appropriation plans and political tensions, for example al-Disi, which straddles the Saudi Arabian–Jordanian border. The existence of inter-country water agreements can be deceptive: most such accords in Asia relate to more mundane issues than sharing waters or sustainably managing transboundary basin resources. Commercial contracts, joint research or flood-control projects, use of river islands, hydropower development, and non-binding memoranda of understanding masquerade as water agreements.

In fact, only four of the transnational river basins in Asia are subject to treaties covering water sharing or other institutionalized cooperation. These are the Mekong (where the non-participation of China, the dominant upper riparian nation, has stunted development of a genuine basin community), the Ganges (between Bangladesh and India), the Indus (between India and Pakistan, with the greatest guaranteed cross-border flows of any treaty regime in the world) and the Jordan (a four-nation basin whose resources are the subject of a treaty arrangement restricted to Israel and Jordan).

The only treaties that incorporate a sharing formula on cross-border river flows are those covering the Indus and Ganges. But even these are far from perfect and often rife with dispute, especially in the Indus basin.

They nevertheless serve useful purposes. In fact, all four Asian treaties demonstrate that inter-country basin arrangements can be concluded even among rival states and that such arrangements can survive political tensions and conflicts.

One imperative is to build Asian norms over shared transnational basin resources, using as a guide the codification of the principles of customary water law by the United Nations Convention on the Non-Navigational Uses of International Watercourses, even though this 1997 convention's entry into force still seems distant.

The only real way to avert or manage water disputes in Asia is to build basin arrangements involving all riparian neighbours. If a dominant riparian state refuses to join, such institutional arrangements will be ineffective.

The arrangements must be centred on transparency, information sharing, equitable distribution of benefits, dispute settlement, pollution control, joint projects and a mutual commitment to refrain from any projects that would materially diminish transboundary flows.

Water institutions, by facilitating constructive dialogue and structured cooperation, help stem the risk that disputes over water sharing or water quality could escalate to open conflict.

Building such regimes is never easy, given the complex physical, geopolitical and economic factors at play, including mismatched levels of economic development and the unilateral harnessing of shared waters by one or more coriparian states. Their legal, institutional and consultative mechanisms are designed not only to forestall interstate competition and conflict, but also to ensure that national water policies serve as a catalyst for social progress and economic growth through a stake in the integrated management of basin resources. Such cooperative arrangements can actually help improve water quality and availability.

Asia has little choice but to improve its water efficiency and productivity levels. Improvements in efficiency of water use in agriculture, energy and industry have stagnated at 1% or less per year for two decades. Greater investment is also needed to upgrade and maintain the water-supply infrastructure; losses from leaks amount to up to 29 billion m^3 of treated water a year, valued conservatively at $9 billion.

Asia's water crisis is opening opportunities for investment and technological innovation in two main areas. One is securing higher water efficiency and productivity gains, including through micro-irrigation systems and industrial water-use efficiency.

The other area is clean-water technologies, including wastewater treatment and recycling, desalination, and cleaning up contaminated or brackish water. These technologies hold the key to containing Asia's mounting water challenges.

Given Asia's exceptionally high water withdrawals for farming, savings will need to come primarily from water conservation and efficiency in agriculture so that more waters can be channelled to industries and cities.

Asian states have little choice but to upgrade their old irrigation systems and promote drip-feed irrigation, which is yet to be widely adopted.

This technology, which directs water flow straight to the root zone of plants, can help slash agricultural water consumption by 50–70% compared to gravity irrigation, and by 10–20% compared to sprinkler irrigation. Agricultural water productivity can also be increased through development of new grain varieties that are more tolerant of drought and flooding.

The Asian experience shows that the more populous a sub-region, a nation, or an area within a country, the greater are its water challenges, with water stress often being accompanied by a fall in water quality. But when water quality is maintained, the scarcity of water can be better managed. For example, Japan and South Korea have low per capita availability of freshwater compared with the global average, yet their good water quality overall better positions them to meet their national needs.

In cases where water quality and productivity have both appreciably increased, conditions of water stress tend to perceptibly lessen. South Korea's per capita water availability is close to Pakistan's, but it has done a much better job of building water quality and improving productivity.

As a result, South Korea, while prone to the ravages of drought, does not face the serious crisis situation haunting Pakistan. There is, in fact, much scope to increase water quality and productivity in many Asian countries, including those with already high efficiency and quality standards, such as South Korea, Japan and Singapore.

Even if energy- and cost-efficient clean-water technologies become available, the cost of water is set to rise sharply in Asia, especially for businesses.

Solar-powered desalination and wastewater recycling will help improve the situation, but the cost of supply is still bound to escalate because of additional infrastructure and maintenance needs. Desalination and wastewater-treatment technologies remain expensive as well as energy- and greenhouse-gas intensive.

WATER CRISIS LOOMS COUNTRYWIDE

Water has become the most commercial products of the century. This may sound bizarre, but true. In fact, what water is to the 21st century, oil was to the 20th century. The stress on the multiple water resources is a result of a multitude of factors. On the one hand, the rapidly rising population and changing lifestyles have increased the need for fresh water. On the other hand, intense competitions among users in agriculture, industry and domestic sector is pushing the ground water table deeper.

To get bucket of drinking water is a struggle for most women in the country. The virtually dry and dead water resources have lead to acute water scarcity, affecting the socio-economic condition of the society. The drought conditions have pushed villagers to move to cities in search of jobs, whereas women and girls have to trudge further. This time lost in fetching water can very well translate into financial gains, leading to a better life for the family. If opportunity costs were taken into account, it would be clear that in most rural areas, households are paying far more for water supply than the often-normal rates charged in urban areas. Also, if this cost of fetching water which is almost equivalent. to 150 million women days each year, is covered into a loss for the national exchequer, it translates into a whopping 10 billion rupees per year.

The government has accorded the highest priority to rural drinking water for ensuring universal access as a part of policy framework to achieve the goal of reaching the unreached. Despite the installation of more than 3.5 million hand pumps and over 116 thousand piped water supply schemes, in many parts of the country, the people face water scarcity almost every year, there by meaning that our water supply systems are failing to sustain despite huge investments.

In India, there are many villages either with scarce water supply or without any source of water. If there is no source of potable water in 2.5 kilometres, then the village becomes no source water village or problem village. In many rural areas, women still have to walk a distance of about 2.5 kms to reach the source of water. She reaches home carrying heavy pots, not to rest but to do other household chores of cooking, washing~ cleaning, caring of children and looking after livestock. Again in the evening she has to fetch water. Thus a rural woman's life is sheer drudgery.

Water is the biggest crisis facing India in terms of spread and severity, affecting one in every three persons.

Even in Chennai, Bangalore, Shimla and Delhi, water is being rationed and India's food security is under threat.

With the lives and livelihood of millions at risk, urban India is screaming for water. For instance, water is rationed twice a week in Bangalore, and for 30 minutes a day in Bhopal; 250 tankers make 2,250 trips to quench Chennai's thirst. Mumbai routinely lives through water cuts from January to June, when some areas get water once in three days in Hyderabad.

Harrowing midnight for a precious bucket of drinking water is a regular feature for many families of Vypuri, an Island off the mainland of Kochi. Women have to queue up in front of the public water taps, being at the lag end of the pipeline system, they get water only after the users ahead in the pipeline finish collecting water. There are nights when water pressure dips so low that some women get it after midnight. They split their day between household chores and collecting water.

Apart from the water scarcity caused by Coca-cola in Plachimada, the other districts in the state are facing a water crisis. For instance, in Kottayam district at some places, the water scarcity is so acute that people hesist to offer a glass of water to the visitor, which hitherto was a common custom.

In the upper Kuttanadu area of the district during summer people collect water from a distance of 3-4 kms. Water supply from public taps is erratic and very often even after standing for an hour in the queue; people are not able to get a bucket of water. Most women and girls in Rajasthan find themselves searching water for much of the year.

They trudge bare foot in the hot sun for hours over wastelands, across thorny fields, or rough terrain in search of water, often life the colour of mud and brackish, but still welcome for the parched throats back home.

On an average, a rural woman walks more than 14000 km a year just to fetch water. Their urban sisters are only slightly better off- they do not walk such distances, but stand in the long winding queues for hours on end to collect water from the roadside taps on the water lorries.

In every household, in the rural areas in Rajasthan, women and girl children bear the responsibilit of collecting, transporting, storing, and managing water. In places, where there is no water for farming, men migrate to urban areas in search of work leaving women behind to fond for the old and the children. Women spend most of their time, collecting water with little time for other productive work. This impacts on the education of the girl child, if the girl is herself not collecting water, she is looking after the home and her siblings when her mother is away.

In brief:

- Water source being open dug well, the quality of water is poor; dirty, saline and has turbidity
- Women have to make at least three trips at 5 am, 11 am and 5 pm
- Sometimes, the number of trips is more
- Total distance traveled is 9-10 km, even higher
- Total Time spent is 6-9 hours
- Total number of pots/buckets is about 3 pots, 30-45 litres (one pot of 10-15 litres per trip)
- Due to long distance, they have to take rest in the middle of the way. Dust storms aggravate their problem
- At some villages water from tubewells is too saline to drink. Even animals particularly cow gets indigestion after drinking this water, so the villagers add water from the dug well. The entire life of women in rural areas like Jaisalmer is spent on water collection and cooking. Even the girls of 8-10 years cannot be spared. They cannot afford the luxury of school. For instance for Pappu a girl of hardly 10 years, water collection has become her main job. In the words of her grandmother "Water fetching is the schooling for Pappu." There are so many Pappus in the villages and dhaanis of Jaisalmer.

In Sriganganagar, the Indira Gandhi canal is the main source for drinking water. However, during the crisis period (either because of no water in the main canal/sub canal or due to the erratic power supply), the rich remain unaffected.

In such crisis women from poorhouse hold draw water from the village diggis, which is totally unfit for any kind of human activity. They use this water not only for washing cloth and bathing but also for drinking. Due to the formation of algae, water becomes greenish and filthy. Women add alum to purify it.

In Orissa drinking water is being privatized. The government first insists on the formation of water associations and conveniently pass the responsibilities on to these association. When this proves inefficient, water distribution rights are given away to private contractors. For example, the Orissa government initially stressed on the formation of Paani Panchayats (water associations).

Later using police the government suppressed these panchayats justifying this by claiming that the villages were not being responsible enough. Titlagarh is the hottest town of India, but it has no water, causing great misery to the women. As the highest temperature, is recorded here 52 degrees centigrade which is also the highest temperature in India.

People called "Titlagarh" as "Tatlagarh", in local language Tatla means hot. In Titlagarh water problem is acute. People are buying water throughout the year for drinking and cooking purpose.

In the month of May and June the rate of water increase three times, from Rs 2 per Dabba to Rs.8 per Dabba (container). This is the picture of urban areas, but in rural areas the problem is worse, where the tubewells all are becoming dry but people have no money to buy water. Due to the water problem some villagers are migrating to other places.

In Uttranchal women are suffering a lot in every village where water problem is severe. Natural sources are drying up which adds the kilometres for women everyday to quench the thirst of their family as well as animals.

Women are the major part of the workforce in Garhwal. They work from early morning to late evening to serve the family. They do all household work from cooking to cleaning and washing clothes and soiled utensils as well as look after their children and animals. Women also collect the water required for cooking, cleaning, washing, bathing and drinking both for human beings and animals.

During the survey in Jaunsar area of district Tehri Garhwal, in villages such as Nagthat, Duena, Vishoi, Gadol, Jandoh, Chi tar, Chichrad and Gangoa, it was observed that water in the region is mostly acidic in nature.

The water problem in Chi tar and Gangoa villages is very severe, where men and women carry water on mules from 8-10 Km to the village. Because of the poor water quality, most of the villagers in the regions are suffering from many diseases related to skin and teeth. Natural resources of water in the area are very few and they are also disappearing very fast. During the survey, Smt. Nisha Devi of Chi tar village explained that they are not getting enough water for their animals so they take their animals to the spring about 2-3 kms away.

In Bundelkhand, women have no work but to collect drinking water on their heads from long distance. The grim situation of water may be best illustrated by one Bundelkhandi saying which roughly translated as "let the husband die but the earthen pot of water should not be broken".

The scenario is worst in Patha in Chitrakut district where women have to travel a long distance to collect water for drinking. Half of the time of women is spent to collect water, which affects their health and the well-being of their children. The paucity of time due to water crisis aggravates the domestic problem.

Instead of solving the water crisis, attempts are being made to create a disastrous situation in the region. Banda city entirely depends on the Ken river. If Ken is linked with Betwa, then it will not affect only Banda, but would also jeopardize the survival of farmers who depend on Ken.

Even in Delhi the water scenario is no better, being worst in Delhi slums. For example Sanjay colony slum of New Delhi has population about 15,000-20,000 with about 4500 households in the locality. Majority of the population is self-employed and are engaged in making daris, mats and other clothes for sale. In this area people collect water from different sources depending on the availability such as DJB tanker, MCD pipe water supply and from Sulabh International. DJB tanker comes daily but it has no fixed time for water distribution. The water that comes from MCD pipe water has fixed time for water supply but it only comes for 1-2 hr in the evening (around 4.30 p.m.). At MCD pipe line people made bore and fetch water from it. If the people don't get water from the above sources they are forced to get it from Sulabh International near Kalkaji temple for which they have pay @ Rs. 2 for 20 litre or so.

The Water crisis is same in West Bengal. In all the districts, the water commons have ceased to exist, and have become open-access resources, with hardly anyone responsible to take care of the resources. In North Bengal, some women reported they had opinions regarding the use of the water body, but their importance in management decisions is cipher. The absence of the community from the management of the water resources is indeed a tragedy, because now the resources are at the mercy of either the market or government officials.

Punjab; the name stands for abundance of water, but the present situation of water resources in the state is highly critical. The ground water availability is drastically hampered. The village ponds are drying day by day. Women in the villages desperately need water. Near Talwandi Sabo, for some villages, the source for drinking water is about 8 km away. Near Jajjal due to contaminated water, women are suffering from a number of diseases including cancer. There have been several deaths attributed to polluted water.

For Maharashtra, water is an abiding concern. In many villages women have to walk more than 3 kilometres everyday to fetch two huge vessels of water illegally from a government reservoir. They have to make at least three trips everyday. The state government do not send tankers to the villagers. At some places, women spend Rs 5 for two canes of water. Images of women carrying the pots of water, walking miles and miles for one single pot are common in the state of Maharashtra.

Women in Maharashtra have carried the water burden both as a result of scarcity and abundance. Drought displacement due to dams and irrigation have contributed to increasing water burden of women. Women in Nandurbar district of North Maharashtra share their woes "forget about getting safe drinking water from wells, we spend most of our time locating streams and springs that quench our thrust".

Many Women came as brides, their hair have gone dry, but the search for water has not ended. Karnataka is facing the worst kind of water crisis. In Bangalore, only 35% of the city gets water on daily basis, the rest on alternative days. In addition to the scarcity, erratic water supply is another problem. In Samadhanagar area, water generally comes in the morning at 11 A.M or in the middle of the night. Both these timings make it very difficult for women to collect water as they leave early in the morning to go to work. In Doddanagar slums in the city, women and children who are also breadwinners of the family spend 3-4 hours filling water, losing their wages. In Hosapalya locality women get severe joint pain in their shoulders, hips and knees due to carrying water pits from water sources outside their colony. In Peenya industrial area, many street fights occur among the women over water. Social conflict and tension is high due to water crisis.

In brief, at an estimate about 150 Million-Woman Days and Rs 10 Billion are lost in fetching water.

2

Water Crisis in Central Asia

INTRODUCTION

Freshwater is a vital element for human life and global civilization. River flows traveling between countries in a common basin has been a source of tension between states, but it has also contributed to unifying regions. The dualistic nature of transboundary waters carries a lesson of international cooperation in an increasingly globalized world. In 2001, former United Nations Secretary General Kofi Annan stated that "fierce competition for freshwater may well become a source of conflict and wars in the future," especially in politically volatile regions like the Middle East. However, many countries in politically unstable regions have found ways to cooperate and have created joint water management regimes to resolve tension over cross-boundary freshwater.

The Transboundary Freshwater Dispute Database (TFDD) at Oregon State University (OSU) has identified 263 water basins that cross national boundaries, which cover over 40 percent of the world's population. Since World War II, over 157 water treaties have been signed between riparian countries to cooperate and deal with complexities of joint water bodies. However, it often requires years of negotiations and support from the international community to craft these agreements. Over the years, effective agreements with processes to settle disputes have been put into effect in the Indus River (India-Pakistan) and the Mekong River Basin (Southeast Asia) and progress is being made in managing tensions between upstream and downstream countries along the Nile River in Africa.

The TFDD has cataloged more than 1800 water related events between countries over the last half century and findings suggest that most interactions between countries were mild and cooperative, rather than leading to open conflict. In fact, the last "water war" was in 2500 BC among rival city-states bordering the Tigris and Euphrates Rivers.Since World War II, two-thirds of water contacts between countries were cooperative and most were verbal, either supportive or negative without any government sanction involved. Water is more likely to lead to localized conflict and violence on an intrastate level rather than between sovereign states. In the broad quantitative study of these events, OSU researchers found that water can act as an "irritant" to degrade relations between countries or as a "unifier" to create a more regional focus on water management in spite of wars and hostile relations between neighboring countries. Over time, effective water agreements share a number of important qualities. These include adaptive management structures, clear and flexible rules for water allocation and management, equal distribution of benefits, conflict resolution and enforcement mechanisms. Moreover, the trend shows that transboundary water agreements are negotiated in an atmosphere shifting from a "rights based" stance to a "needs based" practical approach. It has been crucial to identify shared benefits in transboundary water agreements as was accomplished in the agreement between the United States and Canada in the 1960s. This agreement established flood control for both neighboring states and gave Canada the right to divert water from the Columbia River for hydropower.

In order to govern transboundary waters, the international community needs a global framework convention, which has yet to be accomplished. In 1997, the United Nations General Assembly passed the Convention on the Non-Navigational Uses of International Watercourses. Yet, the convention was never ratified. It faced opposition from upstream countries like China and Turkey and many of its provisions were considered overly vague. Upstream and downstream countries were also conflicted about how it treated basic concepts of international law.

The UN Watercourses treaty was also overshadowed by the decision by the International Court of Justice in 1997, to uphold a twenty year old agreement between Hungry and Czechoslovakia in a case known at the Gabcikovo-Nagymaros Project. The court stopped the post-Communist governments of Hungary and Slovakia from abandoning a management agreement for a system of locks on the Danube River. The ICJ ordered the two riparian countries to increase cooperation including creating a joint regime to manage the project on the Danube River.

Nevertheless, a number of regional transboundary water agreements have emerged in recent years. Prominent examples of such treaties can be found in Southern Africa and Europe. In Europe, the Convention on the Protection and Use of Transboundary Watercourses and International Lakes was ratified by the United Nations Economic Commission for Europe (UNECE) and came into effect in 1996. This treaty is regarded as very robust. UNECE has also developed a number of new programs to increase cooperation, including the International Water Assessment Center, and National Policy Dialogues in former Communist countries.

Active engagement by the international community clearly makes a difference in advancing cooperation among countries over international waters. In a number of cases the World Bank and the Global Environment Facility have helped develop regional water sharing agreements, as have various UN agencies like the United Nations Development Programme (UNDP) and the United Nations Environment Programme (UNEP). It may take decades of engagement and active diplomacy, but the wide range of success in water cooperation has emerged in every corner of the globe. This is an encouraging sign in an age of climate change when water conflicts are likely to grow more combative, which in turn may increase the need for international mediation in water disputes worldwide.

OVERVIEW: SUMMARY OF WATER ISSUE IN CENTRAL ASIA

Central Asia is home to sixty-one million citizens spread across five countries: Uzbekistan, Tajikistan, Turkmenistan, Kyrgyz Republic, and Kazakhstan. There is a high level of poverty in the region. The notable exception, in terms of economic performance, is Kazakhstan, which has relatively low poverty levels and the highest Gross Domestic Product (GDP) per capita due to their large fossil fuel reserves.

Lack of cooperation and regional dialogue in Central Asia is a problem for the region. However, one conflict area deserves special attention: water. Regional cooperation on water management is both a multi-faceted and complex issue. The two main sources of water in Central Asia are the Syr Darya and Amu Darya Rivers, which is the larger of the two. The Amu Darya originates in Tajikistan and flows along the border between Afghanistan and Uzbekistan, and goes through Turkmenistan before returning to Uzbekistan and discharging in the Aral Sea. When combined, the Amu Darya and Syr Darya rivers have about 77 cubic kilometers of water, 96 percent of which is used for irrigation. Other major inter-state rivers include Chu, Talas, Tarim, and Irtysh.

At the heart of the problem of lack of cooperation and dialogue on regional water management are conflicting interests in how these water resources are to be used and whether they are seen as a commodity or public good. Downstream countries, Kazakhstan, Turkmenistan and Uzbekistan, are dependent on irrigated agriculture, whereas upstream countries, Kyrgyz Republic and Tajikistan, are focused on expanding reservoir capacity and hydroelectric power generation.

After the collapse of the Soviet Union in 1991, the newly independent states decided to pursue their own diverging national interests. Although the countries decided to sign the 1992 Almaty Agreement and maintain Soviet Union water quotas, it is now outdated and thus, limited in its effectiveness. Regional and international efforts have failed to find a lasting solution because of the mistrust and low political will to cooperate among the Central Asian leaders. Other contributing factors include crumbling infrastructure due to economic conditions within the countries, unequal distribution of natural resources and climate change.

This report, "Water Crisis in Central Asia: Key Challenges and Opportunities" was prepared for our client, the United Nations

Development Programme (UNDP), to provide an assessment of the key challenges, opportunities and recommendations for increasing regional cooperation with regards to water management. The aim was to propose viable options which could, through increased regional collaboration, lead to an acceptable arrangement that is sustainable and peaceful.

The research chapter was the culmination of the "Practicum in International Affairs," a capstone course of the Graduate Program in International Affairs under the New School for General Studies. The research group was composed of Diana Castillo, Lisa Marie Izquierdo, Mari Stangerhaugen, Bob Nixon, and Gloria Jimenez. The project was supervised by Ambassador Rafat Mahdi, who rendered invaluable support in the completion of this project. In preparation for our research, we met with our client and provided a draft for review before submitting our final product. We also conducted a number of interviews with Permanent Representatives from the Central Asian states and other experts which gave us insight into the complexity and intricacy of the region's water issues.

MAJOR CHALLENGES

Soviet Union Legacy

During the "Great Game" of the 19th century the British and Russian Empires, aware of Central Asia's geostrategic importance as an immense east-west and north-south bridge, competed for hegemony over the landlocked territory. The subsequent history of the twentieth century showed that the region's geopolitical significance remained unaltered. After becoming part of the Soviet Union, the Central Asian Republics became part of a socialist state that aimed to spread a socialist revolution. Likewise, the Soviet legacy in Central Asia should be understood and conceptualized in past USSR policy-making processes: standardization of national language, mass educational system, substitution of "tribal-clan structures" for new identity categories, and repression of religion.

In order to understand the region's current water crisis it is necessary to survey past USSR policies toward the former Soviet Central Asian Republics. In an effort to increase and secure long-term resources, Soviet officials carried out a myriad of policies of domestic reforms as well as a large-scale territorial expansion into Central Asia. From the 1940s onwards, the Soviet era agricultural policies focused primarily on increased output of cotton and rice as a means to reduce reliance on imports of these commodities. These attempts of modernization and self-sufficiency resulted in the transformation of Central Asia's geography, resources, and semi-nomad populations into Russia's sphere of interest.

Most of landlocked Central Asia is located in arid and semi-arid zones. Hence in Moscow the scope for policy-making focused on expanding arable land for agriculture, building massive hydraulic projects, and generating regional hydropower resources throughout Central Asia. Records show more than 1,200 dams were built in the region during the Soviet era, among them is the Nurek Dam, the second largest dam in the world.

The Soviet modernization campaign to transform poor soils into irrigated land for water intensive crops such as cotton, Moscow's "white gold," produced an interdependent economic bloc among the five Soviet-era 'stans.' Furthermore, these developments resulted in the diversion of the Amu Darya and the Syr Darya, which fed the Aral Sea. Vast amounts of freshwater from glaciers in the Kyrgyz Republic and Tajikistan mountain ranges were diverted downstream to Kazakhstan, Turkmenistan and Uzbekistan. During the Soviet period, dams located in the basins of the transboundary rivers were used for the production of hydropower generation, which resulted in an integrated Soviet structure of energy allocation.

During Soviet rule, nature was seen as something to be directed by elaborate engineering. This line of approach to the region inevitably paved the way to irreversible water-related environmental damage to what was once the world's fourth largest lake, the Aral Sea.

Cooperative agreements between the five post-Soviet states, especially the 1992 Almaty Agreement, worked insofar as downstream countries provided the upstream countries with gas and coal in the winter to allow them to generate heat and power without releasing water. Likewise, Kyrgyzstan would discharge the reservoirs along the Syr Darya for summer irrigation. The key here is that all decisions regarding transboundary water management in the Central Asian countries were made top-down by the Ministry of Land Reclamation and Water Management in Moscow, in coordination with the Ministry of Energy, without regard to the Soviet republics' own interests. This led to a widespread belief in the region that Soviet planners deliberately divided resources and unified investment among them so none would be self-sufficient. Jean-Paul Azam and Galyn Makhmejanov argue that, "the credibility of the agreements was always a weak point, since upstream countries wanted to further develop their hydro-power facilities, whereas downstream countries were skeptical of these claims, warning about possible consequences."

REGIONAL POLITICS

Central Asian States

Conflicting political interests and increasing tensions over the use of water have adversely affected regional relations, thus thwarting efforts to promote cooperation on water management in Central Asia. After independence, three out of the five Central Asian leaders came out of the Communist Party and continued the top-down governance used during the Soviet era. Although the region is widely authoritarian, this year the Kyrgyzstan constitution created a parliamentary democracy which balances power between the executive and Parliament. However, it has yet to be seen how effective these efforts will be in the future.

Internal politics with the states of Central Asia is not only affecting the stability within the countries themselves but how they relate to one another. *Foreign Policy* and the Fund for Peace's Failed State Index (FSI) is an annual rating based on 12 social, economic, and political indicators of risk. According to the 2010 Index, three of the Central Asian countries were performing similarly based on these indicators: Uzbekistan (#36), Tajikistan (#38) and Kyrgyzstan (#45). Additionally, the index considered Turkmenistan, Kyrgyzstan, and Uzbekistan to be "in danger" based on their Failed State indicators. Corruption is rampant and political leaders have been involved in the pilfering of national resources as though they were at their sole disposal. The powerful executive offices present an opportunity and pose a challenge as they allow for quick and decisive action, but the lack of political will of the Central Asian leaders, irrespective of the prevailing public sentiment, thwart efforts to cooperate. Moreover, these states have become economic competitors, as they are no longer part of the same economic bloc and can utilize their natural resources to earn export revenue. This has been further intensified through the region's move towards a market economy and the divergent uses of water: agricultural expansion versus increased hydroelectric power generation. Diverging national interests have led to low political will to prioritize regional interests and this lack of a shared vision for a mutually beneficial agreement has prevented effective cooperation.

Divergent approaches to regional water management have also thwarted effective cooperation. The downstream countries favor maintaining old Soviet Union quotas, whereas the Kyrgyz Republic and Tajikistan are in favor of receiving payment for water supplied to the downstream states. The Kyrgyz Republic, Kazakhstan, and Uzbekistan each have constitutions which state that water is a state resource. This debate over water allocation extends once again to water being used for agriculture versus hydroelectric generation. Moreover, downstream countries have claimed that international rivers should be a common good shared by all countries. This illustrates the problem of whether water is a public good or a commodity. Another element to this debate is whether to use domestic or international water law in order to find a resolution to the dispute. Various water agreements have been broken due to the reasons. As these countries pursue often conflicting sovereign interests, the incentive to uphold any agreement will be weak. Moreover, lack of funding and enforcement mechanisms within the agreements further weaken their effectiveness.

Two institutions for cooperation, Interstate Coordination of Water Resources Commission (ICWC) and International Fund for saving the Aral Sea (IFAS), have been limited in their effectiveness in part because of rivalry and conflict over staffing patterns and questions over bias. In the past there have been suspicions that because officials from Uzbekistan were heavily represented, these organizations favored its interests. Dialogue is thus hindered because of mistrust and competition. Further problems of cooperation have been exacerbated by retaliatory actions, such as when Kyrgyzstan suddenly stopped water supplies to Kazakhstan from the Kirov reservoir in April 2010. Eighty percent of its total capacity is used by Kazakhstan for agricultural purposes alone. In addition, in June 2010 Uzbekistan reduced the passage of water from Kyrgyzstan to Kazakhstan in the cross-border Dostyk channel.

Role of Neighboring States

Neighboring countries play a role in Central Asia's water crisis and in regional politics. The Brookings Institute has suggested these countries and others should "use available diplomatic mechanisms to ensure that possible inter-state tensions over the management of scarce water and energy resources in the region are managed effectively" and without conflict. The most prominent neighboring countries affecting regional politics are Russia, China, and Afghanistan.

Russia

Russia has a distinct and dynamic relationship with Central Asia because of its past history. It remains the region's largest trading partner, with revenues totaling more than $21 billion in 2007, but its economic influence has since waned after the recession began. Russia has also been a destination country for many Central Asian migrant workers unable to find employment. Russia's intent in further maintaining its influence in the region occurred when it established its own anti-terrorism rapid action force in Kant, Kyrgyzstan. The country set up the Collective Security Treaty Organization (CSTO), an organization focused on economic and military regional coordination and members include Armenia, Belarus, Kazakhstan, Kyrgyzstan, Tajikistan, and Uzbekistan. According to *Foreign Policy*, this organization is seen as a counter to Chinese and American influence in the region and as an opportunity for Russia to re-establish hegemony in the region.

In terms of water disputes in the region, Russia has been reluctant to get involved. One assessment of Russia's role in water management issues observed that the country had to strike a delicate balance between "reassuring Central Asia's most significant power, Uzbekistan, and safeguarding its own hydroelectric investments in Kyrgyzstan and Tajikistan." While Russia had previously supported the construction of upstream countries' hydroelectric projects, it then switched to a more neutral role when it stated that construction should only proceed after the interests of all states have been adequately addressed. Russian policy aside, it is unclear whether the region would view any Russian arbitration as neutral or credible.

China

China has been described as being part of a new "great game" alongside Russia and the United States for influence in Central Asia. China has mostly played the role of investor by providing funding for oil projects and for the construction of dams, roads, and power transmission lines. According to a *Foreign Affairs* article, China's strategy to secure natural resources has been to court the region with the construction of two major pipelines, one through Kazakhstan and the other from Turkmenistan across Uzbekistan and Kazakhstan. In line with this strategy, China has tried to foster good relationships with the Central Asian states through diplomatic means and by settling many border disputes in the region in order to create more hospitable relations.

Afghanistan

While Afghanistan has been consumed in social and political turmoil, it's agriculturally based economy and potential future development of hydropower is reason to not discount its role. The Amu Darya, an important water source in the region, runs through Afghanistan's northern border and feeds 40 percent of its irrigated lands. Yet poor infrastructure leads to water losses as high as 70 percent. Moreover, an estimated 75 percent of Afghanistan's 34 million people live in rural areas where agriculture is the principle means of livelihood. Hence, the development of its agriculture sector in the future will add even more demand to scarce water resources in the region, thus creating the potential for conflict. Another potential challenge is how the country may pursue development of its own hydropower, as it has only 10 percent of its hydropower potential developed along the Amu Darya. However, Afghan plans to develop its hydropower face opposition from Turkmenistan and Uzbekistan. Lastly is the question over the water distribution of the Amu Darya. Although there are agreements relating to water use, the only one which dealt with water allocation was the Tashkent Agreement of 1987, which excluded Afghanistan. Recently, Tajikistan has led the way for engagement and cooperation with Afghanistan. In 2007 and 2010 two protocols and a Memorandum of Understanding relating to increased cooperation, water use, and capacity building were signed between the countries. Although Afghanistan currently has a limited role, future possibilities for its role to shift as it stabilizes will necessitate further engagement by the Central Asian states.

Distribution of Natural Resources

Overall, Central Asia is blessed with a range of natural resources such as oil, gas, minerals and hydropower, which could drive the region forward socially and economically. However, the distribution of resources favors the downstream countries (Kazakhstan, Uzbekistan and Turkmenistan), which posses oil and gas reserves that are sought after by Russia, China and Europe. The upstream countries (Tajikistan and Kyrgyzstan) have glaciers that produce the water for downstream irrigation and hydro-electricity and also selected mineral resources like gold, rare earth metals and aluminum. The downstream countries have used oil and gas resources, and agricultural exports to boost their national incomes and level of development. Kazakhstan has been the most successful. Upstream countries, especially Tajikistan have few options for development other than exploiting water resources through hydropower development. The two upstream countries are the poorest nations in the region. This unbalanced distribution of natural resources has created the dynamics of the "haves" versus the "have nots'" between the upstream and the downstream countries.

Kazakhstan has done the most to leverage its crude oil resources by linking up to pipelines to China, Russia and Europe. The country has 30 billion barrels of crude oil in proven oil reserves and more oil reserves are expected to be explored soon in the Caspian Sea. The country has doubled its oil production over the last decade, mostly for exports. American and Russian oil companies have been brought to help extract this oil. Kazakhstan also has significant reserves of coal that was developed in the Soviet era, and it continues to be exported to other Central Asia countries. In recent years Kazakhstan has linked up to a number of oil and gas pipelines including the Russian controlled Caspian Pipeline Consortium, the Kazakhstan-China Pipeline and the Baku-Tbilisi-Ceyhan Pipeline, supported by the United States and Europe, seeking to undercut Russian influence over energy supplies to Europe.

Turkmenistan, with major reserves of natural gas is only beginning to enter into the new "great energy game" of playing off Russia, China and Europe and the United States. Over the last decade, Turkmenistan dealt exclusively with Russian pipelines but that is beginning to change. With the 4th biggest globally proven reserves of natural gas, Turkmenistan has inked pipeline deals with Russia and China in 2007. Energy hungry China has become a big customer for Turkmenistan, to the extent of hiring a Russian construction company to finish the natural gas pipeline to China. China is also seen as likely investors in Turkmenistan's state energy companies, fueling further growth.

On the other hand, there are two real restraints to new energy resurgence: the "resource curse" and the growing impact of climate change that are raising temperatures in Central Asia. A growing literature on the natural resource curse in developing countries has emerged in recent years. Resource rich countries like Nigeria and the Democratic Republic of the Congo remain desperately poor and corrupt nations. One variation of the theory is that natural resources especially crude oil both undermine the economy and empower dictatorial leaders to ignore the rule of law.

Kazakhstan is very aware of the downfalls of the resource curse. Since it opened up oil exploration, it set up a natural resources fund, the National Fund of Republic of Kazakhstan that is capitalized with over $20 billion. It is modeled after the Norwegian energy fund and Central Asia's richest state is trying to diversify its economy beyond its current dependence on hydrocarbons. So far, resource funds remain untested in developing countries that rely on energy resources. Ongoing problems with corruption and poor governance can undermine these funds as has happened in Venezuela, where the government has raided the fund over the years.

Climate Change

Global warming is already being felt in Central Asia with melting glaciers in Tajikistan and Kyrgyzstan and rising temperatures in the downstream countries that will have a real impact on agricultural practices. A World Bank report on climate change in Europe and Central Asia observed climate change will inflame even further the current conflict over transboundary flows of water. Climate change acts as a "threat multiplier" for the entire Central Asia water crisis, making it more severe. Since the 1970s, temperature has risen twice as fast in Central Asia compared to global levels. This report noted that increased winter precipitation will be offset by hotter temperatures in the summer causing increased evaporation. A projected 20 percent decline in river runoff in the upstream countries will only complicate the current unsustainable water management practices and increase demand for water in Central Asia. There will also be an increased risk of natural disasters like destructive mudslides in Kyrgyzstan.

Research from the Institute of Water Problems and Hydro Energy at the National Academy of Sciences in Kyrgyzstan found that the ice melted from glaciers has tripled from 1950 levels. In recent decades, upwards of 20 percent of Kyrgyzstan's glaciers have already melted. Rising temperature and water shortages will likely inflict damage on arid soils and harm plant productivity of irrigation-intensive crops like cotton. Climate change is spurring growing desiccation in Central Asia. Food yields could decline by 30 percent. Small farmers will also be the hardest hit from climate change. Tajikistan in recent years experienced recent droughts and extreme weather which had a severe impact on the rural poor. The country in 2008 survived a severe cold winter, with temperatures falling to 20 C below zero for an extended period. This cold weather has damaged many crops, orchards and killed nearly all of the livestock. Moreover, aging energy infrastructure collapsed under the pressure of cold temperatures. Tajikistan experienced a 40 percent decline in food yields after the cold snap and drought.

Kazakhstan with its reliance on coal and oil has made it a leading emitter of greenhouse gases (GHS) along with Turkmenistan and Uzbekistan. Yet, the level of economic growth in these polluting countries has not returned to the 1990s levels, due to the overall industrial decline in Central Asia. On the other hand, Tajikistan and Kyrgyzstan with its reliance on hydropower emit low rates of GHS.

Many countries are now undertaking planning for adapting over the long term to climate change. This process will require developing nations to place greater emphasis on water resources and seek out adaptation funding from the Global Environment Facility, financed by the World Bank. Most experts believe freshwater resources will be one of the areas that will be affected early by climate change. Central Asian countries could be helped by "carbon financed" green investments like small-scale renewable energy technology from the Clean Development Mechanism facilitated by the Kyoto Protocol to fight climate change. The region could also benefit from the growing concern by the international community about the fate of glaciers in the greater Himalayas, which is the source of water for over a billion people in South and Southeast Asia.

There is growing concern that increased climate change could lead to more political instability in Central Asia as seen by the crisis in Kyrgyzstan. In 2007, UK based International Alert placed the entire region in its global list of countries facing potential political instability from the impact of climate change and increased stress on natural resources and food security. Freshwater resources could be one of the first areas hit by climate change. Additionally, social tensions from rising temperatures may raise the risk that weak governance in Central Asia causes.

MANAGEMENT OF WATER SECTOR

The Central Asian countries have some of the largest irrigation schemes in the world, and some 22 million people in these countries depend directly or indirectly upon irrigated agriculture for their livelihoods. Entire communities came into being solely because of irrigation development and settlement schemes during the Soviet era. Today twenty to forty percent of the GDP of these countries is derived from agriculture, almost all of which are irrigated, and without irrigation, much of the land would revert to desert scrub.

Irrigation benefited from massive investment during the Soviet era, but water was not well managed. Water application rates were extremely high, which reduced the quality of farmland through the rising water table and salinization. The irrigation systems were in poor condition even before the Central Asian countries became independent in 1991. Since the collapse of the Soviet Union, the situation has worsened considerably. Both government budgets and farm incomes have fallen dramatically, water management institutions have weakened and institutional structures are generally not strong enough to ensure efficient water management. Thus, much of the infrastructure is fast approaching collapse. Canals are silted up or damaged, gates broken down or non-existent and pumps held together by improvised repairs and parts taken from other machinery. The problem is exacerbated by the shrinking of the Aral Sea, and winter floods caused by excessive reservoir drainage. The United Nations Development Program (UNDP) reports that the Central Asian region loses $1.7 billion a year, which constitutes three percent of the region's GDP from the poor water management that lowers agricultural yields.

COMPETING DEMANDS FOR WATER: IRRIGATION VS. HYDROPOWER

Interdependence

The Central Asian countries have inherited an interconnected and complex hydraulic infrastructure system from the Soviet era. This system was set up to be based upon the construction of large dams and water reservoirs in the mountainous areas of the upstream countries Tajikistan and Kyrgyzstan. This was because of the area's attractiveness of natural conditions and higher water accumulations per unit area in comparison to the conditions of the lowland within the downstream countries, Uzbekistan, Kazakhstan and Turkmenistan. On the other hand, the lowlands were suitable for practicing irrigated agriculture and for growing water intensive agricultural crops, such as cotton, rice and wheat.

In the 1970's a multiyear storage reservoir was constructed in the Kyrgyz region on the Naryn River (that feeds into the Syr Darya River) to even out the dry and wet year flow to effectively support irrigation in Uzbekistan, Kazakhstan and Turkmenistan. Under the Soviet Union's Protocol No. 413 of 1984 in a normal year, 75% of the annual discharge from the reservoir was to be made in summer and discharges in winter could not exceed the remaining 25%. Kyrgyzstan and Tajikistan supplied surplus electricity from their hydropower plants through the Central Asian Power System to the three downstream countries in the summer. In exchange, since the Kyrgyz and Tajik region lacked any significant resources of fossil fuels, electricity was transferred from this power system to enable Kyrgyzstan and Tajikistan to meet their winter demand for electricity and heat. As a result of this system, the countries have become closely interdependent in their water utilization, and the uneven distribution of water resources has raised transboundary reservoir management issues over water allocation among the countries of the region.

The 1992 Almaty Agreement

After the collapse of the Soviet Union, the newly independent Central Asian states agreed to largely continue the Soviet era water sharing agreements, without Soviet era funds and created the Inter-state Coordination of Water Resources Commission which maintained water quotas. The current water sharing within Central Asia dates from the 1992 Almaty Agreement in which the five states agreed to adhere to an "established pattern and principles of allocation", basically codifying existing practices. The Almaty Agreement was signed in haste, only a few weeks after the Central Asian states became independent from the Soviet Union and little thought was given to its long-term consequences. By signing the Almaty Agreement the Central Asian states chose to keep Soviet allocations unchanged, meaning that the bulk of the region's water resources is still allocated to the downstream countries, leaving the upstream countries with little access to the water generated on their territory. Moreover, the Almaty Agreement made no provision for Afghanistan, despite the fact that approximately 6 percent of the flows within the Aral Sea Basin are generated on its territory. Shortly after the Agreement was signed, the upstream countries realized that their water allocation was not sufficient for planned expansions in agriculture. Kyrgyzstan has argued that not only are they denied fair access to water that rises on their territory, they are also expected to pay for the upkeep and maintenance of the dams and reservoirs that control the flow of the Syr Darya, while the downstream countries, especially Uzbekistan, reap the benefits.

Limitations of the 1992 Almaty Agreement

Despite these and other regional and international efforts to ameliorate the water crisis, the only joint agreement signed by all five leaders is the Almaty Agreement from 1992. Yet, in recent years, there have been a number of discussions on its current status and the need to review, revise, and/or replace it. One of the key issues surrounding it is how the upstream states, where Central Asia's water originates, are not given their fair share of resources. Now they are increasing their domestic water usage and decreasing the amount sent to the downstream states. This is a major need to update it, especially as this will have potential to ensure that regional stability is maintained. Another major factor is climate change. The region's main glaciers are shrinking, therefore decreasing the overall water supplies for the region. This highlights the need to acknowledge current water levels so all are ensured they get the amount of water they need. One final issue is Afghanistan, which was excluded from the agreement. This state is of special importance, since once it becomes more stable it will most likely ask for its fair share of water resources.

CENTRAL ASIAN COUNTRIES INITIATIVE FOR LAND MANAGEMENT

This initiative is a collaborative ten year project facilitated by the Asian Development Bank (ADB) to combat land degradation, desertification and declining agricultural yields that impact over 20 million people in the region. All five governments signed a framework agreement with ADB and Global Environment Facility and global partners in 2006. CACILM has received commitments on country level and on the international level to raise $1.4 billion for the initiative. This includes support from international development agencies from Canada, Germany and Switzerland, as well as various United Nations agencies and the World Bank.

CACILM has identified eight national projects in the five Central Asian states and two multi-country projects that focus on land degradation, eco-system stabilization, sustainable agriculture, pastoral management and sustainable forestry. By 2015, the initiative aims to increase private investment and make major improvements in degraded farmland, develop an integrated approach toward land-use planning and train more government workers and citizens in sustainable land management practices. Among the anticipated global environmental benefits of this initiative are a significant reduction in the loss of soils from sand storms, the reduction of soil and pesticide runoff into rivers that run downstream and into transboundary rivers as well as improvements in water availability, which should moderate the harsh climate related to desertification. Other environmental benefits include a reduction in the loss of carbon sinks in soils and forests and a reduction in greenhouse gases created by unsustainable agricultural practices. CACILM is a new initiative and it is too early to evaluate its success or failure, but so far there are good indications of wide participation of all five countries in dealing with the legacy of poor irrigation practices resulting in salinization and water logging which has hurt agricultural yields.

The World Bank

The World Bank (WB) has been heavily involved in Central Asia since each state joined following independence. One type of involvement has been the development of Country Partnership Strategies (CPS) with both Tajikistan and Kyrgyzstan. The CPS identifies key issues affecting the states, such as water and energy, and the best ways to address them by utilizing past experience and knowledge gained from similar projects. Another type of assistance, relevant to this report, is environmental and techno-economical assessments done prior to the commencement of hydropower projects.

The World Bank has also collaborated with potential donors in collecting investments needed for the Central Asian states. One important regional donor is Russia, who recently signed onto two new agreements to expand this role.

The first asks for a $30 million contribution towards improving the region's financial management systems and the other puts $9 billion towards the EURASEC Anti-Crisis Fund, which Tajikistan, Kyrgyzstan and Kazakhstan are part of. Another key regional donor is China, who invested $267.2 million and $58 million towards two electricity lines in Tajikistan.

In recent years, the World Bank launched a new initiative with the five Central Asian governments and regional institutions, such as IFAS, called the Central Asia Energy-Water Development Framework.

This program aims to show each state how to utilize their resources in a socially sustainable and environmentally-friendly manner, with regards to each others' national priorities and regional stability. This initiative has three specific aims: 1) balance energy options while addressing winter energy shortages; 2) strengthen investment in infrastructure to expand energy trade within and outside the region; and 3) work with regional organizations to encourage dialogue among the states and improve water usage for the energy and agricultural sectors. If successful, this program will help the states realize the changes they need to make with regards to these issues, for they are part of the overall problem and have not yet fully been addressed.

As a stakeholder, the World Bank has played a positive role in collecting investments and addressing country specific issues in Central Asia. Also, it is worth mentioning once again the Bank's involvement in building of the Kokaralsk Dam and the Aral Sea Basin Programme 1, as these are just a few of its attempts in addressing the Aral Sea crisis. The Bank may also be able to put one other positive role in the region, depending on the outcome of feasibility study currently being done on the Rogun Dam. The World Bank should be further utilized by the Central Asian states since it seems very interested in helping address the key issues that continue to plague them.

European Union

The European Union (EU) has been engaged with the five countries in Central Asia since they gained their independence, a relationship that has developed significantly over the years and revealed shared economic and security interests. Central Asia's energy resources are of particular interest, as the EU is dependent on external energy sources in order to increase energy security. As a result of this development, in June 2007, the EU adopted the "EU and Central Asia: Strategy for a New Partnership" that marked an upgrade in the relations between the EU and Central Asia.

As part of its Central Asia Strategy, the EU-Central Asia Environmental Dialogue has been established to foster environmental protection and better manage water resources. The EU has increasingly focused on working with the five Central Asian countries to improve the management of lands and forestry resources, and supporting the stabilization of the Aral Sea. To promote and increase capacity building for renewable energy sources and improve energy efficiency, recent activities include trainings and seminars of government officials and financing feasibility studies regarding the installation of small sized hydropower stations and the use of renewable energy sources in the region. The EU is also trying to alleviate the problems arising from the conflicting needs for water access and use between upstream and downstream countries by actively promoting efficient and economic usage of this resource. Several initiatives have been launched to tackle these issues, for example, better use of resources, better management and rehabilitation of irrigation systems and energy transmission lines. The EU has stated that reducing the demand for these resources is a fundamental component of a possible solution.

The work undertaken under the EU Water Initiative, through its main operational instrument- National Water Policy Dialogues- is the centerpiece of EU efforts to achieve the water-related Millennium Development Goals and targets of the Integrated Water Resource Management (IWRM) network. The overall objectives of National Policy Dialogues are to initiate country-specific activities regarding water supply and sanitation, financing strategies and

IWRM to improve regulatory and administrative frameworks, help setting country priorities, identify projects and develop capacity in the region through a dialogue that involves public authorities and representatives of the civil society. National Water Policy Dialogues was launched in Kyrgyzstan in 2008 and Tajikistan and Turkmenistan in 2009.

The EU has in collaboration with UNDP addressed integrated water resource management (IWRM), where the idea is that by looking at national coordination a model for cooperation can be developed. However, it has been pointed out that Uzbekistan has marginalized itself from these multinational projects, making progress difficult, and moreover the EU projects have been largely focused on water quality issues. This does not contribute to resolving the main issue of sharing and allocation of water resources. Although dialogues have been held under the EU Water Initiative, they have mostly been on the national level. In practice, the EU involvement, similarly to efforts by UNDP and the World Bank to some extent, has remained focused on providing technical assistance.

UN Special Programme for the Economies of Central Asia (SPECA)

SPECA was established in 1998 by the presidents of Kazakhstan, Kyrgyzstan, Tajikistan, Turkmenistan and Uzbekistan. Azerbaijan joined in 2002 and Afghanistan in 2005. It is jointly supported and implemented by the UN Economic and Social Commission for Asia and the Pacific (UNESCAP) and UN Economic Commission for Europe (UNECE). What distinguished SPECA from other actors involved in the region, such as the EU and the UNDP is the direct involvement from political leaders and the focus on how important political efforts are in order to solve issues related to the mismanagement of water in the region. At the same time, the program has the "neutral protection" from the UN, which can be beneficial in promoting cooperation. Problems hindering regional cooperation in Central Asia are often political, and SPECA has been able to offer a neutral UN umbrella and a broad range of international legal instruments of which UNECE is the custodian to resolve bilateral and regional disputes.

SPECA states that the "objective of the Programme is to support the Central Asian states in developing their cooperation, creating incentives for economic development and integration into the economies of Europe and Asia." It is working to provide a framework for dialogue and cooperation as well as for broader cooperative initiatives. Its activities include the development of Euro-Asian transport linkages, including the possible extension of railway and road networks into the region as well as the positive development of institutionalized cooperation between the Kazakh and Kyrgyz Governments in the management of water installations on the Chu-Talas Rivers.

SHANGHAI COOPERATION ORGANIZATION (SCO)

The Shanghai Cooperation Organization (SCO) is a permanent intergovernmental international organization established on June 2001 in Shanghai (China) by the People's Republic of China, the Russian Federation, Kazakhstan, Kyrgyzstan, Tajikistan and Uzbekistan.

According to their Charter, the main goals of the SCO are to strengthen relations among the member countries; promote effective cooperation in politics, trade and economy, science and technology, culture, education, energy, transportation, tourism, and environmental protection; make joint efforts to promote peace, security and stability in the region in accordance with the principles of non-alignment, non-targeting and openness.

The Heads of State Council (HSC) is the highest decision-making body in the SCO. It meets annually to make decisions and give instructions on important issues of SCO interest. The Heads of Government Council (HGC) meets once every year to discuss a strategy for multilateral cooperation and priority directions within the Organization's framework to solve pressing issues of cooperation in economic and other areas. The SCO member states represent the voice of three fifths of the Eurasian continent, and with a population of 1.5 billion, make up a quarter of the planet's population. The SCO has an important role to play regarding the water crisis in Central Asia for various reasons:

- With the exception of Turkmenistan, all of the Central Asian countries joined the SCO in an effort to promote good neighboring relations and to strengthen regional cooperation mechanisms.

- All of the goals formulated in the SCO charter fall directly into place with the ongoing water crisis in Central Asia.
- The SCO strategic paradigms cannot be fully achieved as long as regional stability is fractured, particularly in the turbulent Xinjiang province in China and in the Central Asian region.
- Given the SCO political clout in the region, it is by far the institution that stands out with the potential to become a central body to foster broader regional cooperation regime.

Since its inception, the SCO has made various efforts to promote cooperation among the Central Asian states. However, the members' increasingly diverging interests and the absence of Turkmenistan in the SCO continue to represent an obstacle in the achievement of the SCO goals.

CASE STUDIES

Rogun Dam

The building of dams and other water infrastructure has been a major source of tension among the five Central Asian states. No exception to this is the Rogun Dam in Tajikistan, a highly controversial project that dates back to the Soviet Union days. The dam's purpose was to control the flow of the Vakhsh River, a tributary of the Amu Darya, in order to increase agricultural productivity. A technical scheme was developed by 1965 and construction continued until 1976, when most of the diversion tunnels and excavation was completed. However, after the collapse of the Soviet Union in 1991, followed by the Tajik civil war in 1993, and Tajikistan's numerous financial difficulties, the state was forced to abandon the project.

It is estimated Tajikistan currently has 5% of its hydropower potential developed and heavily relies on neighboring Uzbekistan for electricity imports. In response to these key issues, the government has developed a new power sector strategy which aims for the country to be self-reliant by 2017 and have the capacity to export electricity within Central Asia and to South Asia as a source of internal growth. All of this will be possible once the Rogun Dam, which will be the tallest in the world, is completed.

The Rogun Dam project officially resumed in 2008 and will continue developing in a 2 phase plan:

- Phase 1: the dam will be built to 2/3 of its final height (225m), the collecting reservoir will be created, and 2 generators will be installed
  Total cost: $785 million
  Date of completion: 2015; power flow will start in 2014
- Phase 2: complete the dam to its full height of 335m. At full usage it will generate up to 13,000GWh of power and increase the Nurek Dam's power generation to 1,300GWh
  Total cost: $1.67 billion
  Date of completion: 2019; full power output by 2020

To raise capital for the dam's estimated $2.5 billion price tag, the Tajik government set up the Rogun Open Joint Stock Company, which gives the state 75 percent ownership and the other 25 percent to the public. The public will gain its share through the buying of dam shares, which has become a source of controversy within the state. The government says the buying of these shares is every citizens "patriotic duty" to donate to the dam's construction. However, anyone who does not participate may face some sort of retribution. Jobs are scarce and not high-paying, and citizens in the poorest of the Central Asian states are concerned they are being forced to buy something they do not want nor can barely afford.

The government is also attempting to attract foreign investment and so far has secured a $2 billion investment from Russia, part of which is earmarked for projects along the Vakhsh River. However, some international financial institutions do not want to get involved in the project due to opposition from a key downstream state, Uzbekistan. The Uzbek government has raised many complaints, stating the dam will divert water needed for agricultural production and the final height of 335m is of concern due to the area's susceptibility to earthquakes. Some argue Uzbekistan's opposition stems from the possibility that Tajikistan will be able to produce its own electricity and break its dependence on Uzbekistan, which some say Uzbekistan has used as leverage over its neighbors. The rest of the region may then look to Tajikistan for their electricity exports, thus raising Tajikistan's status and influence in the region and providing the basis to demand payment for the usage of its reservoirs.

Tajik officials have tried to disclaim Uzbek statements by asserting the dam will benefit the entire region and contain enough water in its reservoirs to compensate for dry years. These and other statements, however, have not lessened the tension between the states, prompting the World Bank to conduct an evaluation on the Rogun Dam's possible financial, social, and environmental impacts. If, at the end of its 18 month feasibility study, the World Bank finds the dam passes various viability tests, it will organize an international consortium that will provide the Tajik government with the guidance and financial assistance it needs to finish the dam. More importantly, Tajikistan will get some of the international support it has been looking for regarding the Rogun Dam's construction. While visiting the Central Asian states earlier this year, UN Secretary General Ban Ki-moon was assured by both states that they would respect the final outcome of the World Bank's technical assessment and would refrain from taking unilateral action against each other.

Some international institutes, such as the International Crisis Group, are recommending Tajikistan abandon its Rogun plans because the country cannot afford it and the benefits simply do not outweigh the costs. Additionally, downstream states are planning to build reservoirs to counter Tajikistan's control of the Amu Darya, which will only further complicate the relations between the states and future prospects for a more coherent regional management system. Tajikistan has many aspirations regarding the Rogun Dam, including a much needed source of income (electricity exports) and an increase in regional status. Yet, the possible negative effects on its neighboring states need to be highlighted, considering the tense atmosphere regarding each state's use of water.

This is an ongoing issue that may not be resolved until the conclusion of the World Bank's feasibility study, which will also determine the World Bank's success or failure as a third-party mediator. This will depend on the response from Tajikistan and Uzbekistan and if tensions ease between them. The controversy surrounding the Rogun Dam further illustrates the states' interdependence and the need for increased regional cooperation, as neither can make a decision on their own without taking into account how the rest will be affected.

WATER USE IN CENTRAL ASIA

Central Asia lies in the heart of the Eurasian continent and is comprised of the five former Soviet republics – Kazakhstan, Kyrgyzstan, Tajikistan, Turkmenistan and Uzbekistan, as well as of northern Afghanistan and China's Xinjiang Uighur Autonomous Region. All these share basins of the two major rivers in the region: the Amu Darya and the Syr Darya which form the Aral Sea basin. The Amu Darya catchment basin constitutes 62% of the region's surface water resources and the Syr Darya forms the remaining 30%. The Basin's population of over 35 million occupies about 1.5 million square kilometres and population density varies from about 10 persons per square kilometre in the desert plains to over 300 in the valleys and foothills of the mountains (Smith, 1995).

With domination of low-lying deserts, the climate in Central Asia is hot and dry, with low and irregular precipitation. Sharp daily and seasonal differences in temperature are typical, with long hot summers and cool moist winters. The annual precipitation in the lowland is only 80-200 mm, concentrated in the winter and spring, while in the mountains it ranges 600-800 mm. The region has very different climatic zones with distinct water demands for irrigation. Agricultural, industrial and personal needs can only be satisfied through diversion of water from the Syr Darya, Amu Darya and Zeravshan rivers and their tributaries.

The Amu Darya is Central Asia's largest river and has the highest water bearing capacity of the region draining the catchment of 692,300 km^2. It originates in the Pamir mountains and forms the Pyandj river at the Tajik-Afghan border. Near town of Termez in Uzbekistan the Pyandj is joined by the Surkhandarya to form the Amu Darya. The Pyandj is augmented by a number of major tributaries including the Vaksh and Kafirnigan. From its headwaters, the Amu Darya flows 2540 km west across Tajikistan, Uzbekistan and Turkmenistan and finally crosses the Uzbek region of Karakalpakstan to discharge into the Aral Sea. Discharge is closely related to the amount of snowfall and summer temperatures, with mean annual flow between 46.9 and 108.4 km^3 per annum with an average of 78.5 km^3 (O'Hara, 2000).

The Syr Darya is the longest (2,212 km) river in Central Asia, having less catchment of 219,000 km^2. It rises in the mountains in Kyrgyzstan and has two major tributaries: the Naryn fed by over 700 glaciers in the Tien Shan, and the Kara Darya sourcing in the Ferghana and Alay mountains. After confluence in eastern Uzbekistan, these form the Syr Darya which crosses into Tajikistan and then re-enters Uzbekistan and finally flows into Kazakhstan where it discharges into the Aral Sea. Its discharge is smaller than the one of the Amu Darya, ranging from 21.4 to

The Zeravshan, the third largest river in Central Asia, begins in the Pamir mountains in Tajikistan and crosses high mountain valleys before entering the flat plains in Samarkand region of Uzbekistan. As a result of intensive evaporation and consumption, the river gradually disappears in Kyzylkum desert before reaching the Amu Darya. Mean annual flow of the Zeravshan river is 5.2 km^3 (Smith, 1995).

Historical Background

The major states of the 19th century's Central Asia, the Bukhara Emirate and the Khiva and the Kokand Khanates, were put under the control of the Russian Empire by the end of the century, when the Anglo-Russian Agreement curtailed further Russian expansion in the vicinity of the northern borders of British India. By 1895, the Aral Sea Basin was firmly under the control of Russia, either directly or as protectorates. Thus, the scene for the future colonial relationship was set that persisted under the Soviets and indirectly led to the Aral Sea environmental catastrophe.

The 1917 Bolshevik Revolution toppled the Provisional Government (in power between March-November 1917) and proclaimed Russia the Soviet Republic, eventually to be replaced by the Union of Soviet Socialist Republics. The creation of Central Asian states, in their modern borders, was finished by 1924. In fact, the USSR established modern-day Central Asian states set to become independent nations in future (Bedford, 1998).

In 1991, after the Belovezh Agreement was signed by the leaders of the three most powerful Soviet republics – Russia, Ukraine and Belarus, the Soviet Union ceased to exist and the Soviet republics became independent. The independence appeared a somewhat of a shock for the five Central Asian states, as there was little domestic pressure for them to leave the Soviet Union and no real history as independent nations. Closely woven together economically, they had no experience of dealing with important economic decisions, which have always been taken in Moscow. Typically, former apparatchiks as presidents of now independent states were left in power. Nevertheless, necessary cosmetic changes were made such as banning their local Communist parties, reinventing themselves as people's representatives, etc. Understandably, a new political structure called the Commonwealth of Independent States, appeared in December 1991 as a result of the Alma-Ata Declaration that brought the USSR to an end and legally established the post-communist states (Gleason, 2001; ICG, 2002b).

In their description of Central Asian statehood, Menon and Spruyt (1999) give several important particularities of state formation after the collapse of the Soviet Union in Central Asia to keep in mind. The states were formed by Stalin's administrative diktat that assigned largely arbitrary borders to the republics and allotted such territories to "titular nationalities, which is why state boundaries and ethnic composition in Central Asia lack correspondence; Central Asian states are late developers who have traditionally opted for interventionist economic policies and authoritarian government; clan, religious, ethnic and regional affinities here have not been displaced by centralising, high-capacity states; and, finally, these states lack any experience with democratic multi-party systems.

Existing Water Infrastructure

With irrigation agriculture being the largest water consumer in the region, all Central Asian rivers are utilised and heavily managed. Between 1960s and 1980s, an extended network of dams, reservoirs and canals has been built in the Aral Sea Basin. The largest water storage facilities are the Toktogul Reservoir in Kyrgyzstan controlling the flow of the Naryn river, and the Nurek Dam on the Vaksh river in Tajikistan, dubbed "the largest earth-fill dam in the world. Only the Syr Darya basin has 22 operating reservoirs (Toryanikova and Kenshimov, 1999), including the Naryn-Syr Darya cascade of dams which consists of five reservoirs: three upper reservoirs with the over-year regulation - the Toktogul (projected total volume is 19.5 km^3), the Charvak (2.0 km^3), the Andijan (1.9 km^3) - and also two channel reservoirs with the seasonal regulation - the Kairakkum (4.03 km^3) and the Chardara (5.7 km^3), with the aggregate active storage capacity of 24.1 km^3 (Khamidov· et al, 1999). Both rivers have a total of 274 water diversion structures and 612 km of main canals (Elhance, 1997).

However, due to the lack of maintenance and high silt content in the Amu Darya water (up to 6 kg of silt and sand per 1 cubic metre), many important water facilities like, for example, Hauzkhan, Kurtli and Geok-Tepa reservoirs in Turkmenistan, are currently half silted up (Mouradov, 2002). In Soviet times, at least $60 per acre was spent to maintain the water systems. Uzbekistan currently spends less than $25 per acre. Tajikistan, recovering after the civil war, spends $4 (Wines, 2002). As a consequence, of 55 m^3 of water to be used for irrigation, only 38-44 m^3 of water reach the fields and plants actually receive 25-26 m^3 due to the outdated irrigation technology (Yegorov, 2001).

Among the irrigation canals, the Karakum Canal, the world's largest irrigation canal, is the most significant. Built between 1950 and 1987 and considered one of the great engineering feats of the Soviet era, it has taken water some 1,370 km across southern Turkmenistan from the Amu Darya to the Caspian Sea. Though currently in crisis due to the very poor maintenance, the Karakum Canal still supports 3.5 million hectares of rangeland and about 1 million hectares of cropland, providing also power generation, water for industrial and domestic use and partly navigation (Hannan and O'Hara, 1998).

Other canals include: the North and Grand Ferghana Canals transporting water from the Syr Darya to the Ferghana Valley; the

Karshi Canal providing water to 1.2 million hectares in Uzbekistan's Karshi Steppe; the Amu-Bukhara Canal irrigating land in the Bukhara Region in Uzbekistan from the Amu Darya; and the South Hungry Steppe and Kirov Canals irrigating the Golodnaya (Hungry) Steppe from the Syr Darya (Nanni, 1996).

Soviet-built irrigation schemes brought about widespread and rapid land degradation which only in Turkmenistan resulted in land being abandoned at a rate of over 46,000 hectares per annum in the 1970s (O'Hara and Hannan, 1999). Nevertheless, some of the projects are still under construction, for example, the huge Rogun Dam upstream of the Nurek. Given the current location of reservoirs, about 60% of total storage capacity of the Amu Darya and 9% of total storage capacity of the Syr Darya are controlled by Tajikistan, whereas Kyrgyzstan controls 58% of total storage capacity of the Syr Darya largely because of the Toktogul. Downstream Uzbekistan and Turkmenistan have very few water storage facilities and are entirely dependent for water on the upstream countries.

WATER SCARCITY AND ACCESS

The distribution of water in Central Asia is notably uneven. While upstream Tajikistan and Kyrgyzstan enjoy water abundance, downstream nations of Uzbekistan, Turkmenistan and partly Kazakhstan experience sharp water shortages. But the problem is predominantly consumption.

At the heart of economic systems of Uzbekistan and Turkmenistan is cotton, which is the major hard currency earner for those countries. Cotton is a thirsty culture requiring intensive irrigation. With plans to triple cotton and rice production and almost complete dependence on upstream water resources, water overuse is common in downstream riparians and virtually no effort has been made to reduce water use. In addition, people in Central Asia consume 110 to 120 billion m^3 of water per annum for domestic needs, which is several times higher than in the Middle East. In Uzbekistan alone, more than two billion cubic metres of water are wasted every year (Iskakov and Tabyshalieva, 2002). Water is cheap; in some regions its price is about 65 cents per Olympic swimming pool (Wines, 2002). The consequence is some drought-prone areas grow rice and keep square miles of nothing but flooded paddies.

Central Asia has become notorious worldwide as a site of the most dramatic environmental disaster, the Aral Sea Crisis. Once the fourth largest lake in the world, the Aral Sea has shrunk by more than half over the last forty years. The major reason for that was increased discharge of inflowing water for irrigation. Grand Soviet schemes for the production of cotton, rice and other irrigated cultures required huge amounts of water. However, large irrigation canals designed to provide massive agricultural expansion were on arid lands badly suited to irrigation where the soil is often much permeable and seepage is great. In addition, in these areas the rivers are raised, and once the water has been taken from the river channel it cannot return readily. The result of this overexploitation of water resources was that by 1995-1996 total annual inflow to the Aral Sea has dropped to 7 km^3, the surface area of the sea was reduced to 33,000 km^3, and the level had fallen by 37 m. The sea became saline and devoid of fish (Tanton and Heaven, 1999).

Throughout the sea's former basin, water has mobilised deep salt reserves, raised the water table and waterlogged the fields as a result of over-irrigation. In Turkmenistan, 95% of irrigated lands suffer from salinisation, 50% - in Uzbekistan, about 30% - in Kazakhstan, 15% - in Tajikistan. Due to the mismanagement, several new lakes have appeared in the last decades, like the Aidar-Arnasai lake located in the middle course of the Syr Darya and formed in 1969 as a result of the effluent drain from Toktogul and Chardara reservoirs (Sievers, 2002; CAREC, 2002).

Intensive irrigation development in the deltaic areas was also accompanied by increased anthropogenic pressure in form of shrub felling, technogenic erosion and deflation. The period between 1978 and 1982 was marked by intensified process of desertification, as a result of the combination of excessive water withdrawals with a series of dry years (1974-1977). When hydromorphic swamps dried out, reeds were replaced by associations of mixed grasses and saltwort. Between 1982 and 1996, there was a further dramatic reduction in river discharge, with a total stoppage of inflow in case of the Syr Darya. In the driest years, the Amu Darya flow was almost nil. As a result, salt and dust storms became a major new environmental hazard for the area (Saiko and Zonn, 2000).

Despite that, water consumption goes at the same pace as before. The most populated nation in the region (25 million in 2002), Uzbekistan alone uses three-fifths of regional water supplies. In fact, industrial consumption of water in Uzbekistan and Turkmenistan is twice than in Kyrgyzstan and Tajikistan (Smith, 1995). Wasteful use of water on Uzbekistan's very large irrigated area has contributed to a dramatic decline of the combined flow of the Amu Darya and Syr Darya and acted as a major factor in the Aral Sea Crisis.

Uzbekistan showed itself to be a staunch proponent for this wasteful use of water arguing that it is vital for increasing cotton harvests. But excessive water stimulates vegetative growth that does not necessarily increase crop yields and may actually reduce them (Lerman, Garcia-Garcia and Wichelns, 1996). Consequently, agriculture has never been a component of a negotiating set for downstream countries as any sweeping agricultural reform would have resulted in foreign currency losses and Turkmenistan and Uzbekistan perpetuated the cotton monoculture to ensure social, political, and economic stability in the short term (Weinthal, 2001).

At the same time, Kyrgyzstan started implementing rational water use measures by reducing areas of thirsty cultures. As a result, in 2000, out of projected 7,641,600 m^3 of water to be diverted from rivers, 6,866,200 m^3, or 89.8%, was actually diverted, and 4,88,660 m^3, or 86.5%, of projected 5,648,800 m^3 was used for irrigation (Apasov, 2001).

Consequently, water overexploitation is the major reason for downstream riparians' water scarcity. Uzbekistan and Turkmenistan use their water inefficiently and hence they experience water scarcity in a time of water abundance (Wegerich, 2001).

Water Quality

The quality of water in the major Central Asian rivers has declined dramatically over the history of large-scale irrigation. Huge amounts of salt, fertiliser, herbicides, and pesticides found their way to the rivers as the return flow from the fields. Of 36-40 $km^3$of total annual return flow, about 50%, or 18-20 km^3, bring to rivers about 115 million tons of salt and other harmful components, dramatically deteriorating water quality. In the Amu Darya Basin alone, a total of 84 million tons of salt is discharged into the river, transported with the water which is used to irrigate the fields (Kobori and Glantz, 1998; Spoor, 1998; Dukhovny and Stulina, 2001).

The groundwater table has risen and became as well contaminated with high levels of salts and other minerals. Groundwater quality ranges from a maximum of 0.5 g/L of total dissolved salts to 6 g/L, 20 times than in North America (about 300 mg/L). Total dissolved salts in drinking water reach the level of 3.5 g/L, with the salt limit set by the Uzbek government to be 1 g/L. In terms of chemical contamination, about of 65% of drinking water samples taken in Karakalpakstan proved not to correspond to standards (Small, van der Meer and Upshur, 2001).

In the Syr Darya basin, the chemical most commonly found both in river water and in the fields is butifos which has been widely used in the 60s-80s as defoliant with intensity of 1-1.5 kg per hectare. This organo-phosphorous agent with an acute oral toxicity affects central nervous system, liver and kidneys. Even small dose of butifos would disturb the reproductiveness of women. Since 1986, the production and use of butifos has stopped; however, it is still found in the water and at the bottom of the Amu Darya and Syr Darya rivers, as organo-chlorine pesticides (BHC, DDT) are (Ishida et al, 1995).

High levels of pesticides are found in the tissues of fish in the Amu Darya and Syr Darya. Samples of cane, rice, millet and wheat grown around the Syr Darya have been found to contain dangerous levels of benzopyrene, a carcinogen produced by car exhausts, oil and coal furnaces and manufacture of asphalt (Vinogradov and Langford, 2001).

Chemical pollution of drinking water has caused high cancer incidence, and substantial dioxin residues have been found in mothers' milk, particularly in Karakalpakstan. In the midstream and downstream areas of the Amu Darya and Syr Darya, the incidence of waterborne diseases such as typhus, paratyphoid, cholera and viral hepatitis has increased enormously. According to Uzbekistan's Academy of Sciences, only 8 percent of Uzbekistan's rivers are "clean, around 15 percent of river water is of "satisfactory quality, and 41 percent is "bad. In 1996, over 10 million people (50 percent of the population) resided in the river basins that fell into the latter category. Around 36 percent of river water is considered "dangerous or "extremely dangerous, particularly in Karakalpakstan and in the lower delta of the Zeravshan river, where 24 percent of the Uzbek population lives. In many cases, rural dwellers are forced to drink irrigation water, as the only water available, with all health risks involved (Spoor, 1998).

The Aral Sea crisis – or "syndrome as Klötzli (1997) put it – has severely affected the area's human ecology where millions of people are dependent on water and soil that appear to be highly contaminated. A new model of regional co-operation other than that used in the Soviet times was needed to address specific environmental, socio-economic and political problems of the region.

3

South Asia's Water Crisis

A PROBLEM OF SCARCITY AMID ABUNDANCE

In South Asia, home to nearly 1.6 billion people, cities are increasingly feeling the pressure of population growth and urbanization. It is estimated that 22 of 32 Indian cities face daily water shortages. In Nepal's capital, Kathmandu, many local residents have grown accustomed to waiting in queues for hours to obtain drinking water from the city's ancient, stone waterspouts. In Karachi, Pakistan, electricity and water shortages have led to protests and citywide unrest.

"Water, water, everywhere, nor any drop to drink" aptly describes the problem of water in South Asia – a problem of scarcity amid abundance. Transboundary rivers such as the Ganges, Indus, and Brahmaputra have defined the geography, history, and culture of South Asia for centuries and are critical to economic growth, food and energy security, and sustainable development within the region. But over the last few decades, these rivers have come under considerable pressure from industrial development, urbanization, population growth, and environmental pollution. This situation has been compounded by poor domestic management of water resources and increasing variability in rainfall and climate patterns that have made South Asia highly susceptible to floods, droughts, and natural disasters.

While in areas such as trade and energy South Asian governments have made significant progress in opening up and allowing for the movement of goods and people, regional cooperation on water lags behind. Geopolitics and a history of cross-border disputes have meant that transboundary water issues are perceived largely from a perspective of national security. This highly securitized approach has severely limited access to water and climate data in the region. South Asian governments, in particular India and Pakistan, treat hydrological data secret and classified. While some existing bilateral treaties and agreements, such as the Indus Treaty of 1960 or the Ganges Treaty of 1996, do contain provisions for bilateral data sharing, actual data-sharing practices are ad hoc, and the range of information shared is quite limited. It is also worth noting that none of the existing treaties provide for the public disclosure of data or information exchange between governments.

The closed data environment for water and climate information in the region has compromised governments' ability to make informed decisions on the planning, management, and development of what are essentially shared river basins. The lack of information sharing has also affected governments' ability to deal effectively with natural disasters such as floods, earthquakes, and landslides.

On World Water Day, The Asia Foundation released a major new report:"Strengthening Transparency and Access to Information on Transboundary Rivers in South Asia." The report examines the availability and accessibility of hydrological data and information related to three transboundary rivers in Bangladesh, India, and Nepal and tests the efficacy of right-to-information or freedom-of-information laws in accessing this data. The study – conducted with the World Resources Institute and civil society organizations in these countries with support from Skoll Global Threats Fund – highlights some of the key barriers to information access on water and climate issues in the region. The report illustrates that while governments in these countries have enacted laws and policies that seek to open up environmental data and information, in practice, the securitization of information remains a major constraint. Moreover, limited human resources, training, and capacity have undermined the capability of these governments to effectively implement existing transparency laws and policies. Across all three countries, hydrological data and information are not being collected, maintained, or published in a systematic manner. Where data is available, it is often of poor quality, difficult to verify, and provided in a format that is not user-friendly. Taken together, the highly fragmented availability of data makes it difficult to get a complete hydrological picture of the rivers. To discuss some of the broader implications of this study, The Asia Foundation convened civil society organizations, think tanks, international agencies, and donors for a regional forum, "Access to Water and Climate Data in South Asia," on March 23-24 in Kathmandu. Participants debated the issues and challenges in making climate and water data more accessible throughout South Asia, and brainstormed ways to leverage existing information-sharing experiences and practices.

While acknowledging the many constraints to regional data sharing, the forum also highlighted some of the innovative ways in which participating groups are enhancing data access and exchange on water and climate issues. For instance, in the northeastern Indian state of Assam, the environmental NGO Aaranyak and the International Centre for Integrated Mountain Development (ICIMOD) have piloted an innovative community-based flood warning system that uses mobile phones to transmit critical flood related data and information to communities upstream and downstream of the eastern Brahmaputra basin. At a national level, multilateral agencies such as the World Bank and others are supporting governments to improve their data and information management systems while simultaneously building government capacity to better manage these systems. At a regional level, ICIMOD has been working with the governments of Pakistan, Bangladesh, Nepal, and Bhutan to develop a Regional Flood Information System in the Hindu-Kush Himalayas that seeks to facilitate sharing of flood data and information between countries to reduce the vulnerability of affected communities. There are also ongoing efforts to provide the media and private sector with data and information on water related issues. For example, the Third Pole recently launched a new, open source geospatial database – Data.TheThirdPole – to provide the media and other stakeholders with access to a searchable catalog of water-related datasets sourced from different organizations in Asia. Such initiatives testify to the growing demand for more accurate and comprehensive data and information on transboundary water issues on the subcontinent.

The democratization of data, technology, and access has been one of the defining developments of the 21st century. Riding on the wave of this global movement, governments in South Asia have opened up in nearly every sphere, whether enacting transparency laws, disclosing budget and public expenditure information to citizens, or taking the lead in e-governance and other ICT initiatives. Given these developments, and the proliferation of new information and communication technologies, the paradigm of security that has prevented governments from effectively sharing data and information on shared resources is out of date. Water scarcity for many South Asians is already a daily reality, and if we are to go by the UN's latest report, the current situation is only going to get worse unless steps are taken to mitigate the crisis. The sharing of data and information between governments, and between governments and civil society, will be critical to planning for this new and uncertain water future.

THE GLOBAL WATER CRISIS AND THE COMING BATTLE FOR THE RIGHT TO WATER

The three water crises – dwindling freshwater supplies, inequitable access to water and the corporate control of water – pose the greatest threat of our time to the planet and to our survival. Together with impending climate change from fossil fuel emissions, the water crises impose some life-or-death decisions on us all. Unless we collectively change our behavior, we are heading toward a world of deepening conflict and potential wars over the dwindling supplies of freshwater – between nations, between rich and poor, between the public and the private interest, between rural and urban populations, and between the competing needs of the natural world and industrialized humans.

Water Is Becoming a Growing Source of Conflict Between Countries

Around the world, more that 215 major rivers and 300 groundwater basins and aquifers are shared by two or more countries, creating tensions over ownership and use of the precious waters they contain. Growing shortages and unequal distribution of water are causing disagreements, sometimes violent, and becoming a security risk in many regions. Britain's former defense secretary, John Reid, warns of coming "water wars. In a public statement on the eve of a 2006 summit on climate change, Reid predicted that violence and political conflict would become more likely as watersheds turn to deserts, glaciers melt and water supplies are poisoned. He went so far as to say that the global water crisis was becoming a global security issue and that Britain's armed forces should be prepared to tackle conflicts, including warfare, over dwindling water sources. "Such changes make the emergence of violent conflict more, rather than less, likely, former British prime minister Tony Blair told The Independent. "The blunt truth is that the lack of water and agricultural land is a significant contributory factor to the tragic conflict we see unfolding in Darfur. We should see this as a warning sign.

The Independent gave several other examples of regions of potential conflict. These include Israel, Jordan and Palestine, who all rely on the Jordan River, which is controlled by Israel; Turkey and Syria, where Turkish plans to build dams on the Euphrates River brought the country to the brink of war with Syria in 1998, and where Syria now accuses Turkey of deliberately meddling with its water supply; China and India, where the Brahmaputra River has caused tension between the two countries in the past, and where China's proposal to divert the river is re-igniting the divisions; Angola, Botswana and Namibia, where disputes over the Okavango water basin that have flared in the past are now threatening to re-ignite as Namibia is proposing to build a threehundred- kilometer pipeline that will drain the delta; Ethiopia and Egypt, where population growth is threatening conflict along the Nile; and Bangladesh and India, where flooding in the Ganges caused by melting glaciers in the Himalayas is wreaking havoc in Bangladesh, leading to a rise in illegal, and unpopular, migration to India.

While not likely to lead to armed conflict, stresses are growing along the U.S.-Canadian border over shared boundary waters. In particular, concerns are growing over the future of the Great Lakes, whose waters are becoming increasingly polluted and whose water tables are being steadily drawn down by the huge buildup of population and industry around the basin. A joint commission set up to oversee these waters was recently bypassed by the governors of the American states bordering the Great Lakes, who passed an amendment to the treaty governing the lakes that allows for water diversions to new communities off the basin on the American side. Canadian protests fell on deaf ears in Washington. In 2006, the U.S. government announced plans to have the U.S. coast guard patrol the Great Lakes using machine guns mounted on their vessels and revealed that it had created thirty-four permanent live-fire training zones along the Great Lakes from where it had already conducted a number of automatic weapons drills due to fierce opposition, firing three thousand lead bullets each time into the lakes. The Bush administration has temporarily called off these drills but is clearly asserting U.S. authority over what has in the past been considered joint waters.

Similar trouble is brewing on the U.S.-Mexican border, where a private group of U.S.–based water rights holders is using the North American Free Trade Agreement to challenge the long-term practice by Mexican farmers to divert water from the Rio Grande before it reaches the United States.

WATER IS BECOMING A GLOBAL SECURITY ISSUE

The United States

Water has recently (and suddenly) become a key strategic security and foreign policy priority for the United States. In the wake of the terrorist attacks of 9-11, protection of U.S. waterways and drinking water supplies from terrorist attack became vitally important to the White House. When Congress created the Department of Homeland Security in 2002, it gave the department responsibility for securing the nation's water infrastructure and allocated us$548 million in appropriations for security of water infrastructure facilities, funding that was increased in subsequent years. The Environmental Protection Agency created a National Homeland Security Research Center to develop the scientific foundations and tools to be used in the event of an attack on the nation's water systems, and a Water Security Division was established to train water utility personnel on security issues. It also created a Water Information Sharing and Analysis Center for dissemination of alerts about potential threats to drinking water and, with the American Water Works Association, a rapid e-mail notification system for professionals called the Water Security Channel. Ever true to market economy ideology, the Department of Homeland Security's mandate includes promoting publicprivate partnerships in protecting the nation's water security.

But the interest in water did not stop there. Water is becoming as important a strategic issue as energy in Washington. In an August 2004 briefing note for the Institute for the Analysis of Global Security, a think tank that focuses on the link between energy and security, Dr. Allan R. Hoffman, a senior analyst for the U.S. Department of Energy, declared that the energy security of the United States actually depends on the state of its water resources and warns of a growing water-security crisis worldwide. "Just as energy security became a national priority in the period following the Arab Oil Embargo of 1973–74, water security is destined to become a national and global priority in the decades ahead, says Hoffman. He notes that central to addressing water security issues is finding the energy to extract water from underground aquifers, transport water through pipelines and canals, manage and treat water for reuse and desalinate brackish and sea water – all technologies now being promoted by U.S. government partnerships with American companies. He also points out that the U.S. energy interests in the Middle East could be threatened by water conflicts in the region: Water conflicts add to the instability of a region on which the U.S. depends heavily for oil.

Continuation or inflammation of these conflicts could subject U.S. energy supplies to blackmail again, as occurred in the 1970s. Water shortages and global warning pose a "serious threat to America's national security, top retired military leaders told the president in an April 2007 report published by the national security think tank cna Corporation. Six retired admirals and five retired generals warned of a future of rampant water wars into which the United States will be dragged. Erik Peterson, director of the Global Strategy Institute of the Center for Strategic and International

Studies, a research organization in Washington that calls itself a strategic planning partner for the government, says that the United States must make water a top priority in foreign policy. "There is a very, very critical dimension to all these global water problems here at home, he told Voice of America News. "The first is that it's in our national interest to see stability and security and economic development in key areas of the world, and water is a big factor with that whole set of challenges. His center has joined forces with itt Industries, the giant water technology company; Proctor & Gamble, which has created a home water purifier called pur and is working with the un in a joint publicprivate venture in developing countries; Coca-Cola; and Sandia National Laboratories to launch a joint-research institute called Global Water Futures (gwf). Sandia, whose motto is "securing a peaceful and free world through technology and that works to "maintain U.S. military and nuclear superiority, is contracted out to weapons manufacturer Lockheed Martin by the U.S. government, to operate, thus linking water security to military security in a direct way.

The mandate of Global Water Futures is twofold: to affect U.S. strategy and policy regarding the global water crisis and to develop the technology necessary to advance the solution. In a September 2005 report, Global Water Futures warned that the global water crisis is driving the world toward "a tipping point in human history, and elaborated on the need for the United States to start taking water security more seriously: In light of the global trends in water, it is clear that water quality and water management will affect almost every major U.S. strategic priority in every key region of the world. Addressing the world's water needs will go well beyond humanitarian and economic development interests.... Policies focused on water in regions across the planet must be regarded as a critical element in U.S. national security strategy. Such policies should be part of a broader, comprehensive, and integrated U.S. strategy toward the global water challenges.

Innovations in policy and technology must be tightly linked, says the report, no doubt music to the ears of the corporations that sponsored it. gwf calls for closer innovation and cooperation between governments and the private sector and "redoubled efforts to mobilize public-private partnerships in the development of technological solutions.

And, in language that will be familiar to critics of the Bush administration who argue that the United States is not in Iraq to promote democracy, but rather to secure oil resources and make huge profits for American companies in the "rebuilding effort, the report links upholding American values of democracy with the profit to be gained in the process: Water issues are critical to U.S. national security and integral to upholding American values of humanitarianism and democratic development. Moreover, engagement with international water issues guarantees business opportunity for the U.S. private sector, which is well positioned to contribute to development and reap economic reward. Listed among the U.S. government agencies engaged in water issues in the report is the Department of Commerce, which facilitates U.S. water businesses and market research, and improves U.S. competitiveness in the international water market.

BLUE COVENANT: THE ALTERNATIVE WATER FUTURE

Humanity still has a chance to head off these scenarios of conflict and war. We could start with a global covenant on water. The Blue Covenant should have three components: a water conservation covenant from people and their governments that recognizes the right of the Earth and of other species to clean water, and pledges to protect and conserve the world's water supplies; a water justice covenant between those in the global North who have water and resources and those in the global South who do not, to work in solidarity for water justice, water for all and local control of water; and a water democracy covenant among all governments acknowledging that water is a fundamental human right for all. Therefore, governments are required not only to provide clean water to their citizens as a public service, but they must also recognize that citizens of other countries have the right to water as well and to find peaceful solutions to water disputes between states. A good example of this is the Good Water Makes Good Neighbors project of Friends of the Earth Middle East, which seeks to use shared water and the notion of water justice to negotiate a wider peace accord in the region. Another example is the successful restoration of the beautiful Lake Constance by Germany, Austria, Lichtenstein and Switzerland, the four countries that share it.

The Blue Covenant should also form the heart of a new covenant on the right to water to be adopted both in nation-state constitutions and in international law at the United Nations. To create the conditions for this covenant will require a concerted and collective international collaboration and will have to tackle all three water crises together with the alternatives: Water Conservation, Water Justice, and Water Democracy.

4

Water Security

Water security has been defined as "the reliable availability of an acceptable quantity and quality of water for health, livelihoods and production, coupled with an acceptable level of water-related risks." Sustainable development will not be achieved without a water secure world. A water secure world integrates a concern for the intrinsic value of water with a concern for its use for human survival and well-being. A water secure world harnesses water's productive power and minimises its destructive force. Water security also means addressing environmental protection and the negative effects of poor management. It is also concerned with ending fragmented responsibility for water and integrating water resources management across all sectors – finance, planning, agriculture, energy, tourism, industry, education and health. A water secure world reduces poverty, advances education, and increases living standards. It is a world where there is an improved quality of life for all, especially for the most vulnerable—usually women and children—who benefit most from good water governance.

BACKGROUND

According to the Pacific Institute "While regional impacts will vary, global climate change will potentially alter agricultural productivity, freshwater availability and quality, access to vital minerals, coastal and island flooding, and more. Among the consequences of these impacts will be challenges to political relationships, realignment of energy markets and regional economies, and threats to security". It impacts regions, states and countries. Tensions exist between upstream and downstream users of water within individual jurisdictions.

During history there has been much conflict over use of water from rivers such as the Tigris and Euphrates Rivers. Another highly politicized example is Israel's control of water resources in the Levant region since its creation, where Israel securing its water resources was one of several drivers for the 1967 Six Day War.

Water security is sometimes sought by implementing water desalination, pipelines between sources and users, water licences with different security levels and war.

Water allocation between competing users is increasingly determined by application of market-based pricing for either water licenses or actual water.

Fresh Water

Water, in absolute terms, is not in short supply planet-wide. But, according to the United Nations water organization, UN-Water, the total usable freshwater supply for ecosystems and humans is only about 200,000 km3 of water – less than one percent (<1%) of all freshwater resources. And, water use has been growing at more than twice the rate of the population increase in the last century. Specifically, water withdrawals are predicted to increase by 50 percent by 2025 in developing countries, and 18 per cent in developed countries. By 2025, 800 million people will be living in countries or regions with absolute water scarcity, and two-thirds of the world population could be under stress conditions.

Research

According to *Nature* (2010), about 80% of the world's population (5.6 billion in 2011) live in areas with threats to water security. The water security is a shared threat to human and nature and it is pandemic. Human water-management strategies can be detrimental to wildlife, such as migrating fish. Regions with intensive agriculture and dense populations, such as the US and Europe, have a high threat of water security. Researchers estimate that during 2010-2015, ca US$800 billion will be required to cover the annual global investment in water infrastructure. Good management of water resources can jointly manage biodiversity protection and human water security. Preserving flood plains rather than constructing flood-control reservoirs would provide a cost-effective way to control floods while protecting the biodiversity of wildlife that occupies such areas.

Lawrence Smith, the president of the population institute, asserts that although an overwhelming majority of the planet is composed of water, 97% of this water is constituted of saltwater; the fresh water used to sustain humans is only 3% of the total amount of water on Earth.

Therefore, Smith believes that the competition for water in an overpopulated world would pose a major threat to human stability, even going so far as to postulate apocalyptic world wars being fought over the control of thinning ice sheets and nearly desiccated reservoirs. Nevertheless, 2 billion people have supposedly gained access to a safe water source since 1990 who may have earlier lacked it. The proportion of people in developing countries with access to safe water is calculated to have improved from 30 percent in 1970 to 71 percent in 1990, 79 percent in 2000 and 84 percent in 2004, parallel with rising population. This trend is projected to continue.

The Earth has a limited though renewable supply of fresh water, stored in aquifers, surface waters and the atmosphere. Oceans are a good source of usable water, but the amount of energy needed to convert saline water to potable water is prohibitive with conventional approaches, explaining why only a very small fraction of the world's water supply is derived from desalination. However, modern technologies, such as the Seawater Greenhouse, use solar energy to desalinate seawater for agriculture and drinking uses in an extremely cost-effective manner.

MOST AFFECTED COUNTRIES

Based on the map published by the Consultative Group on International Agricultural Research (CGIAR), the countries and regions suffering most water stress are North Africa, the Middle East, India, Central Asia, China, Chile, Colombia, South Africa and Australia. Water scarcity is also increasing in South Asia.

International Competition

More than 50 countries on five continents are said to be at risk of conflict over water.

Turkey's Southeastern Anatolia Project (Guneydogu Anadolu Projesi, or GAP) on the Euphrates has potentially serious consequences for water supplies in Syria and Iraq.

INTRA-NATIONAL COMPETITION

Australia

In Australia there is competition for the resources of the Darling River system between Queensland, New South Wales and South Australia.

In Victoria, Australia a proposed pipeline from the Goulburn Valley to Melbourne has led to protests by farmers.

In the Macquarie Marshes of NSW grazing and irrigation interests compete for water flowing to the marshes

The Snowy Mountains Scheme diverted water from the Snowy River to the Murray River and the Murrumbidgee River for the benefit of irrigators and electricity generation through hydro-electric power. During recent years government has taken action to increase environmental flows to the Snowy in spite of severe drought in the Murray Darling Basin. The Australian Government has implemented buy-backs of water allocations, or properties with water allocations, to endeavour to increase environmental flows.

Blue Peace

Blue Peace is a method which seeks to transforms trans-boundary water issues into instruments for cooperation. This unique approach to turn tensions around water into opportunities for socio-economic development was developed by Strategic Foresight Group in partnership with the Governments of Switzerland and Sweden.

"The Blue Peace is an innovative approach to engage political leaders, diplomats and populations in harnessing and managing collaborative solutions for sustainable water management." –

Foreign Minister Didier Burkhalter of Swirtzerland, speaking at the UN General Assembly

CONVENTIONAL FOSSIL OR NUCLEAR ENERGY BASED DESALINATION

As new technological innovations continue to reduce the capital cost of desalination, more countries are building desalination plants as a small element in addressing their water crises.

- Israel desalinizes water for a cost of 53 cents per cubic meter
- Singapore desalinizes water for 49 cents per cubic meter and also treats sewage with reverse osmosis for industrial and potable use (NEWater).
- China and India, the world's two most populous countries, are turning to desalination to provide a small part of their water needs
- In 2007 Pakistan announced plans to use desalination
- All Australian capital cities (except Darwin, Northern Territory and Hobart) are either in the process of building desalination plants, or are already using them. In late 2011, Melbourne will begin using Australia's largest desalination plant, the Wonthaggi desalination plant to raise low reservoir levels.
- In 2007 Bermuda signed a contract to purchase a desalination plant
- The largest desalination plant in the United States is the one at Tampa Bay, Florida, which began desalinizing 25 million gallons (95000 m^3) of water per day in December 2007. In the United States, the cost of desalination is $3.06 for 1,000 gallons, or 81 cents per cubic meter. In the United States, California, Arizona, Texas, and Florida use desalination for a very small part of their water supply.
- After being desalinized at Jubail, Saudi Arabia, water is pumped 200 miles (320 km) inland though a pipeline to the capital city ofRiyadh.

A January 17, 2008, article in the *Wall Street Journal* states, "World-wide, 13,080 desalination plants produce more than 12 billion gallons of water a day, according to the International Desalination Association."

The world's largest desalination plant is the Jebel Ali Desalination Plant (Phase 2) in the United Arab Emirates. It is a dual-purpose facility that uses multi-stage flash distillation and is capable of producing 300 million cubic meters of water per year.

A typical aircraft carrier in the U.S. military uses nuclear power to desalinize 400,000 US gallons (1,500,000 L) of water per day.

While desalinizing 1,000 US gallons (3,800 L) of water can cost as much as $3, the same amount of bottled water costs $7,945.

However, given the energy intensive nature of desalination, with associated economic and environmental costs, desalination is generally considered a last resort after water conservation. But this is changing as prices continue to fall.

According to MSNBC, a report by Lux Research estimated that the worldwide desalinated water supply will triple between 2008 and 2020.

However, not everyone is convinced that desalination is or will be economically viable or environmentally sustainable for the foreseeable future. Debbie Cook, the former mayor of Huntington Beach, California, has been a frequent critic of desalination proposals ever since she was appointed as a member of the California Desalination Task Force. Cook claims that in addition to being energy intensive, desalination schemes are very costly—often much more costly than desalination proponents claim. In her writing on the subject, Cook points to a long list of projects that have stalled or been aborted for financial or other reasons, and suggests that water-stressed regions would do better to focus on conservation or other water supply solutions than to invest in desalination plants.

SOLAR ENERGY BASED DESALINATION

A novel approach to desalination is the Seawater Greenhouse which takes seawater and uses solar energy to desalinate it in conjunction with growing food crops in a specially adapted greenhouse.

WATER SECURITY AND EMERGENCY PREPAREDNESS

Water security consists of the systems and actions required to protect a water supply from natural disasters, security threats, accidental and intentional contamination, and other vulnerabilities.

Water Utility Security

According to the United States Environmental Protection Agency (EPA), "Improving the security of our nation's drinking water and wastewater infrastructures has become a top priority since the events of 9/11.

Significant actions are underway to assess and reduce vulnerabilities to potential terrorist attacks; to plan for and practice response to emergencies and incidents; and to develop new security technologies to detect and monitor contaminants and prevent security breaches."

One of the most important elements of water security is early and accurate contamination detection. The EPA has issued advisory material and guidelines for contamination warning systems to be implemented in water utilities and supplies. The security challenges that utilities frequently revolve around fast detection, accuracy, and the ability to take fast action when there is a water problem. If contamination is detected early enough, it can be prevented from reaching consumers, and emergency water supplies can be put into effect.

In cases where contamination might still reach consumers, fast and efficient communication systems are necessary. All these factors also point to the need for organized and practiced emergency procedures and preparedness.

Regulation

Since 2002, under the Bioterrorism Act, a water utility supplying more than 3,300 people must take at least the following measures to ensure security of the water supply:

- Conduct an assessment of the facility's vulnerabilities to vandalism, insider sabotage, or terrorist attack, and submit the report to the EPA.

- Show that the facility has an up-to-date emergency response plan, should an incident occur.

More recently, under the Drinking Water Security Act of 2009, the EPA is now required to establish risk-based performance standards for community water systems serving more than 3,300 people.

Cincinnati Water Works, San Francisco, and New York City are among the major water utilities that have taken water security measures at their facilities, such as planning for contamination warning systems.

Water Utility Security Components

Security of a water supply involves a range of elements. Prevention and detection systems include some or all of the following: access to public health and customer complaint data, water quality monitoring equipment, sampling and analysis, cyber-security which includes situation management and IT systems hardware and software, and physical security. Crisis management and recovery, for when critical water events occur, includes flow control and security valves, rapid and effective communication systems, and emergency water supply equipment.

Specific technologies involved in water security are SCADA, GIS (geographic information system), online (real-time) water quality monitoring devices, contamination warning systems, intrusion detection systems (IDS), contamination detection devices, security valves, security cameras and fences, situation management/ emergency management software, emergency supply tanks, manned (or human) security personnel, personal purification devices, and counter-terrorism intelligence.

Notable Water Security Organizations

The Water Information Sharing and Analysis Center (WaterISAC), is the US water sector's security and emergency response information source. This nonprofit service provides US, Canadian, and Australian drinking water and wastewater utilities with the information they need to heighten the protection of water collection and delivery infrastructure. WaterISAC is also a peer-to-peer, business networking platform. Eligible members of the water sector have access to a clearinghouse of government and private documents, guides, best practices, handbooks, and contaminant databases as well as shared data including analysis of successful and failed security incidents within the water sector. These include cyber incidents, physical incidents, and other security related incidents. Many but not all of these are reported to and tracked by WaterISAC. Together, these resources are can be used by utility managers to identify risks, prepare for emergencies, and secure the nation's critical water infrastructure and the environment.

American Water Works Association

International Water Association (IWA), a global network of 10,000 water professionals spanning the continuum between research and practice and covering all facets of thewater cycle.

5

Asia's Water Stress Challenges Growth and Security

Water, the most vital of all resources, has emerged as a key issue that will determine whether Asia is headed toward cooperation or competition. After all, the driest continent in the world is not Africa, but Asia, where availability of freshwater is not even half the global annual average of 6,380 cubic meters per inhabitant.

When the estimated reserves of rivers, lakes and aquifers are added up, Asia has less than one-tenth of the waters of South America, Australia and New Zealand, not even one-fourth of North America, almost one-third of Europe and moderately less than Africa per inhabitant. Yet the world's fastest-growing demand for water for food and industrial production and for municipal supply is in Asia, which now serves as the locomotive of the world economy.

Today, the fastest-growing Asian economies are all at or near water-stressed conditions, including China, India, South Korea, Vietnam and Indonesia. But just three or four decades ago, these economies were relatively free of water stress. Now if we look three or four decades ahead, it is clear that the water situation will only exacerbate, carrying major implications for rapid economic growth and inter-riparian relations.

Yet Asia continues to draw on tomorrow's water to meet today's needs. Worse still, Asia has one of the lowest levels of water efficiency and productivity in the world. Against this background, it is no exaggeration to say that the water crisis threatens Asia's economic and political rise and its environmental sustainability. For investors, it carries risks that potentially are as damaging as nonperforming loans, real estate bubbles and political corruption. Water has also emerged as a source of increasing competition and discord within and between nations, spurring new tensions over shared basin resources and local resistance to governmental or corporate decisions to set up water-intensive industries.

These developments raise the question whether the risks of water conflict are higher in Asia than elsewhere in the world. With Asia becoming the scene of increasingly fierce intrastate and interstate water competition, the answer clearly is yes. Water is a new arena in the Asian Great Game.

In fact, water wars — in a political, diplomatic, or economic sense — are already being waged between riparian neighbors in several Asian regions, fuelling a cycle of bitter recrimination and fostering mistrust that impedes broader regional cooperation and integration. Without any shots being fired, rising costs continue to be exacted. The resources of transnational rivers, aquifers and lakes have become the target of rival appropriation plans.

With a river or groundwater basin often becoming tied with a nation's identity, ownership and control over its resources is considered crucial to national interests. That has helped give rise to grand but environmentally questionable ideas — from China's Great Western Route to divert river waters from the Tibetan Plateau to its parched north and South Korea's politically divisive four-rivers project, to India's now-stalled proposal to link up its important rivers and Jordan's plan to save the dying Dead Sea by bringing water from the Red Sea through a 178-km canal, which is also to serve as a source for desalinated drinking water.

Several factors have contributed to the Asian water crisis, which is leading to river and aquifer degradation. One is that Asia is not only the largest and most-populous continent but also the fastest developing. How the swift economic rise of Asia has brought water resources under increasing pressure can be seen from the fact that most Asian economies now are water-stressed.

The exceptions are few: Bhutan, Burma, Papua New Guinea, Laos, Cambodia, Brunei and Malaysia.

Unlike the fossils fuels, mineral ores and timber that they import even from distant lands, the Asian economies must make do with their own water resources, a significant share of which is in transnational watercourses. This fact only serves as a strong incentive for some nations to try and commandeer internationally shared waters before they leave their national borders. Given the critical role of water in economic modernization, this continent has emerged at the centre of the global water challenges.

Another factor is consumption growth, as a consequence of rising prosperity. The plain fact is that on average Asians are consuming more resources, including water, food, oil and energy. The consumption growth is best illustrated by the changing diets, especially the greater intake of meat, whose production is notoriously water-intensive.

A third factor is the role of irrigation in accentuating the Asian water stress. Asia more than doubled its total irrigated cropland just between 1960 and 2000. Once a continent of serious food shortages and recurrent famines, Asia opened the path to its dramatic economic rise by emerging as a net food exporter on the back of this unparalleled irrigation expansion.

Asia now boasts the leonine proportion of the world's surface land under irrigation. About 70 percent of the world's 301 million hectares of land equipped for irrigation is in Asia alone, making it the global irrigation hub. Just three sub-regions of Asia — South Asia, China and Southeast Asia — by themselves account for about 50 percent of the world's total irrigated land.

It is thus hardly a surprise that Asia leads the world in the total volume of freshwater withdrawn for agriculture. Indeed, almost 74 percent of the total global freshwater withdrawals for agriculture by volume are made in Asia alone.

Water literally is food in Asia. Yet the growth of rice and wheat output in Asia, after the dramatic increases of the previous quarter-century, has actually slowed since the late 1990s, raising concerns that Asian countries will become major food importers, roiling the international market. The international food market is not large enough to meet major import demands from Asia. A fourth factor is that the fastest increase in water demand in Asia is now coming not from agriculture but from the industrial sector and urban households, in keeping with the fact that this continent has become the seat of the world's fastest industrialization and urbanization.

A final factor linked to Asia's water stress is the large-scale impoundment of water resources through dams, barrages, reservoirs and other human-made structures without factoring in long-term environmental considerations.

Dams, to be sure, bring important benefits. But upstream dams on rivers shared by two or more nations or provinces in an era of growing water stress often carry broader political and social implications, especially because they can affect water quality and quantity downstream. Dams can also alter fluvial ecosystems, damage biodiversity and promote coastal erosion and saltwater intrusion.

Asia is not just the global irrigation hub; it is also the world's most dam-dotted continent.

China, the world's biggest dam builder, alone has slightly more than half of the approximately 50,000 large dams on the planet.

Most of the best dam sites in Asia already have been taken. Yet the numerous new dam projects in Asia show that the damming of rivers is still an important priority for policymakers. Such a focus on dam building has only intensified intrastate and interstate water disputes and tensions in Asia, with implications for regional security and stability.

The countries likely to bear the brunt of upstream diversion of waters are those located farthest downstream on rivers like the Brahmaputra, Mekong and Tigris-Euphrates: Bangladesh, whose very future is threatened by climate and environmental change; Vietnam, a rice bowl of Asia; and Iraq, still internally torn. Cross-border water appropriations from the Illy River threaten to turn Kazakhstan's Lake Balkhash into another Aral Sea, which is dying.

So, the big question is: How can Asian nations prevent the sharpening struggle for water resources from becoming a tipping point for overt conflict? To contain the security risks, Asian states must invest more in institutionalized cooperation on trans-boundary basin resources in order to underpin strategic stability, protect continued economic growth and promote environmental sustainability.

The harsh truth is that only four of the 57 transnational river basins in Asia have a treaty covering water sharing or other institutionalized cooperation. These are the Mekong, Ganges, Indus and Jordan river basins. The absence of a cooperative arrangement in most Asian transnational basins is making inter-country water competition a major security risk, increasing the likelihood of geopolitical tensions and instabilities.

With its multitude of inter-country basins, Asia cannot continue to prosper without building political and technological partnerships to help stabilize inter-riparian relations, encourage greater water efficiency, promote environmental sustainability, take on practicable conservation strategies, and invest in clean-water technologies. If Asian states are to address their water challenges, they will need to embrace good practices on the strategic planning and management of water resources.

THE RISKS ARISING FROM ASIA'S WATER STRESS

Water, the most vital of all resources, has emerged as a key issue that would determine if Asia is headed toward cooperation or competition. After all, the driest continent in the world is not Africa but Asia, where availability of freshwater is not even half the global annual average of 6,380 cubic metres per inhabitant.

When the estimated reserves of rivers, lakes, and aquifers are added up, Asia has less than one-tenth of the waters of South America, Australia and New Zealand, not even one-fourth of North America, almost one-third of Europe, and moderately less than Africa per inhabitant. Yet the world's fastest-growing demand for water for food and industrial production and for municipal supply is in Asia, which now serves as the locomotive of the world economy.

Today, the fastest-growing Asian economies are all at or near water-stressed conditions, including China, India, South Korea, Vietnam, and Indonesia. But just three or four decades ago, these economies were relatively free of water stress. Now if we look three or four decades ahead, it is clear that the water situation will only exacerbate, carrying major implications for rapid economic growth and inter-riparian relations.

MOST NUMBER OF DAMS

Asia is not just the global irrigation hub; it is also the world's most dam-dotted continent. China, the world's biggest dam builder, alone has slightly more than half of the approximately 50,000 large dams on the planet.

Most of the best dam sites in Asia already have been taken. Yet the numerous new dam projects in Asia show that the damming of rivers is still an important priority for policymakers. Such a focus on dam building has only intensified intrastate and interstate water disputes and tensions in Asia, with implications for regional security and stability.

The countries likely to bear the brunt of upstream diversion of waters are those located farthest downstream on rivers like the Brahmaputra, Mekong, and Tigris-Euphrates: Bangladesh, whose very future is threatened by climate and environmental change; Vietnam, a rice bowl of Asia; and Iraq, still internally torn.

Cross-border water appropriations from the Illy River threaten to turn Kazakhstan's Lake Balkhash into another Aral Sea, which is dying.

A Way Out

So, the big question is: How can Asian nations prevent the sharpening struggle for water resources from becoming a tipping point for overt conflict? To contain the security risks, Asian states must invest more in institutionalised cooperation on transboundary basin resources in order to underpin strategic stability, protect continued economic growth, and promote environmental sustainability.

The harsh truth is that only four of the 57 transnational river basins in Asia have a treaty covering water sharing or other institutionalised cooperation. These are the Mekong, Ganges, Indus and Jordan river basins. The absence of a cooperative arrangement in most Asian transnational basins is making inter-country water competition a major security risk, increasing the likelihood of geopolitical tensions and instabilities.

With its multitude of inter-country basins, Asia cannot continue to prosper without building political and technological partnerships to help stabilise inter-riparian relations, encourage greater water efficiency, promote environmental sustainability, take on practicable conservation strategies, and invest in clean-water technologies. If Asian states are to address their water challenges, they will need to embrace good practices on the strategic planning and management of water resources.

6

The Compound Water-Energy-Food Crisis Risks in Central Asia

Over 40 representatives of international organizations, including United Nations agencies and international financial institutions, and of bilateral donor agencies, including Russia, met in Almaty at the invitation of the United Nations Development Program (UNDP) on July 21-22, 2008. They reviewed available evidence of the current water, energy and food situation in Central Asia and agreed on a joint response to the risk of what is commonly now referred to as a potential "compound crisis of water, energy and food security facing the region."

At the Almaty meeting, the World Bank reported on the findings of a preliminary situation analysis that it prepared in July 2008 based on readily available information from public sources and regional institutions. Key findings of this preliminary analysis, which focused mostly on Kyrgyzstan, Tajikistan and Uzbekistan, is summarized here with permission from the World Bank, are as follows:

- Precipitation: Tajikistan, west and south Kyrgyzstan and most of Afghanistan received up to 50% less than average precipitation between September 2007 and July 2008; east Kyrgyzstan received around 25% more than average, and Uzbekistan and Turkmenistan received at least that much or more.
- Snow cover: Judging from satellite images, regional snow cover in June 2008 were slightly lower than in June 2006.

- Temperatures: Between April and July 2008, temperatures were significantly higher than average in much of the region, including Afghanistan, but less so in early July.
- River flows: For Amu Darya River, flows in the main upper tributaries were generally somewhat higher than average, in spite of lower than average rainfall in the upper Amu Darya catchment, so probably due to increased snow and glacier melt as a result of high temperatures; downstream Amu Darya River flow was lower than average, but rising towards average flow levels in July 2008. For Syr Darya River, average flows downstream from Toktogul Reservoir were substantially less in 2008 than average, possibly because of low water releases from Toktogul Reservoir.
- Reservoir levels: The principal reservoir on Amu Darya in Tajikistan, Nurek, was much below average levels for much of 2008, but its level was rapidly rising in June and July 2008; it is expected to reach its capacity in full by September. Latest data on the principal reservoir on Syr Darya, Toktogul, in July show that the reservoir level is significantly below the 20-year minimum and is not expected to reach normal capacity this year; reservoirs below Toktogul appear at or above full capacity.
- Vegetation: Vegetation indices (an indicator for crop water stress in rain-fed areas) for Central Asia are somewhat below average overall for Central Asia, but better in some areas (especially in Uzbekistan).

Based on these observations, the current assessment is that the prospects for water availability and crop production in the irrigated areas of Amu Darya basin are likely to be close to normal this year, although rain fed agriculture and livestock in Tajikistan and west Kyrgyzstan may suffer drought conditions. Water availability in the Syr Darya basin downstream of Toktogul could be significantly less than normal this year. Prospects for energy availability in the coming winter could be somewhat better in Tajikistan in 2008/9 compared to the disastrous last winter. In Kyrgyzstan, the energy outlook is serious for the coming winter.

The World Bank also highlighted steps which the governments of Kyrgyzstan and Tajikistan could take to minimize the risk of water and energy related problems: carefully managed release of water this summer, early rationing of power use and imports of power from neighbors this fall, securing fuel and power import supplies for winter use and power tariff increases to help limit demand and generate the financial means to pay for imports.

Overall, the Almaty meeting concluded that while there was at this point no apparent region-wide threat of drought conditions, a combination of factors— chronic water and energy shortages in parts of Central Asia combined with the area-specific drought conditions and hence threats to agricultural production in rain-fed parts of Tajikistan and Kyrgyzstan (and possibly in the areas of Uzbekistan and Kazakhstan irrigated with waters from the Syr Darya), continuing energy shortages in Tajikistan and Kyrgyz, and generally rising energy and food prices—could have serious economic and social consequences for large parts of Central Asia, and especially in the poorest countries, Kyrgyzstan and Tajikistan.

Therefore the participants of the Almaty meeting agreed to commission a quick but comprehensive assessment of water, energy and food security risks in Central Asia under the auspices of UNDP. The terms of references for this assessment have now been issued and applications by experts have been invited (read the Terms of Reference). The assessment is to take stock of the water, energy and food situation and outlook in the region and consider possible responses by Central Asian governments and by the international community. A report is to be prepared by mid-October for presentation at a possible follow-up meeting. In the meantime, UNDP will lead consultations with the concerned Central Asian governments to ensure that their engagement is assured and country-specific information and concerns are fully considered.

In sum, the response of the international community to an apparent threat of a compound crisis of water, energy and food security in Central Asia has been swift. It promises a much-enhanced readiness of the governments of the region and of their international partners to respond with appropriate policies and interventions to minimize the hardships that will likely be experienced by significant segments of the region's population in the coming months. It is also to be hoped, and recommended, that the comprehensive information that has now been compiled as a special effort will be routinely collected and disseminated in the future so as to allow all concerned national and international agencies to be prepared for any pending disaster risks. With the impact of global warming negatively affecting the long-term water, energy and food prospects of the region, this will become an important element of regional disaster preparedness in Central Asia. In addition, of course, it is also critical that other long-term water and energy issues be addressed, including expansion of hydro-power capacity and much greater efforts to use the region's limited and energy resources of the region more efficiently than is currently the case.

UNSUSTAINABLE WATER USE IN UZBEKISTAN'S COTTON INDUSTRY

For generations cotton has remained the driving force behind Uzbekistan's agricultural economy that has made the country the world's 3nd largest exporter of cotton, creating a wealth of foreign exchange for the Uzbek government. Much of the cotton exports are destined for Europe. However, the cotton industry has not prospered without a deep cost, with the legacy of demise of the Aral Sea directly linked to irrigation projects built during the later stages of the Soviet era. Uzbekistan's large "monoculture" cotton industry has come under fire from a variety of international critics for its labor practices, especially is use of child labor as well as for using cotton revenues to enrich the entrenched regime. The country has also bee criticized for resisting major land reform that could give Uzbek farmers more freedom to prosper from access to international markets. Instead the Uzbek government has only modified the state driven system of agriculture it inherited from the Soviet Union.

Cotton and other agricultural goods in Uzbekistan are threatened by a series of environmental and infrastructure risks that will put future rural prosperity and development at risk. The large irrigation system is literally falling apart due to neglect and gross mismanagement. Farmers must struggle to get enough water as leaks and illegal water diversions prevent half of the irrigated water from reaching its intended destination. Crop yields are also suffering from increasing salinization of the soil and flooding of fields and rising groundwater known as water logging. When combined with the future impact of climate change, worsening soil conditions will make farmers' lives increasing difficult in the naturally arid climate. This is an example of a mismanaged water system, and its consequences for regional cooperation and environmental sustainability.

State Run Industry

Unlike several of its Central Asian neighbors, Uzbekistan has held onto much of the Soviet era agricultural system, with centrally directed production quotas and government owned enterprises that control the marketing of cotton to international traders. The system is tightly run from top officials making it subject to many abuses, and international civil society groups have brought complaints of child labor and forced labor used to pick the annual fall cotton crop.

After independence, Uzbekistan moved from the Soviet system of collective farms to a cooperative setup where former state workers owned a share of the new company. Over time little changed in terms of farm management and the leases to the land are still owned by the state.

Likewise, production quotas for cotton still come from the central state officials, and failure to deliver on crop production quotas could lead to severe sanctions. The Uzbek government has only made limited efforts at land reform and developing private farms.

Despite its strategic importance to Uzbekistan, the cotton industry is in relative decline along with the broader agricultural sector. In the first decade of independence cotton production fell by 16 percent. The number of hectares of land committed to cotton has been more than cut in half since Soviet days and crop yields also fell by 17 percent in 2003, as a result of a drought in 2001, according to data from the Food and Agriculture Organization.

Irrigation accounts for 90 percent of Uzbekistan's agricultural production, and uses 85 percent of all water resources in the country, water that is coming from upstream countries via the Syr Darya and Amu Darya river basins. Water use for Uzbek cotton is extremely wasteful as it takes nearly twice the global average of water to grow a kilogram of cotton harvested, due to poor irrigation practices. The irrigated cotton crop has also been a source of tension between Tajikistan and Uzbekistan. Upstream country Tajikistan insists its downstream neighbor must abandoned cotton in favor of less water intensive crops like wheat, corn and vegetables. Uzbekistan argues it has reduced its cotton acreage as far as it can, and moreover that cotton provides its poor rural population with jobs and income. The country also emphasizes that cotton and irrigated agriculture is a vital element in Uzbek culture and ought to be preserved.

Recent droughts during the last decade have raised the question of water use and its intensity for the cotton crop. However, lack of management controls makes monitoring water use at the farm level largely a mystery. German researchers made an estimate water use for crops like cotton, wheat and rice. The study projected major losses of water in cotton fields. Overall, water irrigation on Uzbek farms was viewed as inefficient with water losses approaching 30 percent. The Asian Development Bank is helping with an overhaul of Uzbekistan's water sector. The bank has identified major water management flaws such as overloaded water drainage and high groundwater levels which can damage agricultural land with high salt levels. ADB identified a number of key reforms including a national program to measure water irrigation and establishment of water use fees as an incentive to efficient water use. Uzbekistan says it has experimented with using new drip irrigation technology that is far more water efficient. But to revamp the system for the 1.1 million hectares of cotton could cost $8 billion, far beyond the country's capacity to finance a transition.

Irrigation System in Rapid Decay

The water irrigation and drainage infrastructure is crumbling quickly across Central Asia Construction practices during the Soviet era were inferior and countries failed to pay for the maintenance of the system and farmers are too poor to pay for major repairs.

Making significant repairs to the current irrigation system would cost nearly $24 billion according to a 2000 World Bank estimate. Uzbekistan must find financing from the international community and an early proposal to fund repairs through the state budget was rejected by donor countries. A World Bank field assessment in 2001 found canals were in rapid decline. Many of the irrigation canals and bridges have become structurally unsound. Irrigation infrastructure had deteriorated the most in at the end of canal systems, where farmers struggle to get adequate water and suffer from high salt levels in the water, which destroys the productivity of the soils. Drains are often overgrown and not been repaired for many years.

In Uzbekistan, political influence plays a rôle in who get enough water for crops. Smaller farmers believed the wealthier farms and cooperatives get the water first. This is mostly because the state managed cooperatives grow the strategic crops of cotton and wheat and get top priority in water distribution. Private farmers, who grow a more diverse number of crops are a lower priority for water and suffered during droughts and water shortages. Poor environmental management of the water system has led to salinization of the soil, which harms crop productivity. Higher salt levels come from the irrigated water in downstream countries and higher groundwater levels associated with water logging The Asian Development Bank has noted nearly half of all land in Uzbekistan has become salinized. Cotton yields can fall from a range of 20 percent to 80 percent on highly salinized land. Crop land also been abandoned in growing numbers because it simply become unproductive. A quarter of all farmland in some districts has been taken out of production due to increasing salt levels. Aggressive production targets have also contributed to salinization and lost income for farmers in Uzbekistan. Farmers with degraded soils have trouble meeting state quotas for cotton and wheat. They lose income as yields fall. Meanwhile government production quotas did not change, and sometimes were increased from year to year.

International institutions like the Asian Development Bank and the Global Environmental Facility have responded to the growing crisis of land degradation in Central Asia. A regional strategy was established in 2006 under the Central Asian Countries Initiative for Land Management (CACILM). It aims to boost rural incomes through investments in soil conservation and improved land management. Uzbekistan got a $3 million grant for land rehabilitation for salt damaged areas and improved conservation practices.

UPSTREAM COUNTRIES AND THE NEED FOR ENERGY

Downstream countries depend on upstream countries for water for irrigation purposes, but for the upstream countries, lack of cooperation when it comes to water management is an energy concern. As exporters of water to downstream countries for irrigation, who on their side are rich in oil and gas, Tajikistan and Kyrgyzstan on the other hand are struggling to meet their energy needs for electricity, especially in the cold winter months. They have tried to cope by arranging barter deals with their western neighbors, trading summer water releases and hydropower for coal and gas for fall and winter use. However, as downstream nations began to charge for oil and natural gas imports, the two countries began to alter their hydroelectric facilities' water flows, increasingly hoarding it in the growing months for winter release to generate electricity rather than pay ever rising energy import bills, raising political tensions with their downstream neighbors.

Kyrgyzstan and the Kambarata-2 hydroelectric Plan

In recent years, Kyrgyzstan has been cut short in not having enough power for the winter. Barter arrangements with neighboring countries have also broken down. The responsible intergovernmental bodies for water management is the Ministry of Energy and the Ministry of Natural Resources and the government has embarked on reforms to improve management and transparency in the water and energy sector, that gives hope that workable solutions may be feasible. In 1998, Kyrgyzstan and Uzbekistan signed an agreement to manage the Syr Darya water basin. This agreement governed the Toktogol complex, which permitted Kyrgyzstan to generate electricity. To prevent damaging water releases, a number of barter agreements were created to ship natural gas and coal to Kyrgyzstan in the winter. But these barter agreements were not followed and Kyrgyzstan sought to charge the downstream nations the full use of the water, which caused protests from the downstream countries. The barter agreements could never tackle the core question of water allocation and how to pay for the aging Soviet era dam and irrigation system. There remains a fundamental disagreement over the pricing of water versus other natural resources, which were sold in the region for full market value. Leaders of different countries were also suspicious of each other and did not trust the water agreements, which were promoted by international agencies like the World Bank.

Kyrgyzstan's parliament in 2001 passed a law on water pricing to the downstream countries, maintaining that water was property of the Kyrgyz state. The law also stipulated that downstream countries should pay for the maintenance of the dam and canal system. Uzbekistan and Kazakhstan objected saying it violated international law, and Kyrgyzstan eventually backed down from insisting that downstream countries pay for the full price of the river water. In 2008, Kazakhstan, Tajikistan and Kyrgyzstan signed a new set of barter agreements on supplies of water, oil and coal. The influence of the agreement was limited since Uzbekistan opted out. To complicate matters, Uzbekistan and Kazakhstan pulled out of the regional electrical grid in 2009.

In 2007, Kyrgyzstan resumed construction of the Kambarata-2 project, abandoned in the 1990s. The project was able to draw on a $300 million loan from Russia to help revive the country's economy and infrastructure. The first unit of the Kambarata-2 hydroelectric project will allow Kyrgyzstan to produce an additional 500 million to 700 million kilowatt hours per year of electricity. The country currently generates about 14 billion kilowatt-hours annually, and the increase in power production is destined for export to Russia and China. Kyrgyzstan's ambitions to control the flow of its rivers in order to generate more hydroelectric power are of particular concern to Uzbekistan, its immediate neighbor to the west and the most populous post-Soviet republic in Central Asia. Uzbekistan relies on rivers that originate or pass through Kyrgyzstan and its other mountainous neighbor, Tajikistan, to irrigate its arid cotton fields and farmland.

The Kambarata project is only the first of several projects planned along the Naryn River, which rises in the Tien Shan Mountains and is dammed at Toktogul, the largest reservoir in Kyrgyzstan, before running on to merge with another river to become the Syr Darya. The power plant has received critique from people inside Kyrgyzstan, especially energy experts who argue that the Kambarata dams are too expensive. Instead, Kyrgyzstan must look into developing its coal industry. Both Kyrgyzstan and Tajikistan, however, lack public debate over how water resources must be managed, as leaders make these decisions without the interference of public opinion.

Tajikistan and the Rogun Dam Controversy

Tajikistan is also suffering from chronic mismanagement of water resources. This is especially evident during the winter months, when the country faces electricity shortages and severe cold and darkness. In Tajikistan, the Ministry of Melioration and Water Resource as well as the Ministry of Energy and Industry are the responsible intergovernmental bodies for water management. However, the government and the Tajik Central Bank have come under international scrutiny after the International Monetary Fund (IMF) scandal. The IMF demanded that Tajikistan repay nearly $48 million after it accused the Tajik Central Bank of not providing accurate information about the country's financial state. This led to investors being more cautious about investing in hydroelectric projects. These projects have been a source of tension with Uzbekistan because it claims water supplies will be severely reduced.

One of the more controversial dam projects is the building of the Rogun Dam. Construction of this project began in 1976, but was frozen after the collapse of the Soviet Union. In February 2007 Tajikistan, with support from Russia announced the plan to complete the dam. This would allow the Tajik Republic to overcome its energy crisis through increasing electricity production as well as decrease its dependence on energy imports from Uzbekistan. It is also seen as contributing to the stabilization of Afghanistan through electricity exports. However, Uzbekistan is sternly against any new construction arguing that it will devastate their water intensive economy. Further, they warn against potential environmental damage, particularly to the Aral Sea. Tajikistan sees this opposition to reflect fears that the project will decrease Uzbekistan's leverage over Tajikistan. Energy security is important to both parties, on the one side Uzbekistan wants to retain its leverage and on the other side Tajikistan is seeking greater energy independence.

Downstream Countries and the Need for Irrigation

Uzbekistan is the largest consumer of water resources in the region, which is used for agriculture. Uzbek farmers have been using the water flows from Amu Darya and Syr Darya to irrigate their water-intensive cotton fields since ancient times. Recently there has been an inconsistent supply of water. The year of 2000 and 2001 marked the most severe water-shortage in Uzbekistan recorded over the last two decades devastating their economy. The country is moving away from a highly centralized water management structure to a decentralized system. However, these efforts have not been completely successful. The Main Water Management Department (MWMD) under the Ministry of Agriculture and Water Resources is responsible for the development and management of irrigation and drainage infrastructure. There is ten Basin Irrigation System Authorities (BISAs) responsible for the management of inter-farm irrigation and drainage systems, financed from the state budget. However, the sector is facing financial crisis and is unable to make the necessary investments in the deteriorating sector. In 2000, Uzbekistan gave Water Users Association (WUAs) a management role over irrigation systems to address the hierarchical management of the sector. One of the last institutional reforms was in 2003, changing from an administrative territorial-water management to hydrologic basin water management. Yet, these WUAs have internal problems stemming from favoritism and their role in resolving conflicts and imposing sanctions.

Turkmenistan faces many of the same problems as its downstream neighbor Uzbekistan stemming from a high dependency on water intensive cotton production. The water sector in Turkmenistan is represented by a complex governance system comprising a number of ministries and institutions. The key specialized governmental ministries responsible for water resource management and protection are the Ministry of Water Resources and the Ministry of Nature Protection, but very often authorities share joint responsibilities and functions. In addition to the complicated management structure, there is a lack of interaction and coordination among the ministries and institutions of the water sector.

Considerable efforts have been made in the recent years to modernize the existing infrastructure; still a lot has yet to be implemented. Because functions of water resource management are divided between a number of government agencies, priorities and objectives of these authorities are sometimes different. This makes coordination between them quite complicated. The mismanagement of scarce water resources has severe consequences for the agricultural sector.

As agriculture in Turkmenistan is almost totally dependent on irrigation, proper management of the region's water resources is essential for this industry. One of the major challenges for the management of water in Turkmenistan is that increasing food production is one of the major goals of Turkmenistan's national agricultural policy. This means that irrigation development and agricultural intensification have to be achieved in a general context of limited water resources, creating a need for a more efficient water management system.

Turkmenistan and Uzbekistan have developed a higher dependency on cotton production than Kazakhstan. However, Kazakhstan is also very dependent on irrigation for its agricultural sector which consumes over 70 percent of total supply in the country. A significant problem is that a large amount of the water is lost through inefficient use, leakage due to old infrastructure and pollution. These problems for the most part do not stem from supply shortages but from poor water management. All around the country, almost half the pumps and public taps are turned off permanently because they are worn out or sub-standard. The intergovernmental bodies responsible for water resources management are like the other downstream countries fragmented, under-funded and poorly governed, and budget and staffing cuts has had a dramatic effect on the ability of the authorities to manage water.

The Government of Kazakhstan has embarked on a water resources management project aimed at strengthening the water management organizations within the country by instituting the practice of Integrated Water Resource Management (IWRM).

Aral Sea Crisis

If there is a particular issue that puts a face on the ill-planned Soviet development policies of the past it is the Aral Sea, one of the worst man-made environmental disasters in the world. The crisis first began in the 1950s when the Syr Darya and Amu Darya rivers, which feed the Aral Sea, were diverted as part of the Soviet Union's grand agricultural scheme. Large areas were set aside for cotton production, which meant more water for irrigation and less to replenish the Aral Sea, since it was regarded as expendable. At one point the Aral Sea was the fourth-largest landlocked body of water in the world, occupying an area of about 66,000km and a volume of 1,062 km· Now it has split into two separate bodies: Little Aral Sea, which is in Kazakhstan, and Big Aral Sea, which is in Uzbekistan.

The grand scheme is now in disrepair and continued mismanagement is not addressing the waste of water resources. Further contributing to the Aral Sea's demise is the ongoing usage of the poor agricultural practices from the Soviet Union era. Currently over 80 percent of the land used for crop growing is saline, which requires more water to be used to flood the fields in preparation for the spring planting season.

This water then goes back downstream and is recycled again, further adding to the water and soil's high salt concentration. These poor agricultural practices are mostly done by the downstream states and will only continue due to their high population growth rates and the need to produce large amounts of food. These states are also resistant to diversifying their agricultural sectors to include less water-intensive crops, as they feel any changes to this system will negatively affect their economies.

Climate change is projected to have a negative effect on the crisis, as increasing temperatures and natural evaporation rates are causing the flow of the source rivers to decrease, which means even less water is available to replenish the Aral Sea. A decrease in rainy days has led the coastline to recede and speed up the rate of desiccation, thus exposing toxic salts on the seabed that are from the excessive use of fertilizers and pesticides.

These salts are being carried by dust storms and causing high rates of tuberculosis, anemia, hepatitis, respiratory and eye diseases, and throat cancer for the area's inhabitants. These dust storms are the result of the Aral Sea no longer providing the moisture block needed to prevent these winds from occurring. Also being affected is the livelihood of those who once depended on the Aral Sea as a source of income. Most of the fishing and shipping industry jobs that existed because of the Aral Sea have since been lost and the Sea's high salinity level has led to the extinction of various types of flora and fauna once native to the area.

Efforts to Save the Aral Sea

In 1993, the five heads of state came together to create the International Fund for saving the Aral Sea (IFAS), an organization designed to facilitate regional cooperation in order to address this crisis. IFAS was also created to attract funds from the five states needed to carry out projects and inform the international community about the crisis and gain its support in addressing it. Since its inception, IFAS has partaken in a number of projects, such as the 1993-1997 Aral Sea Basin Programme.

This project's four main objectives focused on stabilizing and rehabilitating the surrounding area, developing better water management strategies, and increasing the ability for regional and national organizations to advance their projects. Another key initiative was the 1998 and 2002 Water and Environment Management Project.

IFAS, in collaboration with the World Bank, attempted to create both a regional and individual strategy with the help of a group of neutral experts. Although this initiative's first two attempts were unsuccessful, there have been discussions on reviving it in order to achieve the goals it set out to do.

Since 1992 Kazakhstan has been attempting to save the Little Aral Sea by building a dam in order to preserve it and bring it back to its former levels. For many years the dam's poor planning and the usage of sand for building material caused it to breach a number of times. But international support from the World Bank helped fund the building of the Kokaralsk Dam, which was completed in 2005. In just a few years the sea level has risen, salinity has been reduced, and fish species have flourished, which has revived the area's fishing industry.

Although some attempts were successful in addressing the Aral Sea crisis, not all have met the same result, especially those by the international community. Analyst Erika Weinthal criticized the international community for responding to the Aral Sea as either a water crisis (World Bank, UNDP, UNEP) or as a water/energy crisis (USAID) but not as a crisis of agriculture. The five states and the international community have rejected any dramatic reform to the agricultural sector in the downstream countries. This move alone could have had the most impact on this crisis, but the political power of the cotton producers is too entrenched to allow this necessary change to finally occur.

The need to modify these agricultural practices due to its effects on the Aral Sea is even more evident now that Uzbekistan's Big Aral Sea is splitting into the Big Aral East and Big Aral West. It is apparent a complete overhaul of the agricultural sector cannot occur with how much these states economically depend on it, but they, along with the international community, need to find a balance between economic needs and the environment before it leads to more problems.

The case of the Aral Sea is one, if not the best, example of the effect that lack of cooperation is having on the region and the disregard the Soviet planners had for the environment while organizing their "grand" scheme. It is interesting to note that once the Aral Sea problem was first realized, the Soviet Union's plan to address it included diverting water from Siberia into the Aral Sea instead of the Arctic. But this would have led to yet another problem and continued the cycle of mistreating nature for human gains. Even though various attempts have been made by the Central

Asian states and the international community to save and revive it, the Aral Sea will never return to its former state and will forever be a constant reminder to the region of its Soviet Union legacy.

REGIONAL AND INTERNATIONAL EFFORTS

Attempts for improved regional cooperation on Central Asia's water issues have been made between the states and with the help of the international community. The following will take a look at some of these key efforts, the extent to which they worked, and how some key aspects may be used for future efforts.

Chu-Talas Joint Rivers Commission

In 2000, Kyrgyzstan and Kazakhstan signed an agreement for joint management on the Chu River (Kyrgyzstan) and the Talas River (Kazakhstan) through the Chu-Talas Rivers Commission. The commission became operational in 2006 and created a new level of cooperation between the two countries. As part of the arrangement, Kazakhstan has agreed to pay for some of the costs of dams in Kyrgyzstan and results have so far shown that Kazakhstan has followed through on its promise. Kazakhstan now pays a reasonable cost for receiving water from the dams on the Chu River, and has thus moved away from Soviet era water quotas. The commission has been praised for providing reliable water forecasts for irrigated agriculture. The Chu-Talas Rivers Commission is regarded as a breakthrough agreement by the United Nations Economic Commission for Europe and is seen as a model for helping resolve larger upstream-downstream water conflicts.

The International Fund for Saving the Aral Sea (IFAS)

One of the unique features of the International Fund for saving the Aral Sea (IFAS) is how the Chairmanship is chosen on a rotating basis and allows each of the five states to hold this position. During the Tajikistan's term as Chairman, President Rahmon's main focus was on the socio-economic and ecological issues of the crisis. These aspects were dealt with during the Summit of Heads in 2002, where all five states signed onto the Dushanbe Declaration, organized the Aral Sea Basin Programme 2, and a UN Special

Commissions was put in charge of coordinating the international community's efforts. IFAS also became a member of various international organizations, created partnerships with world financial institutions and addressed the United Nations (UN) on the current status of the Aral Sea during the 63rd Session of the UN General Assembly dedicated to water and sanitation issues.

In continuing with the rotating of the Chairmanship Kazakhstan will now hold the position from 2009-2011 and relocate IFAS headquarters to Almaty. In May 2010 Kazakhstan held a Donors Coordination Meeting, which further solidified relations with international donors and continued the planning for Aral Sea Basin Programme 3.

The UN declared 2003 as the International Year of Fresh Water and 2005-2015 the International Decade for Actions –Water for Life. In 2008 IFAS received official observer status by the UN. These declarations are of special importance, as the UN is committing itself to helping IFAS in finding a solution to the Aral Sea crisis and giving freshwater issues the international attention it needs.

It will be difficult for IFAS to further its goals if many of the key problems, such as the crumbling infrastructure, climate change, and agricultural practices, are not dealt with as they are still creating barriers in allowing major changes to be made in saving the Aral Sea. Also, instead of continuing to fund the same types of projects, the international community could help fund projects on these key issues, especially in updating the infrastructure, since the Central Asian states do not have the funds needed for that kind of project. Although IFAS has had some high and low points, it has served as a platform in promoting regional cooperation between the five states in addressing a key issue that affects them all.

UNDP Integrated Water Resources Management (IWRM)

IWRM is a management system of surface, ground and return water that takes into account the "different economic sectors and hierarchical levels of water use, involves all stakeholders into decision-making, and promotes efficient use of water, land and other natural resources for the sake of sustainable satisfying water requirements of eco-systems and human society." This initiative views regional coordination as critical in addressing increased demand for water, climate change, and conflicting interests for water usage. A large component of this approach is that public participation is crucial and that countries need to take a legal, financial, holistic and integrated approach to water management. IWRM has been in practice for centuries, but was only officially recognized internationally in the Dublin Declaration in 1992. IWRM was implemented in Central Asia under the Soviet Union during which time Basin Water Organizations were established for "Amu Darya" and "Syr Darya."

In 1996, the Central Asia IWRM Resource Center was founded in order to build capacity of the region on sustainable water use. UNDP's 2005 report "Bringing Down Barriers: Regional Cooperation for Human Development and Human Security" recommended the need to "establish a regional Water-Energy Consortium to manage the abundant regional water and energy resources for greater efficiency, human development and regional stability." The same year, the Central Asian countries attempted to set up a *water* and energy consortium (WES) to advance IWRM in the region. Again in the late 2000s, the states attempted to form a Water-Energy Consortium (WEC) but this effort failed due to Uzbekistan withdrawing from negotiations, a move motivated by its isolationist policy. So far these initiatives have been considered largely ineffective.

Currently, UNDP in collaboration with the European Commission has initiated *Promoting IWRM and Fostering Transboundary* Dialogue in Central Asia, a $5.4 Million project based out of Almaty, Kazakhstan. *This project is working in* Kyrgyzstan and Tajikistan, to develop and implement IWRM Strategies at the national and basin levels, as well as increasing dialogue and cooperation between Kazakhstan and China on the Ili-Balkhash. Regionally, the program is trying to build capacity and trans-regional coordination. This project is facing little resistance as countries welcome technical assistance. While the project is addressing critical issues of water usage and management, it is limited by its mandate to stay out of politics, a large cause of the lack of cooperation in the region. An additional challenge IWRM faces is that water managers become responsible for short and long term environmental and social impacts of their management decisions.

This in turn necessitates legislation to address the socio-economic components of water resources. The attempts to integrate IWRM in National Water Policies have overall been unsuccessful. The Johannesburg Declaration called for Kazakhstan to be the first country in the region to prepare a National IWRM and Water Efficiency Plan (WE) and it completed its plan in December 2005. As of 2008, only Kazakhstan has an IWRM national plan in place, whereas the other four countries in the region are still in the preparation phase with their plans.

Central Asia as a whole ranked lowest on the indicator of monitoring, information management, and dissemination, and lower stakeholder participation- all strategies that could promote IWRM, compared to East and South East Asia. These IWRM and WE plans would address the inefficiency of water use, a contributing factor to the water crisis, and should be developed and implemented by the rest of the countries.

TRANSBOUNDARY WATER DISPUTES IN CENTRAL ASIA

Over the last decades, there has been a growing speculation about the likelihood of an acute conflict or even war over freshwater resources.

Scholars increasingly point out that the 21st century might see the battles fought due to water scarcity. Indeed, water is the only resource having no substitute, and the demand for it is constant and burning. All forms of the Earth's life, including humans, need water to survive. The fact that we inhabit the 'water planet' soothes little as only less than 3% of total water resources on the Earth are freshwater. Its distribution is obviously uneven, with some nations suffering severe droughts every year and the others blessed with water abundance.

It is no wonder then that through the whole history of human race, water allocation and quantity fuelled tensions between various states, with particular role played by transboundary river resources. And although history shows that full-scale wars over water, proving to be neither strategically rational nor hydrographically effective, have never been fought (Wolf, 1998), water continues to be a source of intense disputes worldwide.

The problem grows harder when it comes to the relationships between two or more countries over river water as a result of the "internationalisation of a basin through political change. The number of international basins has grown from 214 in 1978 to 263 today. These international basins cover 45.3% of total land surface, affect about 40% of the world's population, and account for about 60% of global river flow.

Nineteen basins are shared by 5 or more riparian countries, with only the Danube being shared by 17 riparians, whereas five basins – the Congo, Niger, Nile, Rhine and Zambezi – are shared by between 9 and 11 countries (Wolf, 2001).

In this situation, such long-negotiated instrument of international water law as the 1997 UN Convention on the Non-Navigational Uses of International Watercourses, is of little help as it provides for equally contradictory 'equitable use' and 'no significant harm' principles: while the former is favoured by upstream countries, downstream riparians insist on emphasising the latter because it protects their own rights.

It is also difficult to enforce the Convention in the absence of any international enforcing mechanisms. More importantly, the Convention hardly weighs out a variety of political, social, economic, demographic and environmental factors that encompass each shared river basin.

Negotiators whose task is to provide timely diplomatic intervention, or apply means of the so-called 'preventive diplomacy', in order to avoid the escalation of a dispute into open conflict need to be aware which basin is prone to water conflict well in advance. To do that, they need to identify potential indicators of conflict that incorporate a wide range of physical, social, economic and environmental variables, including those which can be analysed within a Geographic Information System (GIS), and to develop a comprehensive model to explore specific linkages between them. In particular, this method can be applicable in those cases of internationally shared rivers where progress towards successful resolution of a dispute was slow or unachievable.

Considering all factors having influence on the river basin regime is becoming crucial to elaborate meaningful and workable framework to provide resolution to the growing water conflict.

Since the collapse of the Soviet Union, Central Asia has become a tangle of unresolved transboundary water disputes. Water is the most critical resource in Central Asia and it "has more often been the source of competition rather than the focus of conservation (Hogan, 2000b).

The absence of mechanisms to handle the water problems has already resulted in various accusations of improper water use. Consequently, the whole region becomes the site of potential conflict that requires a framework which should incorporate a great many variables to identify the proneness to water conflict and to allow for the possibility of preventive diplomacy.

Such method which has never been used towards the specific problem of Central Asian water disputes can provide solutions based on a more holistic approach to natural resources, while recognising the historical, geopolitical and natural characteristics of the region.

This study seeks to identify potential indicators of water conflict and analyse some of them within the Geographical Information System (GIS).

Unlike other studies that involve global level analysis, the thesis will focus on Central Asia's regional and basin specific information. An attempt to answer a question of what indicators better point to water conflict will be taken.

Hypothesis

The study aims at testing the working hypothesis that proneness of a specific river basin to water conflict can be identified through a variety of indicators representing physical, political, environmental and socio-economic processes occurring in this specific region, thus providing better chance for using preventive diplomatic actions.

Methodology

The study's methodology is based on the concept of international river basins offered by the Transboundary Freshwater Dispute Database (TFDD), Oregon State University (TFDD, 2002). The database contains a large collection of water treaties and agreements and is a sound foundation for transboundary water conflict research. For the purposes of this study, the Amu Darya Basin is examined. Taking the basin as a unit of research, the proposed study offers a model of relationship between water resources and social, political, economic and environmental patterns in Central Asia. There is also chance to explore the use of GIS such as ESRI Arc View for social research. A parallel analysis of water conflict related variables focuses on finding combinations of indicators that provide an indication of potential water conflict.

7

Challenges to Water and Security in Southeast Asia

THE GLOBAL WATER AND SANITATION CHALLENGE

In her March 22, 2010 World Water Day Speech, Secretary Clinton stated that "water represents one of the great diplomatic and development opportunities of our time." She noted that, "It's not every day you find an issue where effective diplomacy and development will allow you to save millions of lives, feed the hungry, empower women, advance our national security interests, protect the environment, and demonstrate to billions of people that the United States cares, cares about you and your welfare. Water is that issue."

By 2025, nearly two-thirds of the world's population will be living under water-stressed conditions, including roughly 1.8 billion people who will face absolute water scarcity (a level that threatens economic development as well as human health and well-being). Water scarcity and poor water quality will increase disease risks, undermine economic growth, limit food production, and become an increasing threat to peace and security.

More than 260 watersheds worldwide are shared by two or more countries. As water becomes scarce, tensions over shared resources are likely to rise – both within countries and among countries. Promoting joint management and using water to build trust and cooperation in conflict-prone regions are important tools in reducing the risks of future conflicts. The effects of climate change will only exacerbate these challenges. Perhaps the most profound effects of climate change will be the shrinking of glaciers and rivers. Water availability will change as will the likelihood of extreme floods and droughts. These extreme events can affect more people than all other natural disasters combined.

The Greater Mekong sub-region is one of Asia's areas most vulnerable to the impacts of climate change because of the large numbers of people living in floodplains and low-lying coastal areas and because the people and economies of the region depend strongly on agriculture and ecosystem services.

The region's extraordinary biodiversity is also at risk from both the direct and indirect impacts of climate change.

As we know from our own experiences with the wetlands and marshes of large river systems such as the Mississippi, the management of these systems can have far-ranging societal and ecological impacts.

Sustainable river management in the face of climate change is of great concern to us, as well as for those living in large watersheds around the world.

To help strengthen U.S. engagement in Southeast Asia, Secretary Clinton announced the Lower Mekong Initiative (LMI) in July, 2009 on the margins of the ASEAN Post-Ministerial Meeting. The LMI aims to engage Cambodia, Laos, Thailand, and Vietnam by helping build regional capacity in the areas of environment, health, education, and infrastructure in order to facilitate multilateral cooperation among the four countries on issues of mutual concern, such as the common challenge of effective water resource management

Also in response to this challenge, Secretary Clinton has asked Under Secretary for Global Affairs Maria Otero and U.S. Agency for International Development Administrator Rajiv Shah to identify specific steps we can take to strengthen the United States' capacity to respond to watershed management and climate change. We are also establishing a joint steering group under the leadership of Bureau of Oceans, Environment, and Science Assistant Secretary Kerri-Ann Jones.

THE COMPLEXITY OF THE MEKONG SYSTEM

Hydrologically, the Mekong River is one of the most complex river systems in the world. It is the longest river in Southeast Asia, stretching 2,703 miles through six countries, nearly twice the length of the Colorado River. Its watershed supports between 65 and 80 million people, providing over $2 billion dollars in revenue from wild fisheries alone.

The large flows of the Mekong — nearly as large as those of the Mississippi — vary widely according to available precipitation. The basin has a wet season and a dry season. During the wet season, only about 16 percent of the flows come from China. During the dry season months, this share rises to 40 percent. Due to the complexity and extent of the Mekong system, drought and flood events rarely affect the entire reach equally.

Within the Lower Basin are ecologically unique features that play crucial roles in regulating the flows of the Mekong: the Tonle Sap Lake, Cambodia's most important fishery, and, below that, the wide reach of the Delta, which produces about 52 percent of Vietnam's rice and most of its aquaculture fish and shrimp exports.

Located in the Cambodian floodplain, the Tonle Sap Lake is filled by the monsoon rains. When it overflows, it can temporarily reverse the flow of the Mekong. The surge in water storage in the lake is enormous, increasing from 1-2 million acre-feet in the dry season, to 40 - 60 million acre-feet in the wet season, enough to cover the state of New Jersey in 10 feet of water.

The injection of nutrient-rich sediments also creates one of the world's most productive ecosystems and the world's largest freshwater fishery. Through this natural action of seasonal storage, the Tonle Sap Lake regulates the flows of the Mekong, moderates flood events, provides crucial flows during dry months, and prevents the incursion of sea water within the Delta.

The Mekong Delta supports about half of Vietnam's total production of rice and provides food security for its population. Vietnam is one of the world's richest agricultural regions, the second-largest exporter of rice worldwide, and the world's seventh-largest consumer of rice. The Mekong River and its tributaries are crucial to rice production in Vietnam. A total of 12 provinces constitute the Mekong Delta, containing 17 million people, 80 percent of whom are engaged in rice cultivation. According to the United Nations Development Program in Vietnam and Vietnam's Ministry of Agriculture and Rural Development, the rice industry is under serious threat due to the 2010 heat wave, climate change, and upstream Mekong River development.

Strong Riparian Dependence on the Mekong

The inhabitants of the Mekong River Basin depend heavily on the river. Irrigated agriculture and fishing engage 85 percent of the workforce within the Basin, and for most farmers the river is critical to their survival. Many farmers rely on fishing to supplement their incomes and provide nourishment. In every Mekong country fish are the most important source of animal protein; for many, the principal source of protein in their diet. Poverty still challenges the region, and those who are heavily dependent on the natural resource of the Mekong are the first to suffer from any environmental changes.

It is important to note that, while the region is still home to over 20 million people living in poverty, it also holds great capacity for growth and economic opportunity. For example, U.S. exports to Vietnam have tripled in the last three years, with two-way trade reaching nearly $16 billion in 2009. Regional economic growth in 2009 was 6 percent; proving the region's economy to be very resilient during the recent economic downturn.

Hydropower Plans

One result of increased development is that the countries of the Mekong Basin are increasingly turning to hydropower as a solution to their growing energy needs. Construction of dams on the Mekong River may pose immediate and long-term threats to the food security and livelihoods of tens of millions of people in the Lower Mekong Basin. However, awareness of these threats is rising rapidly due to the confluence of an extended drought this year and a concerted push by interested parties, including the United States through the Lower Mekong Initiative, to highlight the possible adverse affects of dam construction. The impetus behind the Mekong dam projects is the creation of a regional electrical grid that will facilitate the development of the Mekong Basin. In the future, the Mekong and its tributaries could support an elaborate, interlocking electric power generation grid supplying Laos, northern Thailand, parts of Cambodia, and much of Yunnan Province in China. The economic stakes for dam construction are high, and the states of the Mekong Basin are eager for the developmental benefits they can obtain.

All dams have an impact on the flow and natural ecology of rivers and streams, but in certain cases the developmental and environmental tradeoffs in terms of electric power and navigation can be justified. In the case of the 11 mainstream dams planned by Cambodia, Laos, and Thailand on the lower half of the river, disruption of the food security of 60 million people who depend on the river could be among the serious consequences resulting from damming the Mekong River. A single misplaced dam on the lower Mekong could block the path of migratory fish species that supply up to 80 percent of animal protein in the local diet. A reduction in freshwater flows caused by poorly designed dams could also increase the salinity of the river water, thus adversely affecting the rice crop.

The ambitious plans for investment in infrastructure should be grounded in a comprehensive analysis of where these investments would provide the highest return and what their hydrological impact would be. In the Lower Mekong region there is generally little analysis of soil and water quality, or other constraints to food production, when river modification is being considered. Often hydropower development plans have been plagued by weak oversight of required environmental and social impact assessments.

On the upper stem of the Mekong, China's eight-dam cascade in Yunnan Province, four of which are completed, will certainly disrupt some of the river's natural functions as well as give China some degree of control over the timing and amount of river flows. But the greatest downstream ecological impact may be caused by downstream infrastructure development and would be felt in Cambodia's Tonle Sap Great Lake and Vietnam's Mekong River Delta. Mainstem dams, including two planned by Cambodia itself, may degrade the Tonle Sap, and the Delta may also suffer major consequences due to the loss of vital silt replenishment.

Hydropower remains a valuable energy resource, so long as the cost-benefit tradeoffs are fully understood and responsibly addressed. Many development projects must weigh the tradeoffs between the opportunities presented by new economic infrastructure — such as roads, bridges, and dams — and the full impacts to ecology and local livelihoods. The sale of electricity generated by dams provides a source of foreign revenue for countries with few existing alternative options for economic growth, but this may be unsustainable and comes with potentially significant environmental and social costs.

System Under Stress

The Mekong River system is already beginning to show signs of strain brought about by multiple competing uses. Although much attention has focused on the impact of future dams, more immediate environmental threats exist through overuse and pollution from industry, wastewater, and agriculture.

Maintaining water quality in the Mekong is key to sustaining the health and productivity of the populations dependent on it. High salinity levels are prevalent in the Delta, mostly during the dry months as diminished flows of the Mekong are unable to push back against sea water incursions. Moreover, agricultural runoff, municipal wastewater, industrial effluent, and sulphate-rich soils have resulted in elevated levels of acidity and eutrophication of the Lower Mekong watershed.

The Lower Mekong countries have recently started to address the issue of water pollution, but the region is plagued by lagging enforcement and monitoring. Upstream sources of water pollution, as well as domestic wastewater continue to degrade the health of the river. Certain municipalities, for example, discharge the majority of their untreated sewage directly into the river.

While the state of the Mekong environmental system is threatened by existing pollution and future development, the few completed monitoring studies have found that the effect of pollution on Mekong fisheries has been limited thus far. While the current impact of development along the Mekong is also limited, future threats to fisheries, water quality, and human health are most likely to come from human interference in the form of dams, increased transportation, additional habitat destruction from land-use changes, and continued water pollution.

The State Department has provided some small grants to a network of universities in the region to study the levels of pollution in the river. This effort has enhanced collaboration among research institutions within the four nations in the Mekong Basin. More studies are needed to fully understand development's effects on the Mekong's fragile biodiversity and to strengthen nascent research partnerships.

Beyond the impact of human activities in the watershed affecting the Mekong River Basin, climate change will undoubtedly add to the list of challenges. Changing rainfall patterns, glacial melting, and greater hydrological variability may increase the likelihood of floods and droughts. Given an average elevation of around five feet, sea-level rise poses a grave threat to the Vietnam Delta.

Local Politics and Water Politics

Shared water issues among the Mekong countries are managed through a series of overlapping legal and institutional arrangements, such as navigation agreements. Effectively managing transboundary water is a significant challenge, particularly for riparian nations with different levels of economic development and past animosities. Facing these difficulties, the Mekong River Commission has steered regional watershed development since 1995, emphasizing avenues for cooperation, strategic planning, and continued dialogue.

Under the 1995 Mekong Agreement signed by the Governments of Cambodia, Laos, Thailand and Vietnam, the Mekong River Commission (MRC) has provided a framework for addressing transboundary water resources in the region. Its structure has allowed for needed flexibility and resiliency as hydrologic and economic realities shift. Major foreign donors to the MRC include Germany, Australia, Sweden, and Denmark.

Since 1995, the MRC has widened its scope. While remaining a forum for cooperative discussions, it has moved from large-scale basin planning to include small-scale resource development and the establishment of a knowledge base in lower-basin hydrology. Although not a regulatory agency, the Mekong River Commission builds knowledge and technical capacity for member states through providing assistance and recommendations.

In the future, the MRC will be forced to address difficult issues of water allocation and basin management. Hydropower development and analysis of water flows during the dry season must be discussed to craft adequate cooperative solutions. Responses to floods or droughts require strengthened communication between riparian countries. These problems are not easy, but cooperative solutions are possible.

In response to these challenges, Secretary Clinton launched the Lower Mekong Initiative (LMI) in 2009 to help address regional issues, with a particular focus on the environment, health, education, and infrastructure. The LMI seeks to facilitate effective, coordinated responses to challenges that are inherently regional in nature through working level visits, training workshops, conferences, and scientific and technological exchanges.

U.S. leadership and increased attention on the LMI has had an impact on how other regional players view these issues. Recently, China agreed to share more of its operational data with the Mekong River Commission and has allowed a visit by Mekong River Commission officials to China's Yunnan province to look at two of the four dams. Japan has also increased its involvement in the region, pledging $5 billion in assistance at the Japan-Mekong Summit last October.

U.S. Policy Regarding Transboundary Water Security Issues

The unfortunate reality is that there will always be disputes over water. Our involvement includes emphasis on building solutions that consider the environment and climate change, health, education, infrastructure, and economic growth. Through our support of multinational solutions, we hope to foster an environment that will preempt instability and minimize the potential for violent conflict. In analyzing the potential for conflict, we look at factors that are driving tensions, as well as factors that can defuse tensions.

In the Mekong region we see only a few factors with the potential to contribute to conflict. Those factors are unilateral development of upstream infrastructure, bilateral development of downstream infrastructure, changing environmental conditions, and historical tensions in relations between Mekong countries. These instigating factors are to a large extent countered by some important mitigating factors. First, the Mekong countries recognize that they need to act in concert in the stewardship of the Basin. The Asian Development Bank (ADB) and other donors are helping to foster this collaboration. In addition, the MRC is a regional institution which has recently made significant strides and includes representation and support from each of the Basin countries. While much needs to be done to ensure the institution can effectively advance sound water resources management across the Basin, it provides a solid foundation for regional assessment, planning, and discussion. In our view, the MRC's existence greatly minimizes the likelihood of violent conflict among the Mekong states.

While the United States has a long history of engagement with the countries of Southeast Asia on a bilateral basis, there is an increasing awareness of the growing number of issues that transcend national boundaries. The countries of the Lower Mekong region share a variety of common concerns, including transboundary water management, infectious diseases, and vulnerability to climate change. Our Lower Mekong Initiative seeks to support a common regional understanding of these issues and to facilitate an effective, coordinated response.

In order to build regional capacity and cooperation, the State Department is working with other U.S. government partners to develop innovative programs under the auspices of the LMI. "Forecast Mekong," a computerized decision-making tool the U.S. Geological Survey is developing with State Department support, will provide policy makers in the Mekong countries with the information they need to make good decisions on managing the Mekong waterways, including predicted effects of hydropower dams on water flow. This information will be made available on the Internet so that scientists and researchers, based in the region and around the world, can also access the data and the analysis capability. Also created under the auspices of the LMI is a "sister-river partnership" between the Mekong River Commission and the Mississippi River Commission that will help to build the capacity of the Mekong River Commission and to support its efforts to incorporate water-related concerns into regional decision making.

USAID is also working to strengthen the capacity of the Lower Mekong countries to assess the environmental impacts of hydropower development at both the project and basin levels. Through the Asia Development Bank (ADB) and Greater Mekong Sub-region Initiative, USAID will support partnerships between the countries to conduct Strategic Environmental Assessments for hydropower projects. In addition, USAID, in partnership with ADB, MRC and the Worldwide Fund for Nature, has developed a sustainable hydropower development assessment tool, which will soon be piloted in various sub-basins within the watershed.

The United States has an important role to play here. We can inform regional policy and decision making, build local capacity, and promote sustainable development by sharing advanced science and technology capabilities. Our goal in this area is not to determine the outcome of these discussions, but to give policymakers the tools they need to make informed decisions about development of the river.

Finally, in concert with other technical agencies of the U.S. government, USAID and the State Department are making significant investments in the health, environment, and education sectors. In addition to existing bilateral activities, we are further developing our regional programming as well. I would like to highlight the Secretary's announcement of $3 million from USAID for the study of climate change impacts on the Mekong Basin. Let me share a rough sketch of what we hope to accomplish with this money.

USAID will support the development of a regional adaptation strategy across the Lower Mekong. It will engage local institutions and conduct studies to assess vulnerabilities of the ecosystem as well as hold dialogues with a variety of stakeholders to gain support for a regional approach. Further into the program, we look to implement pilot projects and build platforms for sharing of information. Through an integrated and regional approach we will be able to build local and national government capacity for long-term planning founded on sound science and advanced technology.

These programs incorporate U.S. expertise into a regional plan to address some of the key water and development challenges these countries face. They also foster cooperation among the countries in the region to work together for a common purpose.

REGION'S GREAT RIVERS MAY BE THREATENING SOUTH ASIA'S PEACE

Spent half a century picking a living from Wular lake high in Indian-controlled Kashmir. Today he is lucky if he scoops a fish or two out of the soupy mess. Push a boat into the knee-deep lake and the mud raises a stink of sewage. A century ago Wular and its surrounding marshes covered more than 217 square kilometres (84 square miles), making it one of Asia's larger freshwater lakes. Now, thanks to silt and encroachment, the extraction of water by nearby towns and tree planting on the shore, it measures only 87 sq km and is shrinking.

Compared with much of South Asia, Kashmir, a disputed territory in northern India, has many rivers and relatively few people. But even here fresh water is running short. To see how contentious this can be, drive half a day south to where the Baglihar dam is rising up. An enormous wall bisects the valley, dressing it in white spray, and three huge jets of water blast from its sluices.

Half complete, the dam is already a local wonder that tourists gape at. It generates 450MW for the starved energy grid of Jammu and Kashmir. Once the scheme fully tames the water, by steering it through a tunnel blasted into the mountain, the grid will gain another 450MW.

The river swirls away, white-crested and silt-laden, racing to the nearby border with Pakistan. But there Baglihar is a source of bitterness. Pakistanis cite it as typical of an intensifying Indian threat to their existence, a conspiracy to divert, withhold or misuse precious water that is rightfully theirs. Officials in Islamabad and diplomats abroad are primed to grumble about it. Pakistan's most powerful man, the head of the armed forces, General Ashfaq Kayani, cites water to justify his "India-centric" military stance.

Others take it further. "Water is the latest battle cry for *jihadis,*" says B.G. Verghese, an Indian writer. "They shout that water must flow, or blood must flow." Lashkar-e-Taiba, a Pakistani terror group, likes to threaten to blow up India's dams. Last year a Pakistani extremist, Abdur Rehman Makki, told a rally that if India were to "block Pakistan's waters, we will let loose a river of blood."

Assorted hardliners cheer them on. A blood-curdling editorial in *Nawa-i-Waqt,* a Pakistani newspaper, warned in April that "Pakistan should convey to India that a war is possible on the issue of water and this time war will be a nuclear one."

Upstream such outbursts are usually dismissed as proof that troubled Pakistan is, as ever, spoiling for a fight. Water is merely the latest excuse. India is not misbehaving, says Mr Verghese placidly. It fails to take all it is entitled to from cross-border rivers in Kashmir. Run-of-the-river dams like Baglihar consume nothing, since water must flow to run turbines. Such a dam, he says, merely briefly delays a river.

Indians point out, too, that Pakistan enjoys a rare guarantee: the Indus Water Treaty, struck in 1960 by far-sighted engineers and diplomats who saw that after the partition of land, water had to be shared out too. The treaty, which has survived three wars, details exactly how each side must use cross-border rivers. Mostly this applies to the tributaries that flow from Kashmir to form the massive Indus river, Pakistan's lifeblood.

If Indians abide by the treaty, then in theory at least they cannot be misbehaving. They see Baglihar as proof of co-operation, not a threat. When Pakistan objected to the dam's design, India accepted international arbitration, the first case in the treaty's history. Outside experts studied the dam and ordered small changes. But in effect they said it posed no threat to Pakistan. And last year the dispute was officially ended by the two governments.

Downstream, however, few sound satisfied. "The Baglihar decision...allowed a reservoir on a river coming into Pakistan, and now a precedent is set," laments John Briscoe, a water expert formerly of the World Bank who advises Pakistan. The Pakistanis fear Indian control over the headwaters of the Indus. And Indian bureaucrats fuel these fears with obsessive secrecy about all water data.

Bashir Ahmad, a geologist in Srinagar, Kashmir who studied the Baglihar dam, gives grim warning about the Indians' future intentions: "They will switch the Indus off to make Pakistan solely dependent on India. It's going to be a water bomb." A less excitable report in February by America's Senate offered a similar assessment: "The cumulative effect of [many dam] projects could give India the ability to store enough water to limit the supply to Pakistan at crucial moments in the growing season." Dams are a source of "significant bilateral tension", the report concludes.

More dams are to come, as India's need to power its economy means it is quietly spending billions on hydropower in Kashmir. The Senate report totted up 33 hydro projects in the border area. The state's chief minister, Omar Abdullah, says dams will add an extra 3,000MW to the grid in the next eight years alone. Some analysts in Srinagar talk of over 60 dam projects, large and small, now on the books.

Any of these could spark a new confrontation. The latest row is over the Kishanganga river (called the Neelum in Pakistan) as each country races to build a hydropower dam either side of Kashmir's line of control. India's dam will divert some of the river down a 22km (14-mile) mountain tunnel to turbines. To Pakistani fury, that will lessen the water flow to the downstream dam, so its capacity will fall short of a planned 960MW.

Pakistan also claims (though the evidence is shaky) that 600,000 people will suffer by getting less water for irrigation. Again it insisted on international arbitration at The Hague. In September, to Pakistani delight, India was ordered to suspend some of its building for further assessments to be made. But India still looks likelier to come away happy in the end, as the treaty foresaw and permitted the Indian design, and India is likely to finish its dam ahead of Pakistan in any case, by 2016 rather than 2018.

WHEN CHINA'S UPSTREAM

Countries downstream have genuine reasons to fret. Pakistan is exposed. Like Egypt it exists around a single great river, though the Indus is nearly twice the Nile's size when it reaches the sea. It waters over 80% of Pakistan's 22m hectares (54m acres) of irrigated land, using canals built by the British. In turn that farming provides 21% of the country's GDP, as well as livelihoods for a big proportion of its 180m people. Many of them are already thirsty.

On average each Indian gets just 1,730 cubic metres of fresh water a year, less than a quarter of the global average of 8,209 cubic metres. Yet that looks bountiful compared with each Pakistani's share: a mere 1,000 cubic metres. Worse yet, South Asia's fresh water mostly falls in a few monsoon months. The dreadful floods this year and last showed that untamed and unpredictable rivers can be both resource and threat.

More rows between India and Pakistan are certain. India may keep on dismissing them as Pakistani bluster, an easy thing to do if you are upstream. But India is downstream in another highly tricky area: its border with China.

Tension already exists over the status of India's Arunachal Pradesh state, which China refuses to recognise. A quarrel over rivers in the region could serve as a focus for wider disputes about territory. A measure of the recent slump in relations came when, to the fury of India's authorities, China blocked an attempt by the Asian Development Bank to prepare for a dam project in Arunachal Pradesh. And one of India's largest rivers, the Brahmaputra (Tsangpo in China), flows south from the Tibetan plateau and into Assam not far from the disputed land.

Angry Indian politicians, activists, bloggers and journalists claim that water-starved China (with 8% of the world's fresh water but 20% of its population) has plans to divert the Tsangpo/ Brahmaputra to farmers in its central and eastern regions. Feelings are running so high that India's prime minister, Manmohan Singh, felt obliged to issue a statement on August 4th saying that China's leaders had assured him there were no such plans afoot. And though a few run-of-the-river hydroelectric schemes are being built upstream on the Tsangpo, none of these could change the river's course. Cool heads point out that speculation about China channelling the torrent from near the border, at a spot known as the Great Bend, looks fantastical, at least at present.

Chinese engineers would need to use nuclear explosions to have a chance of making tunnels through a series of ridged mountains to get water east from the Great Bend. Although plans have existed since the fourth century to take water from China's west to the east, and the scheme was pushed by Mao Zedong, the engineering, at least for now, appears to be technically impossible. Yet broader Indian strategic fears—the fact that the Chinese control the Tibetan plateau, which is the source of water for parts of densely populated northern India—will evaporate no more easily than Pakistani fears of India.

An Ever-thirstier Region

The scarcity of water in South Asia will become harder to manage as demand rises. South Asia's population of 1.5 billion is growing by 1.7% a year, says the World Bank, which means an extra 25m or so mouths to water and feed: imagine dropping North Korea's entire population on the region each year. Greater wealth in South Asia brings with it a soaring demand for food, especially for water-intensive meat and other protein. Industry and energy-producers also use water, though unlike farms they return it, eventually, to the rivers.

Worse, overall supply will not only fail to keep up with rising demand but is likely to fall (unless a cheap way is found to turn sea water fresh). The Himalayan glaciers are melting. A Dutch study last year of the western Himalayas reckoned that shrunken glaciers will cut the flow of the Indus by some 8% by mid-century. Flows may also get less regular, especially if glacial dams form, withholding water, and then collapse, causing floods.

Others give even scarier predictions. Sundeep Waslekar, who heads a Mumbai think-tank, the Strategic Foresight Group, which has picked water as a long-term threat to Asian stability, sees a "mega-arc of hydro insecurity" emerging from western China along the Himalayas to the Middle East and farther west. The strain of bigger populations, diminishing water tables and a changing climate could all conspire to produce a storm of troubles. South Asia is especially vulnerable: Mr Waslekar sees a cut of 20% in total available fresh water over the next two decades.

The greatest threat of all would be from any change to the monsoon, which delivers most of the region's fresh water each summer. Here, again, worries arise. Indian meteorologists who have studied rainfall data from 1901 to 2004 have noted signs in recent decades of more dry spells within the peak monsoon months. If these lead to weaker, or less predictable, monsoons in future (though this year's was about normal) the consequences for farmers could be dire.

When the Water ran Out

In any case, the cost of running short of water is already becoming clearer. The*Lancet*, a British medical journal, reported last year that up to 77m Bangladeshis had been poisoned by arsenic—the largest mass-poisoning in history. It was the result of villagers pumping up groundwater from ever deeper aquifers. The same poison is now entering crops and more of the food chain.

Filthy water and bad sanitation spread diseases, such as diarrhoea and cholera, which kill hundreds of thousands of Indian children every year, says Unicef, the UN's children's agency. Several South Asian rivers, suffering from weaker flows, have become a sludge of human and animal waste, dangerous to drink and wash in and unsafe even for watering crops.

All over the region water tables are dropping as bore holes drive deeper. In the dry season even some of the larger rivers slow to a trickle. Knut Oberhagemann, a water expert in Dhaka, Bangladesh, says that the flow of the mighty Ganges where it enters Bangladesh is at times a pitiful few hundred cubic metres a second, so low that "you can walk across the river". When the same river, at this point called the Padma, reaches the coast, it is often so feeble that the sea intrudes, poisoning the land with salt.

The same problem curses the delta of the Indus in Pakistan. There a semi-desert was turned into some of the most fertile land on earth by British-built irrigation canals. But as the sea encroaches on low, flat land, rivers at times are flowing backwards, laments a local environmental activist. Take away the fresh water—around 60% of which is now lost to seepage and evaporation because of the bad management of those canals—and the desert will eventually come back.

Save or Snatch

Governments in South Asia can respond to growing scarcity in one of two ways. The first is to improve the way they use the water they have, both by managing it better and by co-operating with one another. The second is to try to grab as much water as they can from their neighbours.

Better management of irrigation canals and better farming techniques would help hugely to cut waste. In Pakistan bitter rows between provinces have long scotched coherent planning. Wealthy Punjab, a big farming province, is routinely accused by downstream Sindh (and by others too) of taking an unfair share of the water.

And Pakistan badly needs more dams to control floods, store monsoon water and make electricity (China is said to have offered to help Pakistan build a series of big dams, and has already sent engineers to help speed along the new one on the Neelum/ Kishanganga). Only about 10% of the potential hydropower of the Indus has been tapped so far, and only 30 days' average river flow can be stored (by contrast, the Colorado in America has dams to store 1,000 days'-worth).

Many governments are at least thinking in terms of dams and co-operation. Mr Waslekar reckons that 60-80 big dams (mostly for energy) will be built in South Asia in the next two or three decades, at a cost of hundreds of billions of dollars. In many cases—as for example in mountainous Bhutan, where the economy gets a huge boost from selling hydropower to India—this can foster economic and diplomatic co-operation. India has visions of one day persuading unstable but immensely water-rich Nepal to follow suit. The country is the source of more than 40% of the Ganges's water, and Indian analysts talk dreamily of 40GW of hydropower potential waiting to be used.

Other cross-border water deals are pending. Cosy ties with Bangladesh's government mean that India can more easily build dams on some of the several dozen rivers that cross their shared frontier. In September Mr Singh visited Dhaka to sign a deal with Bangladesh to allow the latest hydro dam to go up on the Teesta river.

Though the deal was postponed at the last minute by a row with a regional Indian leader, it now looks set to go ahead. However there are bitter memories in Bangladesh of an earlier deal, on the Ganges, which allowed India to put up a barrage to block the river's flow in the dry season.

Tentative signs of wider co-operation exist. China issues twice-daily reports on the Tsangpo river flow in the flood season, separately to India and to Bangladesh. This could be seen as encouraging, if the two giants of the region wished to consider getting together over water. Indeed if full-scale friendliness were ever sought, an immense opportunity awaits.

Mr Verghese points out that the Tsangpo/Brahmaputra falls 2,450 metres (8,000 feet) over a few kilometres in China just before it reaches the Indian border. Send it through a 100km tunnel from the Tibetan plateau down to Assam and an enormous 54,000MW could be generated. One day its power could light not only much of north-east India and Bangladesh, but nearby Myanmar and beyond. Such a mega-structure would become a keystone for regional co-operation.

It will almost certainly never be built. Analysts have suggested that, given the generally dire relations between South Asian countries, water will provoke clashes rather than co-operation. A 2009 report for the CIA concluded that "the likelihood of conflict between India and Pakistan over shared river resources is expected to increase", though it added that elsewhere in the region "the risk of armed interstate conflict is minor".

And a Bangladeshi security expert, Major-General Muniruzzaman, predicts that India's "coercive diplomacy", its refusal to negotiate multilaterally on such issues as river-sharing, means that "if ever there were a localised conflict in South Asia, it will be over water."

SAFEGUARDING SOUTH ASIA'S WATER SECURITY

IN today's era of globalization, the line between critic and hypocrite is increasingly becoming blurred. Single out a problem in a region or country other than one's own, and risk triggering an immediate, yet understandable, response: Why criticize the problem here, when you face the same one back home?

Such a response is particularly justified in the context of water insecurity, a dilemma that afflicts scores of countries, including the author's United States. In the parched American West, New Mexico has only ten years worth of drinking water remaining, while Arizona already imports every drop. Less arid areas of the country are increasingly water-stressed as well.

Rivers in South Carolina and Massachusetts, lakes in Florida and Georgia, and even the mighty Lake Superior (the world's largest fresh-water lake) are all running dry. According to the U.S. Environmental Protection Agency, if American water consumption habits continue unchecked, as many as 36 states will face water shortages within the next few years. Also notable is the fact that America's waterways are choked with pollution, and that nearly twenty million Americans may fall ill each year from contaminated water. Not to mention that more than thirty U.S. states are fighting with their neighbours over water.

Such a narrative is a familiar one, because it also applies to South Asia. However, in South Asia, the narrative is considerably more urgent. The region houses a quarter of the world's population, yet contains less than 5% of its annual renewable water resources. With the exception of Bhutan and Nepal, South Asia's per capita water availability falls below the world average.

Annual water availability has plummeted by nearly 70% since 1950, and from around 21,000 cubic metres in the 1960s to approximately 8,000 in 2005. If such patterns continue, the region could face 'widespread water scarcity' (that is, per capita water availability under 1,000 cubic metres) by 2025. Furthermore, the United Nations, based on a variety of measures – including ecological insecurity, water management problems and resource stress – characterizes two key water basins of South Asia (the Helmand and Indus) as 'highly vulnerable'.

These findings are not surprising, given that the region suffers from many drivers of water insecurity: high population growth, vulnerability to climate change, arid weather, agriculture dependent economies and political tensions. This is not to say that South Asia is devoid of water security stabilizers; indeed, its various trans-national arrangements, to differing degrees, help the region manage its water constraints and tensions. This paper argues that such arrangements are vital, yet also incapable of safeguarding regional water security on their own. It asserts that more attention to demand-side water management within individual countries is as crucial for South Asian water security as are trans-national water mechanisms.

To understand the importance of trans-boundary water arrangements in South Asia, one must first bear in mind a paradox: the region is poorly integrated, yet linked together by water co-dependencies.

Consider, first, that the World Bank has declared South Asia the world's least integrated region. According to the Bank, South Asia has the world's worst railways and road density, while only sub-Saharan Africa has worse electricity and sanitation systems. Predictably, intra-regional trade accounts for just 5% of the region's total international trade, and less than 2% of gross domestic product. Not surprisingly, South Asia's regional organization, SAARC, is not nearly as dynamic as regional groupings like the European Union or the Association of South East Asian Nations.

Second, that many of the region's countries depend on the same rivers – and, by extension, neighbouring upper riparians – for their water supply. India, Bangladesh and Nepal look to the Brahmaputra, while both Pakistan and India are beholden to the rivers of the Indus basin. Bangladesh and Pakistan, both lower riparians, must obtain great majorities of their water resources (91% and 75%, respectively) from beyond their borders.

Conversely, China, while not a geographic entity of South Asia, is an upper riparian for many of the key rivers flowing into South Asia. India is both a lower (in the case of the Brahmaputra) and upper (in the case of the Indus) riparian. This means, hypothetically, that any flow-diverting Chinese activities on the Brahmaputra could alarm India, Nepal and Bangladesh, and in turn trigger Indian flow manipulations on the Indus, with implications downstream for Pakistan. Such a dynamic creates a hydro domino effect: one nation's water policies can spark a chain reaction throughout the region.

Another notable factor about South Asia's interconnected water geography is that many major rivers originate in or pass through politically contested or tense areas. The Tibetan plateau – where the mighty flows of the Salween, Brahmaputra, Indus, Sutlej, and other rivers all spring to life, providing water to 1.5 billion people downstream – is controlled by China, and abuts India's water-rich Arunachal Pradesh state, which China covets and has sparked Sino-Indian tensions. The rivers of the Indus basin, of course, flow through the Kashmir region – an unending source of Pakistan-India tensions. No wonder that many of South Asia's riparian pairings (India-Pakistan for the Indus, and India-Bangladesh for the Brahmaputra and the Ganges) reflect the region's most troubled bilateral relationships.

In effect, South Asia's water relations play out amid a volatile backdrop of shortage, dependency and geopolitical tension.

A nation's upper riparian status by no means guarantees water security. China, an uber-upper riparian, suffers from a full-blown water crisis. The North China plain – one of the country's 'economic and social cores' generating more than 20% of its grain supply, according to China scholar David Pietz – is frighteningly water-scarce, with a per capita availability of 225 cubic metres per year. India, meanwhile, contains about 20% of the world's population, but only about 4% of its water. A 2010 Asian Development Bank report projects that the country could suffer from water shortages of as much as 50% by 2030.

Faced with current shortages, policymakers in upper riparian states frequently opt for supply-side solutions. Water generation measures may ease water stress internally, yet they often exacerbate regional tensions. India and China, to generate desperately needed water resources for both agriculture and energy, often resort to dam construction and other large engineering projects. Many of these are run-of-the-river and hence do not prevent flows from continuing downstream. Still, dams are a delicate matter. China's insistence that its South to North Water Diversion Project will not divert flows from the Brahmaputra is met with skepticism in India. Additionally, even run-of-the-river dams and other hydro projects threaten lower riparians' water and food security. For example, if India builds all its envisioned hydro projects on the western rivers of the Indus basin, Pakistan's agriculture could be deprived of up to a month's worth of river flows – enough to ruin an entire planting season.

Lower riparians also opt for large, supply generating projects. Pakistan's water resources policy has been dominated by dam building for decades, and the country's Water and Power Development Authority (WAPDA) plans to construct five dams, three large canals, and five hydropower facilities by 2025. As a lower riparian, these national engineering projects will not impede river flows into downstream countries. However, they upset riparian communities, who risk being displaced. Supply-side efforts also aggravate regional and provincial tensions, which are high in many South Asian countries. The furious debate surrounding Pakistan's Kalabagh dam, for example, has pitted supporters in Punjab against opponents everywhere else in the country. This internal discontent feeds into the domestic instability that so concerns Pakistan's neighbours.

In Pakistan, water insecurity also spawns different manifestations of militancy. In recent years, the Pakistani Taliban, aware of Pakistan's precarious water situation, has attacked the country's largest earth-filled dam, the fabled Tarbela. More recently, extremists in Punjab have issued violent threats, angrily blaming India for 'stealing' Pakistan's water and vowing aggression against India unless it ceases such 'theft'. It is perhaps not coincidental that while Pakistan based extremists have been largely absent from the latest uprising in Jammu and Kashmir, they have been increasingly vocal in their accusations of India's alleged water theft. These extremists regard their India blame game as an expression of nationalism – an attempt to draw attention away from divisive debates within Pakistan about dam construction and toward a unified front on confronting India. Water may well be supplanting Kashmir as the militants' chief rallying cry.

Another response – more potential than actual, at least at this point – is for desperate citizens to flee to more water-secure nations. According to a Strategic Foresight Group estimate, water scarcity will contribute to the displacement and migration of 50 to 70 million people in India, Bangladesh, Nepal and China by 2050. To be sure, water strain takes a devastating toll on human security inside upper and lower riparian nations alike – as evidenced by the livelihood-shattered Pakistani fishermen along the disappearing Indus plain and the water starved, suicidal Indian farmers in parts of India.

However, migration is a particularly worrisome threat for lower riparians, with the potential not just to uproot millions of people, but also to imperil regional stability. Bangladesh offers a vivid example. As an impoverished, highly populous, lower riparian that depends on other countries for nearly all its water needs, it is deeply vulnerable to Indian or Chinese activity on rivers upstream and to glacial melting in the Himalayas. And as a low-lying nation, it is susceptible to rising sea levels and monsoon flooding. This array of water problems, according to some observers, could hasten mass Bangladeshi migrations into India's volatile East, with politically explosive implications.

The combustible mix of water vulnerability, geopolitical tensions, and supply-side responses with ripple effects across borders constitutes a recipe for disaster – and figures to become even more explosive in the coming decades as the region's population growth soars and Himalayan glacial melt accelerates. Several nightmare water-driven scenarios come to mind:

Indus Basin War. Militants in eastern Pakistan, vowing to avenge India's 'theft' of Pakistan's water from the Indus basin's western rivers, launch terror attacks in India. New Delhi dispatches troops to its western flank, and threatens to shut-off western river flows into Pakistan.

Sino-Indian Water Showdown. China, in response to Indian defensive upgrades in and near Arunachal Pradesh, the water-rich northeastern Indian state that Beijing has long claimed, seeks to reclaim a strategic advantage by slowing the flow of the Brahmaputra into India's Assam state – an impoverished bastion of separatist militancy that is also an important area of agricultural production.

Environmental Refugee Crisis. As glacial melt in the Himalayas runs its course, river flows slow to a trickle, and lower riparian Bangladesh experiences rampant water scarcity, Bangladeshis migrate en masse to more water secure but politically volatile eastern India – deepening instability in the latter as violent factions target these new arrivals, and long entrenched separatist militants exploit the unrest by launching their own attacks.

These hypothetical scenarios, and the bubbling cauldron of water insecurity and political tensions that makes them impossible to dismiss, crystallize the importance of trans-boundary water arrangements with the ability to manage, if not reduce, the region's water based tensions.

Numerous trans-boundary rivers in South Asia are governed by treaties. These include the Mahakali (to which India and Nepal are party), the Ganges (involving India and Bangladesh), and the Indus (comprising India and Pakistan). The Mahakali accord is meant to promote the river's integrated development, though various disagreements have prevented the treaty from being properly implemented. The Ganges agreement is also constrained by several disagreements, particularly over the Farakka Barrage, which Bangladesh believes has reduced downstream flows of the Ganges.

Nonetheless, none of these countries has ever gone to war over water, and the treaties are surely a major reason why. The Indus Waters Treaty (IWT) allocates the Indus basin's western rivers to Pakistan, and the eastern rivers to India (India is authorized to draw on the western rivers for agricultural purposes, so long as this use does not involve storage). It deserves particular attention, given that it is repeatedly lauded as a magnificent example of international cooperation and conflict management. Such rhetoric is warranted. The two parties, despite their rocky relations, truly make a commitment to uphold the treaty's provisions. The IWT emphasizes transparency, particularly in terms of data exchange and notification of plans to undertake hydro projects. Sure enough, in 2010, India allowed Pakistan to inspect several under-construction Indian hydropower projects on the western rivers. The two nations have also agreed to set up a telemetry system to measure river flows.

Additionally, only once in the treaty's 50 year history have the accord's mechanisms for dispute resolution been put to the test. This was a period between 2005 and 2007, when a neutral expert (appointed by the World Bank, as per the IWT's stipulations) weighed in on the concerns of Pakistan about the Baglihar dam, a project being constructed by India on one of the Indus basin's western rivers. The expert ruled against Pakistan on several technical points – particularly when he stated that a gated spillway was necessary – yet agreed with it on others (such as on the issue of power intake levels). While many on both sides undoubtedly found ways to oppose the outcome, it is undeniable that the dispute was settled peacefully. In June 2010, both governments concurred that the Baglihar dispute had been definitively resolved.

In 2010, Pakistan decided to bring some technical concerns about the Kishanganga dam (a hydro project being constructed by India in Jammu and Kashmir) to an international court of arbitration. While the outcome of this latest case is far from clear, the Baglihar precedent suggests the arbitration process for Kishanganga should be similarly smooth.

Despite its successes, many observers fear the IWT's increasing vulnerability. This derives in part from the long-standing grievances harboured by both countries about the treaty. Indians believe it curtails the storage rights of Jammu and Kashmir, and hampers the development of hydro projects on the western rivers. Indeed, India's participation in the treaty is both economically and politically risky – given that the energy-starved nation must forego opportunities to harvest hydroelectric resources, and given the resentment these cautious hydro development policies breed among Kashmiris.

Pakistan, meanwhile, resents its inherent vulnerability as the lower riparian (even though the IWT allots it 80% of the total

Indus basin river flow). For many in Pakistan, the country with the lowest per capita water availability in Asia, entrusting its water security to its deeply mistrusted neighbour is profoundly unsettling.

Furthermore, worries about population growth and climate change effects (particularly the melting of Himalayan glaciers) are fuelling calls for a revised treaty that takes such trends into account. There are also recommendations that the treaty be expanded, so that it includes the other two Indus basin riparians, China and Afghanistan. Those advocating this latter view argue that a four-party treaty would reduce the possibilities of region-wide conflict, and promote basin-wide ecological sustainability.

Some experts contend that the 'dividing the resources' mentality of the IWT is no longer tenable, and that Pakistan and India should move toward a more cooperative 'share the resources' paradigm. Ahmad Rafay Alam, one of the most eloquent articulator of this view from the Pakistan side, argues that the two nations should determine 'whether it is in the economic, social or political interest of both riparians to cooperate on water, rather than be antagonistic over it.' For example, instead of railing against Indian run-of-the-river dam projects on the western rivers, power-starved Pakistan should consider buying the electricity they generate – a more affordable investment than buying power from pricier indigenous gas-powered rental power projects.

This paradigm can be applied to a broader geographic area as well. Bhutan and Nepal are blessed with ample hydroelectric potential; India could therefore invest in energy resources in these countries just as Pakistan could in India.

Some experts make more modest suggestions about improving trans-national water arrangements. They believe that regional water security is best attained not by changing the architecture or philosophy of regional water agreements, but instead by strengthening mechanisms for cooperation and transparency within existing arrangements. In other words, instead of crafting a new IWT, the parties should make even greater commitments to respect the treaty's current provisions on transparency. A core component of this viewpoint is the need for more data sharing on river flows, hydro project plans, and glacial melting. This emphasis on transparency is a chief feature of U.S. government policy on transnational water arrangements. Policymakers in Washington, when describing South Asian water arrangements, repeatedly underscore the same terms: good communication, data sharing and joint management.

Some modest steps have already been taken along these lines. India and Pakistan recently agreed to several information sharing measures. Additionally, China and India have agreed to share data on glacial melt. Still, much more can be done, and it is here that the international community can play a key role. International academic conferences and other forums facilitating the exchange of information about water constitute one way to boost water transparency. Technology sharing is another avenue.

The United States, for example, can share its new METRIC system – a new water measurement tool developed by academic researchers that has already helped resolve a fight over water in the Arkansas river, and could similarly be deployed in the Indus basin. Similarly, America could provide satellite data that document water availability. It is sometimes observed that there are no international water treaties or other global mechanisms to promote water cooperation. The international community's participation in water data sharing exercises, in South Asia and elsewhere, can serve as a modest corrective.

Champions of trans-boundary water transparency argue that by fostering greater data sharing, riparians' mutual suspicions can be reduced, paving the way for greater water cooperation. It is important to note, however, that greater water transparency can easily backfire, and even undermine riparian relations. As one study concludes, revelations of 'inequitable Indian water stewardship on Indus tributaries' could exacerbate the volatility of India-Pakistan relations. One might then argue that nations with delicate relations may in certain cases be better served by not revealing inflammatory water data, and should instead maintain opacity.

This raises a critical point: Advocating for more trans-boundary water openness, pushing for 'resource sharing' paradigms, and proposing more inclusive treaties all presuppose a level of political cooperation that may not exist in South Asia. After all, it is easy to propose the formation of a new Himalayan Rivers Commission to govern water management in this sub-region, as was done in 2010. However, it would be much more difficult to implement such an arrangement, which would necessitate the close cooperation of nations harbouring major trust deficits toward each other.

So the question invariably arises: How can South Asia's trans-national water arrangements be enhanced in such a troubled political environment? One answer is to look within, and to muster better efforts to improve internal water governance. This is because sounder water management inside countries can create a more favourable political climate for the pursuit and achievement of lasting external water cooperation. Better internal water management can serve as a catalyst for effective regional water governance.

It is common to attribute water problems exclusively to politics. It is often said that India-Pakistan water tensions are just one facet of a long troubled bilateral relationship. Similarly, one frequently hears that India-China disagreements over water are rooted in the larger competition between the two rising powers for influence over South Asian territory and resources. And India's water disagreements with Bangladesh and Nepal too are said to be part of a long history of poor political relations.

Such views are accurate, yet incomplete. After all, across the United States and Australia, regions and states bicker over river water allocations – yet these tensions have little to do with politics. Neither Colorado and Kansas in the United States, nor Victoria and Queensland in Australia, are at risk of going to war; they simply disagree about how to properly divide up river flows. As such, their squabbles demonstrate an inability to efficiently manage existing water resources. In South Asia, where the availability of water resources is more precarious, this poor water governance is a chief cause of water insecurity.

In South Asia, water insecurity is not solely a function of resource shortages. To be sure, much of it is running low on water.

However, excluding some arid portions of the region, very little of South Asia is actually water-scarce. The resource is precious, yet present. South Asia's water problems are very much rooted in the wasteful and inefficient management of the region's available water supplies.

Pakistan is arguably the worst culprit. Water infrastructure and transmission systems – the canals and pipes that have helped make the Indus river system the world's largest contiguous irrigated area – are literally falling apart because they have not been properly maintained. As a result, millions of gallons of water are lost to leakage every day. In urban areas, wastewater treatment facilities are nearly non-existent – hence the country's great cities are notorious for fetid surface water resources that sicken and kill hundreds of thousands every year.

Meanwhile, Islamabad offers few incentives to the population to use water saving technology. The lack of subsidies for drip irrigation, for example, compels farmers to use traditional, water wasting flood irrigation. Furthermore, the government has made little effort to diversify crop production. This is unfortunate, given that Pakistan's most intensively produced crops – and those that fetch the greatest profits for small farmers – are also the most water guzzling.

Then there are the structural factors that exacerbate Pakistan's water mismanagement. Thanks to the nation's feudal land setup, a small landed elite owns most rural land, while the majority of the rural population is landless. In a country with few water laws or rights, land ownership determines water access.

As a result, most of Pakistan's rural population struggles to obtain water. In theory, mechanisms such as *warabandi* – the colonial-era water distribution system meant to ensure farmers equal access to irrigation water – and provincial level water arbiters such as the Indus River System Authority (IRSA) are meant to compensate for such inequalities. In reality, they fail miserably. Warabandi is exploited by politically connected large farmers, while IRSA is rarely taken seriously, and its edicts about provincial river flow allocations are routinely ignored. Given this gloomy domestic water situation in Pakistan, it is clear why not only militants, but also the country's government, have chosen to externalize blame over the border. After all, bringing attention to its dysfunctional domestic water management would essentially be an acknowledgment that Islamabad is to blame for its water crisis. While Islamabad is much less prone to blame India than it was several years ago (in fact, in 2010, Pakistan's minister for water and power acknowledged that India rarely prevents river water from flowing into Pakistan), it rarely admits that the country's water problems are largely internally rooted.

Pakistan is not the only poor water manager in South Asia; India's water governance is similarly troubled. India is home to 'dilapidated' pipes and pumping stations that cause more than one-third of New Delhi's fresh water (and at least 40% of most Indian cities' total water resources) to be lost to leakage. The Yamuna river is choked with 'faecal bacteria', and this sewage has increased 'thousands of times' over the last decade. Water intensive rice and wheat crops are championed by the government through price guarantees to farmers. And per capita storage availability – the *sine qua non* for dam efficiency – has plummeted in recent years to levels found in Africa's poorest nations.

Poor internal water management has grave implications for public health, food security and the environment. Sometimes the effects can be catastrophic. Consider this summer's flooding in Pakistan. If the country's water infrastructure had been sturdier and better maintained, raging rivers would have been better contained and the damage wrought by the deluge may not have been as extensive.

Perhaps the most disturbing implication is the strain on groundwater resources. With poor internal water management regimes causing surface water to be wasted, lost or contaminated across the region, South Asians are increasingly digging deeper – literally – to alleviate their water insecurity.

In the context of agriculture – by far, the sector that consumes the most water across South Asia – the increasing inefficiency of highly subsidized, state-run irrigation systems have driven farmers to mine groundwater, which they have more control over and is more readily available. Even back in 2000, nearly 70% of

Bangladesh's irrigation, and more than 50% of India's, was served by groundwater resources.

Yet groundwater depletion goes beyond the agricultural sector. According to the World Bank, India is the world's most voracious consumer of groundwater. This heavy consumption is reflected in a 2009 study by several U.S. scientists, which found that groundwater levels fell by about four centimetres per year between 2002 and 2008 across three states in northwestern India – including the breadbasket of Punjab. These areas could conceivably exhaust their entire groundwater supply within the next few decades.

Pakistan, too, is increasingly groundwater-reliant. Lahore – the country's second-largest city – is completely dependent on it for drinking water needs, and groundwater tables have fallen by as much as sixty-five feet in some areas of the metropolis. Worse, wastewater is now infiltrating the city's groundwater, choking it with arsenic.

Groundwater – once a pristine, untapped resource – is now being extracted intensively throughout South Asia. In effect, with this onslaught on South Asia's groundwater, the last bastion of regional water security has been breached. And as groundwater becomes increasingly short and scarce, South Asia may be compelled to return to rapidly dwindling surface water resources and to compete ferociously for the ultra-precious supply that remains – a terrifying prospect, and particularly for lower riparians.

Faced with domestic water problems, and mistaking mismanagement for shortages (or intentionally cloaking mismanagement in the guise of shortages), governments succumb to their supply-side fancies, and construct more dams and reservoirs. Such actions, as noted earlier, fan provincial tensions, and, in the case of upper riparians, anger downstream neighbours. Herein lies the troubling link between poor water management at home and trans-national water cooperation: the former prompts governments to take actions that threaten the latter.

Whether such actions outweigh the risks of imperilling trans-national water cooperation is debatable. This is because many supply-side coping strategies are neither efficient nor sustainable. One of Pakistan's top water experts, Simi Kamal, has calculated that the quantity of water projected to be generated by the nation's under-construction Diamer-Basha dam pales in comparison to the amount that would be freed up simply by repairing and maintaining Pakistan's leaky canal system.Additionally, Pakistan's dams, like India's, are rapidly losing storage capacity.

Such considerations give way to another unsettling reality: So long as internal water management remains poor, the benefits accruing from deeper regional water cooperation will be strictly political; from a water resources standpoint, little will improve. Take the case of Pakistan. Assume, for a moment, that increased cooperation enables Pakistan to succeed in getting India to release more water downstream. What would be the result? Many Pakistanis would argue that their water problems would be solved: parched farmland saved, children's thirst quenched, and lost water livelihoods restored.

In reality, however, none of this would happen. Instead, more water would mean more inefficiency: More water lost to leaky canals and pipes, wasted in irrigation, showered on water-guzzling crops, and contaminated by urban waste. Indeed, if nothing is done to improve internal water governance, allowing more water to gush into Pakistan would simply intensify the country's water crisis.

South Asian nations need to focus more on demand-side solutions to domestic water problems. These include water conserving technologies, crop diversification, better investments in infrastructure maintenance and wastewater treatment, and a stronger embrace of rainwater harvesting (a conservation method that has already caught on quite strongly in parts of the region). Such policies are less expensive, and potentially more efficient, than traditional supply-side water engineering projects like large dams. Some encouraging signs are emerging from India, where there has been some debate about the merits of emphasizing sugar-bean cultivation over that of sugarcane, which is notoriously water wasting. There has also been discussion about embracing water saving mechanisms such as the direct seeding of rice.

If such demand-side management policies are implemented successfully, South Asian nations would become more judicious in their use of existing water resources, and therefore less threatened in the short-term by the spectre of scarcity. Upper riparians would, presumably, be less likely to initiate new hydro-generation projects that upset their downstream neighbours.

Lower riparians, meanwhile, would have less incentive (and fewer grounds) to stoke tensions with their upstream neighbours by accusing them of water theft.

As a result, trans-national water arrangements would be threatened less, and the calmer political climate would enable riparians to make more substantive progress on the data sharing and transparency essential for better South Asian water security. None of this, it should be noted, would necessitate drawing up new treaties or other water agreements.

To be sure, new demographic and environmental realities may well call into question the continued relevance of decades-old trans-national water arrangements. Still, these mechanisms need not stop functioning simply because of the presence of factors not at play fifty years ago. One study of the Baglihar dam case observes that the issue was 'addressed bearing in mind the technical standards for hydropower plants as they have developed in the first decade of the 21st century, and not as perceived and thought of in the 1950s when the [IWT] was negotiated.' A precedent has effectively been set for new conditions to be taken into account when interpreting the existing treaty, without needing to incorporate such conditions into an altogether new or revised treaty.

This is just one more reason for South Asian nations to redouble their efforts to ameliorate internal water management. Trans-national water arrangements can also stand to improve, yet they are not in desperate need of reform and revision. Rather, it is the water governance of the region's individual countries that so urgently needs to be fixed. In effect, South Asian water policies must adopt a new approach – one that, in the words of noted water expert Ramaswamy R. Iyer, embraces the 'responsible, harmonious, just, and wise use of water.' With population growth and climate change continuing apace, the stakes have never been higher, and the costs of inaction never starker.

GROUNDWATER RESILIENCE TO HUMAN DEVELOPMENT AND CLIMATE CHANGE IN SOUTH ASIA

Globally, groundwater is recognized as an important natural resource with great economic value. In many developing nations, groundwater abstraction has accelerated resource development over the past 20 years and led to major social and economic benefits. Estimates show that freshwater represents nearly 2.5 percent of the Earth's total water content, of which around 30 percent is groundwater and the rest includes ice and glaciers, surface water, and soil and atmospheric water. Thus groundwater represents a significant proportion of the Earth's freshwater content, and in many countries groundwater is the only reliable source of freshwater.

Approximately one-fifth of the Earth's total freshwater resources can be found in South Asia – the home of around 1.7 billion people. During the monsoon surface water is abundant throughout the region; during the dry season surface water scarcity is common. A vast amount of freshwater is stored as groundwater beneath the densely populated floodplains of the Ganges, Brahmaputra and Indus River systems. In the dry season or when the monsoon is delayed, this storage is critical. It can also be a safer alternative to often-polluted surface water year-round. For these reasons, groundwater is the main source of domestic, industrial and irrigation water supplies throughout South Asia.

A safe and sustainable water supply is essential for improving public health, and achieving economic growth and food security in the region. Currently, groundwater resources are facing degradation due to a range of problems, such as overexploitation, mismanagement, and natural and anthropogenic contamination. The strategic importance of groundwater for global water and food security will further intensify under climate change.

Groundwater-fed irrigation has become the mainstay of irrigated agriculture over much of India and Bangladesh, Punjab and Sindh provinces of Pakistan, and the Terai plains of Nepal. Traditionally, surface water from ponds and rivers had been used to provide both drinking and irrigation water supplies in all South

Asian countries. However, over the last few decades groundwater has largely replaced surface water-fed water sources. In Bangladesh, currently 97 percent of drinking water and nearly 80 percent of irrigation water come from groundwater. The use of groundwater for irrigation in India and Pakistan is approximately 60 and 35 percent respectively. By volume, India is the biggest groundwater user in the world. A recent estimate shows that in India, Bangladesh, Pakistan and Nepal combined the annual groundwater withdrawal is nearly 250 km – approximately 35% of the world's total groundwater withdrawal. A substantial proportion of this groundwater is used to produce rice, the staple food of South Asia. Recently, Bangladesh has made significant progress towards becoming self-sufficient in food grains, primarily through groundwater-sustained agriculture. It has long been taken for granted that shallow groundwater used for irrigation and drinking water supplies in Bangladesh is fully recharged during the monsoon season. However, recent studies reveal that the volume of groundwater storage is rapidly declining in many parts of Bangladesh and India because groundwater is not being recharged at the same rate as it is used.

Intensive and unsustainable use of groundwater in South Asia, particularly in northern India and central and northwestern Bangladesh, has led to rapid depletion of aquifers in recent years. NASA's GRACE (Gravity Recovery and Climate Experiment) satellite observations have been used to show that northern India has lost approximately 109 km3 of groundwater between 2002 and 2008. Over the same period, India's neighbor Bangladesh, which has 4.5% of India's landmass, has lost nearly 3 km^2 of its groundwater due to over-abstraction. It is reported that sustained groundwater depletion has contributed substantially to global sea-level rise ; groundwater depletion in Asia is estimated to have contributed to a global rise of 2.2 millimeters over the period 2001 to 2008. Recent sea-level rise in the Bay of Bengal has been attributed, at least in part, to over-abstraction of local groundwater to supply irrigation and municipal water over the last few decades.

Another concern is the deterioration of groundwater quality due to both natural processes and anthropogenic activities. In large parts of Bangladesh and several northeastern states of India, shallow groundwater is contaminated with high concentrations of naturally occurring arsenic. Nearly 100 million people in the Indian sub-continent are currently exposed to dangerous levels of arsenic in their drinking water supply. High concentrations of naturally-occurring fluoride is another threat to public health affecting nearly 66 million people in southern and northwestern India. Although, arsenic and fluoride contamination is not as big a problem in coastal Bangladesh, highly saline groundwater is a major public-health concern, particularly for maternal health. Similar concerns exist in other deltaic areas of South Asia. Although sources of high salinity in coastal groundwater are difficult to identify, it has been shown that the reduction of flow through the lower Ganges and rising sea levels are partly responsible.

How will climate change affect South Asia's groundwater resources in future? Unlike surface water, groundwater is more resilient to climate change and slow to respond to any change. However, some specific aspects of climate change can greatly influence the timing and magnitude of groundwater recharge and quality, such as a shift in monsoon season, heavy rainfall events, increased evaporation, increased runoff and rising sea levels. Elsewhere, it has been shown that episodic heavy rainfall events favor more rapid groundwater recharge in central Tanzania. Heavier rainfall events are also projected to occur in South Asia but the potential impact on groundwater recharge remains unanswered. Sea level rise can cause coastal fresh groundwater at shallow depths to be gradually replaced by saltwater. This process can accelerate through over abstraction of groundwater in many of the growing coastal cities of South Asia.

The degradation of groundwater resources by human development and climate change is increasingly disturbing drinking and irrigation water supplies globally. The problem is not exclusive to South Asia, but it is perhaps most critical in what is the world's most densely populated region. Public health, food security, industrial growth, and ecosystems all are currently at greater risk than ever before. More public investment will be needed to manage the growing demand for drinking, industrial and irrigation water supplies. Alternatives are needed and improved efficiency of use is required. Many past development projects in South Asia did not take into consideration the declining state of groundwater. Governments need to recognize the social and economic importance of protecting aquifers from further deterioration. Public awareness and education are also essential. Lastly, more scientific research is necessary, particularly in complex coastal environments. Continually improving our knowledge of groundwater systems in South Asia, and the threats they face, is a key step in protecting this precious natural resource.

INDUS WATERS TREATY (INDIA-PAKISTAN)

The Indus Waters Treaty between India and Pakistan has been described as one of the most successful water sharing treaties ever accomplished. It is a unique treaty because it was able to get two countries with historically hostile relations to reach an agreement that has been in place since 1961. The treaty is also unique because of the role the World Bank played in brokering the agreement. It is therefore worth looking into for possible lessons for a future solution for the Central Asian countries.

The waters of the Indus basin begin in the Himalayan Mountains of Indian held Kashmir. The water flows from the hills through the arid states of Punjab and Sind, converging in Pakistan and emptying into the Arabian Sea south of Karachi. Developments over the last century have created a large network of canals and storage facilities that provide water for more than 26 million acres - the largest irrigated area of any river system in the world.

The partitioning of the Indian subcontinent created a conflict over the entitlement of waters of the Indus basin. The newly formed states could not come to an agreement over how to share and manage what was essentially a unitary network of irrigation. Also, the geography of partition was such that the source rivers of the Indus basin were in India. Pakistan felt threatened by the prospect of Indian control over the tributaries that fed water into the Pakistani portion of the basin, as it threatened the country's main source of water to cultivate its land. This was a classic conflict situation between upstream and downstream riparian countries, and it was exacerbated by a lack of trust and intense territorial animosity between the two sides. Even though both countries tried to settle the matter bilaterally several times after partition, no lasting agreement was reached until the World Bank got involved as a mediating entity.

The World Bank volunteered to act as a benign go-between, but it did not intend, at least initially, to split the existing canal system and the basin unity. The World Bank's initial proposal was to have the Indus irrigation scheme administered as one unit by the two parties, irrespective of the new borders drawn as a result of the partitioning of the sub-continent. However, both parties turned down this proposal. After several years of negotiating, the two parties made progress towards an understanding that involved dividing the six rivers between the two parties. In addition, Pakistan was to receive financial assistance to construct storage reservoirs. This was to compensate for loss of water after rivers were divided.

The Indus Waters Treaty and the role of the World Bank

The Indus Waters Treaty was signed in 1960 and divided the six rivers comprising the Indus river system between the two countries. India was granted the three eastern tributaries (Ravi, Beas, and Sutlej) and Pakistan assumed the flow of the three western rivers (Indus, Jhelum, and Chenab). A unique feature of the Indus Waters Treaty is that it is the only international waters-treaty co-signed by a third party, namely the World Bank. The World Bank signed the Treaty for certain specified purposes stated in the Treaty: Article V "Financial Provisions" deals with India's contribution to Pakistan for the replacement works to be constructed as a result of the termination of Pakistan's water rights to the Eastern rivers. India's contribution was made to the World Bank and credited to the Indus Basin Development Fund. Besides the contribution from India, the Fund consisted mostly of grant funding from a number of donors and World Bank loans. The Fund was used to finance the replacement works that Pakistan needed in order to end its reliance on the Eastern rivers and to augment the flow of the Western rivers. The funding for Development Fund is a very important aspect of the Treaty. The solution to get funding from the international community for replacement works, and not make India pay for it all, was the tipping point that made India accept the agreement,

RESOLVING THE BAGLIHAR DISPUTE THROUGH THE WORLD BANK

The procedural role of the World Bank was recently exercised when Pakistan approached the World Bank in 2005 stating that a dispute had arisen with regard to the Baglihar hydropower plant India was constructing on the Chenab River.

Although the Chenab River was allocated to Pakistan, India was allowed certain uses of the Western rivers, which include run-off-river hydropower plants.

It was the first time since the Treaty was signed that the Bank had been called upon by one of the parties to exercise its role and responsibilities under the Treaty with regard to a dispute settlement. In 2005 the World Bank informed the two parties that it had appointed Mr. Raymond Lafitte, a Swiss national, an engineer and professor, as the Neutral Expert to address the Baglihar difference. The Neutral Expert was able to deliver a decision that was accepted by the two parties and the Bank has been credited for its ability to play a fair, transparent and continued constructive role in its appointment of the Neutral Expert.

This case study can be related to the water dispute in Central Asia. It illustrates how shifting borders and the creation of independent states exacerbated what was initially an intra-national issue. It is also interesting to note that because hostility, mistrust and competing interests makes it hard to come to an agreement between the countries themselves, a possible solution could be the positive, active, and continuous involvement of a third party. The active participation of the World Bank was crucial to the success of the Indus Waters Treaty. The Bank offered a strong leadership role as well as providing support staff, funding, and, perhaps most important, its own proposals when negotiations reached a stalemate between India and Pakistan. It is therefore important to consider the Indus Waters Treaty as a potential model for environmental cooperation in Central Asia.

MEKONG RIVER BASIN (SOUTHEAST ASIA)

Foreign Policy Association, 2010

The Mekong is the longest river in Southeast Asia, the seventh longest in Asia, and the twelfth longest in the world. It originates in the Tanghla Shan Mountains on the Tibetan plateau, passes through southern China, Myanmar, Laos, Thailand, Cambodia, Viet Nam, and ends in the Indian Ocean. Roughly 70 million people of which some 62 million reside in the Lower Mekong Basin (almost all of Cambodia and Laos, one-third of Thailand, and one-fifth of Viet Nam) depend on the Mekong river system for their own subsistence. It is projected that in the following years, there will be an increase in the total number of people who depend on the Mekong River for food, water and transport.

Given the importance of the Mekong River Basin to all six riparian states, in 1957 the Mekong Committee was created. Whereas many inter-state water treaties have been designed in midst of potential open conflict, the Committee emerged during a time of relative peace in the region. Since its inception, the Committee has operated in conjunction with many other international, regional and national organizations working in the Mekong River Basin. However, in 1995, Cambodia, Laos, Thailand and Vietnam signed the Agreement on the Co-operation for the Sustainable Development of the Mekong River Basin (MRC), making it the only legally constituted regional organization mandated from the highest political level to represent the interests of riparian states in Mekong River matters. In 1995 the MRC agreed to focus its efforts into three areas of priority. These are:

- Developing rules for the cooperative use of water through the Water Utilization Program.
- Basin Development Planning, facilitating cooperative sustainable development of water related resources.
- Environmental monitoring.

The MRC excels as a resilient paradigm that has withstood the test of time albeit with challenges: lack of accurate, timely data on Mekong River water quantity and quality: inadequate and incomplete policy and regulatory frameworks vis-à-vis the Basin's complex ecosystems and habitats, and weak enforcement capabilities. Another challenge that threatens the goals of the MRC is that the People's Republic of China and the Union of Myanmar are only dialogue partners to the MRC. Thus management of dams and downstream flows that severely affect the other Mekong countries are not given priority by the former two states. It is important to note that China has stressed that its eight dams would help, and not hinder, the MRC goals. Presently, China is reluctant to join the MRC, refuses to share more hydrological data related to the Mekong, and to be more transparent about its Mekong dams plans.

Interestingly, the Mekong water system, similarly to the Amu Darya River and Syr Darya River in Central Asia, has an ominous colonial legacy of large-scale exploitation by the French that supplied the large demand for Europe's industrialization process.

Notwithstanding the later, cooperation among the riparian Mekong countries has been a compelling force behind a common purpose: the promotion and coordination of integrated basin development through regional cooperation.

In spite of the fact that each of the riparian Mekong countries may have their own set of interests in the Mekong water and resources, they established a remarkable foundation to equitable sharing of common water resources by focusing on three elements. First, provide each country in the Mekong sub-region with equitable access to an important source of renewable energy- hydropower potential. Second, the MRC, fully aware of the importance of agriculture in the region, promotes a socio-economic agenda that focuses on greater efficacy of irrigated agriculture, diversification of the sector, and better quality of life for majority of rural population. The Mekong River is said to be the force behind the agricultural sector of Southeast Asia, and meets more than half of total water demand in the region. Third, given the Mekong River geographical dynamics, the MRC agenda focuses on developing transportation hubs among the riparian countries, which could facilitate regional and international trade, transparent borders, regional integration, and overall better regional relations between neighbors.

Relevant to the current water crisis in Central Asia is the way the water resources of the Mekong River Basin has been conducive to regional cooperation since 1957.

The MRC framework illustrates that joint water management agreements among riparian countries have an operational and effective role with regard to securing and promoting regional concord and development. The main lesson learned regarding the MRC is that an international water treaty among the Central Asia states is plausible, so long as the leadership at the highest political level put forward genuine resolve to settle any regional water-use disputes. The MRC framework should be an excellent example for the Central Asian countries should they decide to pursue a water cooperation agreement with special focus on equitable sharing of common water resources, so as to ensure the betterment of their own people. That is, with or without the involvement of an acceptable and neutral third-party mediator.

8

Food, Water, and Energy Security in South Asia

INTRODUCTION

Food and water are essential for human existence and energy is the key to human development. Access to these resources and their sustainable management are the basis for sustainable development. Recognizing that efficient use of these limited or declining resources is essential to sustainability, the global community has turned its attention to the concept of the food, water, and energy nexus. The World Economic Forum 2011, the Bonn2011 Nexus Conference, the sixth World Water Forum, and World Water Week 2012, to mention a few, have urged an integrated approach to food, water, and energy security. The Rio + 20 declaration 'The Future We Want', which stresses the need for a balanced integration of economic, social, and environmental issues in economic development, also stresses the need to address society's core issues of food, water, and energy security in a manner that reduces the adverse impacts on nature–water, biodiversity, air, and climate. The nexus approach recognizes the interdependencies of water, energy, and food production and aims to systemize the interconnections to provide a framework for assessing the use of all resources and to manage trade-offs and synergies.

The concept of the food, water, and energy nexus is extremely relevant to Asia as the region has to feed two-thirds of the world's population (4.14 billion people) and accounts for 59% of the planet's water consumption. Ensuring food security and providing access to safe drinking water and modern energy for all remains a key challenge for Asia's sustainable development. The challenge is especially great in the South Asian countries–Afghanistan, Bangladesh, Bhutan, India, Maldives, Nepal, Pakistan, and Sri Lanka–where more than 40% of the world's poor live and some 51% of the population is food–energy deficient. With just 3% of the world's land, South Asia has about one-fourth of the world's population (1.6 billion people). Rice and wheat, the staple foods in the subregion, require huge amounts of water and energy. Freshwater, once abundant, is under growing stress due to the increased demand for competing uses, and climate change is creating additional uncertainties. About 20% of the population of South Asia lacks access to safe drinking water. The increase in water stress and water demand raises questions about how to ensure enough water for growing food without losing hydropower for energy security. The energy required to make water available for crop production, for example through groundwater pumping, is in serious shortage; per capita energy consumption in this region is among the lowest in the world, only 300 kg of oil equivalent, which is just one-third of China's 2001 per capita consumption. With a large and rising population, limited land resources, inadequate energy supply, and growing water stress, South Asian countries face a common challenge of how to produce more food with the same or less land, less water, and increased energy prices.

Ecosystems the Missing Link in the Food, Water, and Energy Nexus

The nexus approach provides a framework for addressing competition for resources and enhancing resource use efficiency with a cross-sectoral focus. However, the nexus discourse has yet to appreciate the value of ecosystems, their functions, and their services in water, energy, and food production. Food and freshwater services critically depend on the flow and services from ecosystems. The ecosystem functions and services provided by mountains, for example " including freshwater, energy, biodiversity, forest products and services, food and medicinal products, and fish and other aquatic products " are central to food, water, and energy security. The Hindu Kush Himalayas provide ecosystem services that are critical for water, energy, and agricultural sustainability and productivity in South Asia. All of the subregion's major rivers and their numerous tributaries originate in the Himalayas. About 1.3 billion people in South Asia (the mainland population) rely on freshwater obtained directly or indirectly from the Hindu Kush Himalayan (HKH) mountain systems.

Figure Options

Failure to recognize the value of HKH ecosystems results in inadequate measures to manage the headwaters of the subregion's rivers, their catchments, watersheds, and vital natural resources, posing a serious threat to the sustained flow of ecosystem services critical for food, water, and energy security in the HKH and downstream.

The Regional Dimension

Many ecosystem resources such as water from transboundary rivers are used and managed at multiple scales " local, national, and regional " and governed by diverse stakeholders. Much of the food, water, and energy nexus debate so far has focused on intersectoral coordination for efficient use of competing resources; the emphasis has been on integrating policies, mainly for water pricing and withdrawing subsidies to reduce energy demand for water in agriculture or for construction of big infrastructure to store water to support the growing demand for water and energy for irrigation. So far, few systematic efforts have been made to understand the spatial and regional dimensions of the nexus, in other words to examine the spatial patterns of resource availability and use, how resources flow, upstream–downstream linkages, and the potential benefits of addressing challenges through regional and river-basin approaches. The nexus approach has also paid little attention to the upstream–downstream linkages of ecosystem services, biophysical and socio-economic interdependencies, and the importance of cross-scale coordination in managing nexus challenges. Since different countries have different resource endowments and face different challenges in managing the nexus, upstream–downstream coordination can tap the potential of synergies in transboundary river basins. In South Asia the food, water, and energy nexus has a strong regional dimension, with upstream actions often having downstream effects. For instance, floods generated in Nepal also result in floods in India; glacial lake outburst floods in China can affect hydropower stations in Nepal; erosion in one country deposits sediment in another; and hydropower potential in one country serves markets in another. Approaching the food, water, and energy nexus from an ecosystem-based regional perspective, which takes into account the transboundary nature of HKH ecosystems and rivers, offers opportunities to enlarge planning horizons, increase economies of scale, identify trade-offs, and maximize synergies in food, water, and energy.

This paper explores the food, water and energy nexus in the Hindu Kush Himalayan region and South Asia from a regional dimension using an ecosystem perspective, focusing particularly on the role of HKH ecosystem services in sustaining food, water, and energy security in downstream areas. It begins by assessing the issues and challenges in food, water, and energy security in South Asia. The contribution of HKH ecosystems to food, water, and energy security in South Asia, while the following section enumerates the challenges of sustaining these vital mountain ecosystems. The article concludes by suggesting some policy measures to promote food, water, and energy security in South Asia and the HKH region. This study relies predominantly on information drawn from secondary sources, including books, reports, and journal articles. Some information has been drawn from research by the authors and ICIMOD's research experience in the HKH region over the past 30 years.

KEY CHALLENGES OF THE FOOD, WATER, AND ENERGY NEXUS IN SOUTH ASIA

South Asia is one of the most dynamic regions of the world in terms of population growth, economic progress, urbanization, and industrialization. The demographic, economic, and environmental changes in South Asia have increased the demand for natural resources and intensified their uses, which has serious implications for food, water, and energy security in the subregion. The key features and challenges of food, water and energy security.

Table : Key indicators related to agriculture, water, and energy security in South Asia.

Indicators	2007[a]	2050 projection
Population (millions)	1520	2242
Population density (per km^2)	352	–
Annual population growth rate (%)	1.5	0.53
Population below USD 1.25 a day (million)	596 (2005)	14.1
Poverty ratio (below USD 1.25 a day)	40.3 (2005)	–
Per capita GDP growth (%)	3.6 (1995"1997)	–
Undernourished people (millions)	331	93
Undernourished population (%)	21.8	4.2
Population without access to safe water (millions)	269	–
Total land area (million km^2)	4.47	–
Cultivable land area (million km^2)	2.19	–
Cultivated area (million km^2)	2.04	–
Arable land (million ha)	204	213
Irrigated area (million ha)	104.3 (2000)	135.2
Total rainfed area	98 (2000)	110
Annual growth rate in irrigated area (%)	1.6	0.1
Cultivated area (% of total area)	93	–
Cultivated land (ha per person)	0.12	0.08
Cultivated land irrigated (%)	39	–
Contribution of irrigated agriculture in total food production (%)	60–80	–
Fertilizer consumptions (millions tonnes)	27	59
Fertilizer consumption (kg/ha)	210	256
Agriculture growth rate (%)	2.4	1.3
Crop production growth rate (%)	2.1	0.9
Cereal production growth rate (%)	1.9 (1997)	–
Irrigated cereal yields (tonnes/ha)	2.7 (2000)	4.1
Per capita cereal consumption (kg/person/year)	169 (1997)	–
Cereal demand (million metric tonnes)	241 (2000)	476
Livestock production growth (%)	3.2 (2007)	2.2
Milk and dairy products growth rate (production)	4.1	2.0

Milk and dairy products growth rate (consumption)	4.1	2.0
Total water withdrawal (km^3)	1023.40	–
Annual water withdrawal by sector (%)		
Agriculture	91	–
Municipalities	7	–
Industry	2	–
Total water consumption in agriculture sector (km^3)	1479 (2000)	1922
Total water withdrawal for irrigation(km^3)	1095 (2000)	1817
Per capita water withdrawal (m^3)	631	–
Agricultural use (% of total withdrawal)	82.30	–
Total irrigated area (million ha)	88. 60	–
Total irrigated area (%)	47.48	–
Irrigation		
Surface water contribution	36.7 (2009)	–
Groundwater contribution	54.7 (2009)	–
Energy use per capita (kg of oil equivalent)	515 (2009)	–
Household with no access to electricity (%)	63	–
Households using traditional biomass for cooking (%)	65	–
Electricity consumption in agriculture sector per tube well (kWh)	8100 (2001)	–

Increasing Population and Declining Agricultural Land

In the half century from the late 1950s to 2010 the population of South Asia almost tripled from 588 million to 1621 million. With high population growth and industrial development, per capita agricultural land has been declining sharply over the years. Between 1980 and 2010, per capita arable land fell from 0.11 to 0.05 ha in Bangladesh, 0.23 to 0.13 ha in India, 0.15 to 0.08 ha in Nepal, and 0.24 to 0.12 ha in Pakistan.

It is estimated that in 2025 there will be 2.2 billion people in South Asia, and with the increased population cereal demand will rise to 476 million tonnes as compared to 241 million tonnes in 2000. The projected cereal demand rises to 550 million tonnes if higher incomes are taken into account.

Stagnating or Declining Food Production

Although total food production is increasing because of additional area brought under irrigation, the growth rate of food production has slowed down in many parts of South Asia, and per capita food consumption has remained stagnant even though per capita incomes have registered impressive growth in recent years. Climate change may further exacerbate the situation. According to the Intergovernmental Panel on Climate Change, crop yields in South Asia may decrease by up to 30% by 2050 without changes in practices.

Low levels of consumption have contributed to persistent hunger and malnutrition. Despite impressive economic growth in the last decade, South Asia is home to over 40% of the world's poor (living on less than USD 1.25 a day) and 35% of the world's undernourished. More than 56 percent of the world's low-birth-weight babies are born in South Asia.

Increasingly Water- and Energy-intensive Food Production

About 39% of the cropland in South Asia is irrigated, and irrigated agriculture accounts for 60"80% of food production. Agriculture consumes about 90% of the water and about 20% of the energy used in South Asia. Although in the early 1960s the major source of irrigation was surface water, the contribution of groundwater has been increasing steadily and has now overtaken surface-water irrigation in some countries. At present groundwater's contribution in irrigation is 79% in Bangladesh, 63% in India, 19% in Nepal, and 21% in Pakistan. In total about three-fifths of the region's irrigation water comes from groundwater.

WATER AND ENERGY SCARCITY

Water, once considered abundant, has become increasingly scarce. Per capita water availability in Pakistan, for example, fell from 5000 m^3 per annum in 1951 to 1100 m^3 per annum in 2006 and is predicted to drop closer to 1000 m^3 by 2010. Water stress is also growing in India, with per capita water availability falling from 1986 m^3 in 1998 to 1731 m^3 in 2005 and projected to decline to 1140 m^3 in 2050. India is already extracting groundwater 56%

faster than it can be replenished. Climate change is likely to have serious implications for water availability in the dry season. As about 70% of South Asia's cereal production comes from irrigated agriculture, water scarcity may affect food production unless appropriate measures are taken.

Increased extraction of groundwater has increased demand for energy and lowered the groundwater table in many parts of the HKH region, especially the northwestern Himalayas. This has created a serious concern for the entire region as the shortage of water and energy has severely constrained not only agriculture but also overall economic growth and human wellbeing. For instance, energy shortage in Pakistan is causing a loss of about USD 1 billion per annum along with a loss of 400,000 jobs. The situation is similar in Bangladesh, India, and Nepal and is challenging overall macroeconomic stability. It is estimated that in 2011"2012 about 50% of India's export earnings were spent to import crude oil to meet the energy demand. Similarly, about 35% of export earnings in Pakistan are needed for the import of petroleum products.

Impacts of Burning Biomass for Energy

Inadequate access to modern energy and the prevalent practice of burning biomass for cooking and heating also has impacts on the food, water, and energy nexus in South Asia. About 70% of the population in South Asia uses biomass such as fuelwood, crop residues, and animal dung as the main source of energy for cooking and heating. In traditional burning practices, incomplete combustion of biomass contributes to emissions of atmospheric black carbon " aerosol particles that absorb solar radiation and release the energy as heat, contributing to atmospheric warming. When black carbon is deposited on ice and snow it reduces the albedo of these surfaces, increasing the absorption of heat; it is thus thought to be accelerating melting of Himalayan glaciers. Black carbon particles also influence cloud formation. Scientific studies suggest that the haze referred to as the atmospheric brown cloud might have a significant effect on rice and wheat yields in South Asia through reduction of solar energy to the surface and change in rainfall. Thus, by accelerating the melting of the

Himalayan glaciers and influencing light and rain, black carbon could affect water availability and food and energy security in South Asia.

Moreover, diversion of animal wastes from fertilizers to fuel use has serious implications in the food, energy, and water nexus. Cattle dung, rich in organic matter, was used traditionally as manure in agriculture and also provides food for a wide range of animal and fungus species which are recycled into the food chain. Its increasing use as fuel for cooking in rural areas leads to loss of soil nutrients, affecting crop production. In India, about 30% of rural energy consumption is derived from animal wastes; annually, 300 to 400 million tonnes of cattle dung are used as fuel for cooking.

In Bangladesh, where 60% of rural energy comes from biomass, household consumption of biomass fuel is 219 kg per month, of which 42 kg is cow dung. In Pakistan about 50% of cattle dung is used as fuel. Biomass is also the main source of fuel in Afghanistan and Nepal, and cattle dung is increasingly being diverted from manure to fuel.

South Asian soils are very poor in organic matter, and with the reduced use of cattle dung in crop fields and the increased use of inorganic fertilizers, the organic matter content in soil is declining. In Bangladesh, for instance, the average organic matter content of topsoils has gone down from about 2% to 1% over the past 20 years. In Pakistan, soil carbon ranges from 0.52% to 1.38% and most soil series have less than 1% carbon. In India, the use of dung as fuel has resulted in an estimated loss of nitrogen to crops of 3 kg per hectare per year. About 11 million hectares of South Asian cropland suffer from nutrient depletion and land degradation, which has led to stagnation or even decline in the productivity of the rice–wheat system. Finally, the diversion of cattle dung from farm manure to fuel has accelerated the use of chemical fertilizers, whose production is highly energy intensive " again, having an impact in the food, energy, and water nexus.

THE ROLE OF THE HINDU KUSH HIMALAYAS

From a nexus perspective the essential question is whether water and energy constraints can be overcome to grow adequate food for the growing population without degrading the natural resource base.

Water

Rice and wheat are the staple foods in South Asia; about 50% of dietary energy comes from these two crops. But these crops require huge amounts of water – about 1000 tonnes to produce 1 tonne of grain. Their production depends on the availability of water in the dry season and on irrigation facilities, which depend on water from the Hindu Kush Himalayas. These mountains are the source of Asia's 10 largest rivers including the Brahmaputra, Ganges, Indus, Mekong, Yangtze, and Yellow Rivers, which are a lifeline for more than a billion people, almost half of humanity. These rivers and their numerous tributaries are the main sources of freshwater in South Asia. They provide water for drinking, irrigation, fisheries, navigation, and hydropower and support terrestrial and aquatic ecosystems.

The world's largest irrigation concentration is in the Indo-Gangetic plain. In Pakistan, food, water, and energy security depends heavily on the state of the Indus River. The Indus irrigation system, the world's largest contiguous irrigation system, irrigates about 14.3 million hectares of farmland, representing about 76% of the cultivated area in Pakistan; it enables the production of more than 80% of the food grains of Pakistan and cash crops, in particular cotton. Agricultural water withdrawal in Pakistan is 170 billion cubic metres per year.

Similarly, the Ganges River system is the main source of freshwater for half the population of India and Bangladesh and nearly the entire population of Nepal. The Ganges and Yamuna canal systems irrigate vast areas of India by using surface and groundwater received from the Himalayas. Almost 60% of India's irrigated area of 546,820 km^2 is in the Ganges basin. Water use for irrigation in the Ganges basin is about 100 billion cubic metres per year.

The Brahmaputra River supports irrigation, hydropower, and fisheries for a vast part of Bangladesh, Bhutan, and India. Almost 6000 km^2 are irrigated using 1.4 billion cubic metres of water per year. Afghanistan's food and water security heavily depends on the Amu Darya. More than 5 billion cubic metres of water per year are drawn from this river and its tributaries in northern Afghanistan to irrigate 385,000 ha of farmland.

Himalayan freshwater resources: The Hindu Kush Himalayan mountain system is often called the 'third pole' or 'water tower of Asia' because it contains the largest area of glaciers and permafrost and the largest freshwater resources outside the North and South poles. About 30% of the world's total glaciated mountain area is in the HKH region. Estimates of glacier area vary considerably; one estimate suggests the glacier area in the HKH region is 114,800 km^2. A study conducted by ICIMOD inventoried 54,000 glaciers in the HKH covering 60,000 km^2. Himalayan ice reserves are estimated to be equivalent to about three times the annual precipitation over the entire HKH region. During summer and early autumn, meltwater released from glaciers, ice, and snow feeds the rivers reaching downstream, increasing their run-off and recharging river-fed aquifers. Glaciers provide a natural antidote for hydrological seasonality, providing water during the dry season when it is most needed.

However, the role of meltwater varies through the region: In the northwestern and far-eastern Himalayas more than 50% of the annual discharge comes from snow that falls during the winter westerlies. By contrast, the central Himalayan rivers generally receive less than about 25% of their annual discharge from snowmelt, and are instead fed mainly by summer monsoon rainfall. It is estimated that about 50"80% of the inflows in the Indus River system is fed by snow and glacier melt from the Hindu Kush Karakoram part of the HKH. With over 5000 glaciers, the upper Indus basin has a glaciated area of about 15,000 km^2, which corresponds to about 2700 km^3 of stored ice, equivalent to about 14 years of average Indus River system inflows. The Hindu Kush Karakoram and western Himalayas are the source of about 90% of the lowland flow of the Indus River and its tributaries.

Groundwater: Although estimates of the Himalayan contribution to downstream groundwater recharge are limited, a recent study claims that it may be substantial. Andermann et al. (2012) report that groundwater flow through bedrock is approximately six times the annual contribution from glacial ice melt and snowmelt to central Himalayan rivers. Groundwater is an invisible ecosystem service of the Himalayas; it is vital for irrigation in the entire agricultural landscape of HKH countries, in addition to serving other human uses and sustaining wetland ecosystems. Further study, therefore, is needed to determine the potential role of HKH watershed management in reducing runoff and increasing infiltration to ensure groundwater recharge downstream.

Energy

From a nexus perspective, the major challenges facing South Asian countries relate to supplying enough energy for increased food production and other economic activities as well as domestic use without increasing carbon intensity. Hydropower from the HKH mountain systems can enhance energy security in South Asia, provide quality energy for agriculture and food production, reduce to some extent the vulnerability and impacts of fluctuations in supply and prices of fossil fuels (especially imports), and provide local, national, and global environmental benefits through the reduction in consumption of fuelwood and fossil fuels. Harnessing the huge untapped hydropower resources in the region could fuel industrialization and economic growth as well as strengthen food security.

Hydropower and clean energy potential in Himalayan rivers: The Himalayan topography and rivers with abundant rainfed and snowfed water resources provide an opportunity for generating an enormous amount of hydropower. The hydropower potential of the HKH region is more than 500 GW. The contribution of hydroelectricity to total commercial energy is about 50% in Bhutan, 17% in Nepal, 13% in Pakistan, 6% in India, and 4% in Afghanistan; and to the total electricity supply is about 100% in Bhutan, 92% in Nepal, 74% in Myanmar, 33% in Pakistan, 17% in India, and 16% in China.

The hydropower potential of the Brahmaputra River is one of the largest among the world's rivers – more than 296.8 TWh. The location where it drops 2300 m from the Tibet Autonomous Region of China to Assam in India has immense potential. The

Brahmaputra's theoretical hydropower potential is estimated to be about 83,000 MW in Nepal, 21,000 MW in Bhutan, and almost 59,000 MW in northeast India. The Ganges–Brahmaputra–Meghna river system is estimated to have about 200,000 MW of hydropower potential, of which half or more is considered to be feasible for harnessing. Nepal has identified 28 potential reservoir sites with an aggregate gross storage capacity of 110 billion cubic metres. Biswas (2004) notes that Nepal and Bhutan could harness this hydropower potential at a relatively low cost compared to alternative energy sources. The 1986 Brahmaputra Master Plan of India identified 18 storage sites in northeast India, five classified as large, with a total gross storage capacity of 80 billion cubic metres. Several multipurpose projects with large reservoir storage capacities have been identified in India in the Brahmaputra and Meghna basins. One large storage site (Tipaimukh) has been identified in the Meghna (Barak) system with a gross storage potential of 15 billion cubic metres.

In the Indus River system in Pakistan, 800 potential sites have been identified. The collective potential of hydropower in the Indus River system is about 60 GW, but only 6720 MW (11%) have been realized.

The Ganges and its tributaries also have huge potential for hydropower development and trade. A recent study conducted by the World Bank suggests that about 25,000 MW of electricity could be generated in the Ganges basin through upstream storage of water in 23 dams, and that this could provide benefits worth of USD 5 billion per year with little trade-off.

Of the total hydropower potential in India, 79% (117,329 MW) is in the Himalayan region. However, only 12,543 MW has been developed, with another 12,375 MW in development.

In Afghanistan, hydropower contributes more than 54% of the total power supply. The upper Amu Darya and Panj Rivers in Afghanistan are estimated to have about 20,000 MW of hydropower potential. Ten hydro projects with a total capacity of more than 10,000 MW have been identified. However, present utilization is only 256 MW. Micro-hydropower: In addition to the potential on a large scale, Himalayan streams and rivers also offer ample opportunity for generating hydropower at small and medium scales. Nepal and Pakistan have good experience with micro-hydropower plants (less than 100 kW capacity), especially in relation to community involvement in planning, construction, and operation. These countries also have a significant industrial base that produces the required electro-mechanical equipment. In northern Pakistan, under an initiative of the Aga Khan Rural Support Programme, communities in remote mountain valleys built 240 micro hydro plants between 1990 and 2005, with a total capacity of more than 10,000 kW. A Clean Development Mechanism (CDM) project was registered with the CDM Executive Board in October 2009 to develop 103 new micro and mini hydropower plants in Pakistan with a total capacity of 15 MW at a cost of USD 18 million.

India has also initiated small and micro-hydropower development in its Himalayan region. By 2006, 3,434 MW had been installed in Himachal Pradesh, Uttaranchal, Assam, West Bengal, Sikkim, and Bihar, contributing about 13.2% of renewable power.

OTHER ECOSYSTEM SERVICES

Climate regulation: The Himalayan mountain system creates conditions conducive to agriculture by regulating microclimate as well as wind and monsoon circulation in the Himalayan region. Because of their altitude and location, the Himalayas block moisture-laden monsoon winds from travelling further northward and thus facilitate timely and heavy precipitation (snow and rain), saving South Asia from the gradual desiccation that afflicts Central Asia (NAS, 2012). During winter, the mountains pose a barrier to storms coming from the west, and as a consequence receive snow at higher elevations and rainfall at lower elevations and in the adjacent plains of northern India (GoI, 2010). The Himalayan ranges also prevent frigid and dry arctic winds from blowing south into the subcontinent, keeping South Asia much warmer than other regions at corresponding latitudes around the globe.

Soil fertility: In addition to providing surface and groundwater, Himalayan rivers carry soil and nutrients to downstream areas, making floodplains in South Asia, particularly the Indo-Gangetic plain, fertile and contributing substantially to productivity of agriculture and aquatic resources.

Agro-biodiversity: The Himalayas are important storehouses of agro-biodiversity, which is fundamental for agricultural sustainability and human wellbeing in South Asia and beyond. Over 675 edible plants and nearly 1743 species of medicinal value are found in the Indian Himalayan region alone (Singh, 2006).

Aquatic resources: Both tropical and Himalayan cold-water fish are important sources of nutrition and food security in the HKH region and downstream. The Himalayan river systems harbour some of the richest fish biodiversity resources in the world. Connecting Himalayan headwaters with the sea, they serve as biological corridors for migration of fish and other aquatic species, thus supporting biological diversity and livelihoods. The Ganges river system alone hosts around 265 species of fish. Because of the perennial water from mountain snow and ice in the Ganges and the Brahmaputra, India and Bangladesh stand second and third respectively in the world in terms of inland fisheries production (Hussain, 2010). Subsistence and semi-intensive fisheries also support the livelihoods of a huge population. A total of 2.5 and 0.4 million fishers in India and Bangladesh respectively rely on fishing in Himalayan rivers for income, food security, and nutrition (FAO, 2012). The Koshi River, a major tributary of the Ganges, has 103 fish species and contributes about half of Nepal's total fish production of 33,000 tonnes per year; more than 30,000 people depend on fishing in the Koshi and other rivers in Nepal for their livelihoods (Sharma, 2008).

CHALLENGES OF SUSTAINING HIMALAYAN ECOSYSTEMS FOR FOOD, WATER, AND ENERGY SECURITY

Throughout the Himalayas, the growing demand for resources, widespread poverty, and the strong profit motive of commercial enterprises, and inadequate incentives for sustainable management have led to unsustainable use of resources (Singh, 2006). Rapid population growth " with South Asia's population projected to increase from 1.36 billion in 2000 to 2.31 billion in 2050 (Lal, 2007) " has increased demand for food, fodder, grazing land, water, and other natural resources in the mountains and downstream. Rapid urbanization " at an annual rate of 2.87%, as compared to 2.34% worldwide (Sardar, 2012) " is also increasing the demand for water, energy, and food. The urban population of South Asia has grown from 73.95 million in the 1950s to 485.79 million in 2010. Urbanization has resulted in changed food preferences and higher demand for meat and other water and energy intensive foods. These demographic pressures and higher demands, along with increased connectivity and other socio-economic factors, are resulting in changes in land use and land cover and intensified resource use patterns in the upland areas.

The HKH region suffers severe land degradation, in particular deforestation and forest degradation, erosion, landslides, overgrazing, biodiversity loss, declining productivity, and desertification. Rangelands have been converted to rainfed farming, marginal lands have been used for quick-return commercial farming, and minerals have been extracted without adequate environmental protection.

Forests have an important role in replenishing groundwater and maintaining the volume of river water in the dry season, sequestering carbon, and supporting agriculture. Most of the forests in the central Himalayas were heavily degraded during the last century as a result of the growing demand for timber and fuelwood and inadequate management (Haigh et al., 1990). The southeastern Tibetan plateau, once covered by coniferous forest, was denuded of forest by the middle of the twentieth century (Cui et al., 2007). Similarly, most of the forest lands in the Indus basin have been converted to other uses for short-term gains (, 98). Forest degradation poses significant challenges to local people's livelihoods and food and energy security as they depend heavily on forest for fuelwood, fodder, and other non-timber forest products (Rasul et al., 2008).

Forest degradation and the loss of vegetation have made the Himalayan watersheds more vulnerable to erosion, which has led to loss of soil and nutrients, siltation of rivers and reservoirs, and increases in the incidence and severity of flooding. The Koshi River in Nepal carries an annual load of 119 million cubic metres of silt, which is equivalent to 2 mm of topsoil depth over its entire catchment (Laban, 1979). Siltation is not only causing river beds to rise; it is also affecting the water infrastructure, reducing the life of reservoirs and dams for hydropower, irrigation, and flood control, thus affecting energy and food production (Tiwari, 2000). Watershed degradation is also resulting in decreased groundwater recharge and consequent drying up of springs, streams, and other water sources. This has caused shortage of water for drinking, irrigation, and other livelihood activities in the Himalayas.

The changes in the headwater regions also have downstream impacts in the Indo-Gangetic plain in terms of silting of river beds, increased incidence of floods, and decreased water discharge in rivers. It is estimated that 2400 million tonnes of silt are being transported to Bangladesh every year.

So far adequate measures have not been taken to protect the vital Himalayan ecosystem resources through coordination between upstream and downstream stakeholders. Although mountain communities bear the cost of conservation in foregoing more productive alternatives, their efforts bring them few benefits because of a lack of institutional mechanisms and policy arrangements for sharing the benefits and costs of conservation (Thapa, 2001 and Singh, 2006).

These challenges highlight the importance of urgent action to protect and sustainably manage Himalayan ecosystems to ensure food, water, and energy security in the HKH region and South Asia.

Discussion

With limited land resources, growing water stress, increasing energy demand, unstable energy prices, and poor socio-economic conditions, South Asian countries face serious challenges as to how to provide adequate food and nutrition, access to modern energy, and safe water and sanitation to a burgeoning population without degrading the natural resource base. The nexus approach provides a framework for better understanding of the interdependencies of the food, water, and energy sectors and linkages between upstream and downstream countries as well as better insights into how to address such challenges by maximizing synergies and managing trade-offs.

Analysis of the role of Himalayan ecosystem services in ensuring food, water, and energy security in South Asia, one of the key characteristics of the nexus in South Asia is that food production in the region has become increasingly water and energy intensive. While the demand for food, water, and energy is growing tremendously, land, water, and other natural and environmental resources are in decline, so that increased food production in South Asia will have to come from the same or even less land. Another distinctive feature of the food, water, and energy nexus in South Asia is the high economic and environmental dependence on upstream resources. The Himalayan ecosystems are critical for ensuring food, water, and energy security not only in the HKH region but also in downstream river basins. As water, nutrients, and other ecosystem services flow downstream from the Himalayas, the land use and management practices at the headwaters and in Himalayan watersheds affect the quantity and quality of water, energy, and other resources critical for sustaining agriculture and food security downstream.

The widespread burning of biomass for fuel could also affect water availability and food and energy security in South Asia. Although the causes of accelerated melting of snow, ice, and glaciers in the Himalayas are not fully understood, growing evidence suggests that black carbon could be one of the factors responsible for this phenomenon.

The interdependencies in food, water, and energy security in South Asia thus highlight the need for intersectorally integrated solutions, while the crucial role of the Himalayas underlines the need to address the issues from an ecosystem perspective.

Mountain communities are the custodians of vital resources and their actions have important implications for the condition of the headwaters and watersheds. So far, however, no effective mechanisms have been developed to provide adequate incentives for communities to conserve mountain natural resources. Lack of appropriate incentives or other policy and institutional mechanisms has resulted in increased degradation of headwaters and emissions of black carbon along with declining agricultural productivity, with serious implications for downstream communities. Ecosystem degradation in Himalayan headwaters and watersheds could jeopardize the food, water, and energy security in South Asia.

Despite the urgent need for clean energy to meet the growing demand for food, water, and energy, the hydropower potential of the Himalayan rivers has remained under tapped. Acute energy deficit in Bangladesh, India, and Pakistan and huge hydropower potential in Bhutan and Nepal suggest an opportunity for synergies that could be obtained by exploiting the hydropower potential of the Himalayan rivers in a collaborative and integrated manner. Optimal utilization of Himalayan water for energy, irrigation, navigation, and fisheries can contribute significantly in achieving food, water, and energy security in South Asia in the long run.

It may be argued that the exploitation of hydropower in upstream areas might affect water availability for irrigation downstream and thus intensify food " energy trade-offs. However, hydropower generation is a non-consumptive use, so it does not necessarily reduce water availability downstream; the water used for hydropower can also be used for irrigation if it is properly managed. Arguably, upstream storage of monsoon water for hydropower may augment downstream water availability in the dry season (Rasul, 2014). This perspective is supported by a detailed World Bank study in the Ganges basin which found that huge hydropower benefits can be obtained with a very small trade-off in irrigation (Sadoff and Rao, 2011). In harnessing hydropower potential, of course, it is essential to address any potential adverse impacts on the environment, ecology, and society (Biggs et al., 2013) and to ensure equitable benefit sharing following the framework set out by the World Commission on Dams (WCD, 2000).

The potentials cannot be realized without coordination and collaboration across countries, as most of the Himalayan rivers flow through more than one country. At present, cooperation between upstream and downstream countries is minimal, and its absence is a major constraint in addressing the nexus challenges (Rasul, 2014). To address the challenges of food, water, and energy security, it is therefore necessary to identify synergies across boundaries at the basin level (Crow and Singh, 2009). For example, the Aswan Dam on the Nile River not only contributes to mitigating drought and flood damage but also supplies electricity to half of the rural communities in Egypt, supports the fishing industry, and has created new livelihood opportunities.

Conclusions and Policy Recommendations

The findings of this study suggest that ecosystem services and their upstream–downstream linkages, particularly in the region's transboundary river basins, are an integral part of the food, water, and energy nexus. In a transboundary river basin " where resource flows transcend national boundaries, and where management practices and conservation initiatives upstream have impact in downstream areas " the synergies and trade-offs in food, water, and energy cannot be optimally managed unless a basin-level approach is taken. The Himalayas are a regional public good, and it is the common interest and shared responsibility of all in South Asia to protect the Himalayan ecosystems for the benefits of the region. To address the nexus challenges, a two-pronged approach is needed: first, to enhance cross-sectoral coherence and second, to improve management of the Himalayan headwaters, watersheds, forests, rangelands, soils, and farmlands on which the sustainability and stability of flow of ecosystem services depend. The following are some broad recommendations.

- Harmonize policies among the three sectors, taking into account interdependencies of resources across both sectors and scales, upstream and downstream, as well as the role of Himalayan ecosystems in long-term security of water, energy, and food in the region.
- Integrate planning and management of water, energy, land, forest, ecosystems, agriculture, and food security to reduce intersectoral externalities, tap synergies and co-benefits across sectors and scales, enhance resource use efficiency, and reduce environmental impacts.
- Manage demand for water and energy through regulation and introduction of incentives for efficient use of water and energy for food production.

- Strengthen coordination mechanisms among upstream and downstream countries to maximize synergies and minimize trade-offs in resource use, and take a river basin approach to protect Himalayan ecosystems, catchments, watersheds, and headwaters and to harness the potential of water resources, as the benefits of sustainable watershed management transcend national boundaries.
- Develop appropriate incentives such as payments for ecosystem services and mechanisms for sharing the benefits and costs of conservation to encourage local communities to use and manage the headwaters sustainably.
- To sustain the ecosystem services of the Himalayan glaciers in providing fresh water to downstream areas, control black carbon emissions by providing clean energy options to rural people (such as as micro and macro hydropower, efficient stoves for burning biomass, and biogas) and by improving kiln efficiency in the brick making industry.
- In exploiting hydropower potential, take the ecological, environmental and social implications of hydropower development seriously into account. Detailed studies of technical and economic feasibility are required to identify potential hydropower areas and to demarcate fragile zones where heavy construction must be avoided, for example at high altitude and in vulnerable watersheds.
- Establish a cooperation framework for multiple uses of water (for irrigation, energy, navigation, fisheries, and domestic uses) and for appropriate benefit sharing.
- Finally, as knowledge and understanding of the dynamics of the food, water, and energy nexus and the possible areas of trade-offs and synergies are limited, support integrated modeling research and the development of a nexus knowledge base to support decision-making in addressing trade-offs and promoting synergies among the concerned sectors.

9

China's Growing Water Crisis and Security Risk

What is the biggest challenge that China faces? Corruption, the gap between the rich and poor, and the rapidly aging population often top the list of answers to this question. Yet a closer look suggests that the greatest threat may well be lack of access to clean water. From "cancer villages" to violent protests to rising food prices, diminishing water supplies are exerting a profound and harmful effect on the Chinese people as well as on the country's capacity to continue to prosper economically. While much of the challenge remains within China, spillover effects — such as the rerouting of transnational rivers and a push to acquire arable land abroad — are also being felt well outside the country's borders. China's leaders have acknowledged the severity of the challenge and have adopted a number of policies to address their growing crisis. However, their efforts have fallen woefully short, as they fail to include the fundamental reforms necessary to turn the situation around. Meanwhile domestic pressures, as well as international concerns, continue to mount.

DEVELOPMENT RUN AMOK

China's water story begins with a challenging reality: The country's per capita water resources just exceeded more than one-quarter that of the world average, and the distribution of those resources throughout the country is highly uneven. Northern China is home to approximately 40 percent of the country's total population and almost half its agricultural land, and produces more than 50 percent of GDP. But it receives only 12 percent of total precipitation. Southern China, in contrast, receives 80 percent of China's total precipitation, yet skyrocketing levels of water pollution dramatically reduce the south's natural advantage.

The spectacular economic growth that has made China the envy of the world has only exacerbated the challenge. Resources, particularly water, are consumed without consideration for future demand. Industry and agriculture are notoriously profligate water consumers: Industry, which accounts for about one-quarter of China's total water consumption, uses anywhere from four to 10 times more water per unit of GDP as other competitive economies. Water used for energy is a singularly important drain on China's scarce resources. By far, the largest portion of China's industrial water use is devoted to energy: The process of mining, processing and consuming coal alone accounts for almost 20 percent of all water consumed nationally. Hydropower raises the bar even further. Already the largest producer of hydropower in the world, China plans to triple hydropower capacity by 2020. According to Ma Jun, the director of the Chinese NGO Institute of Public and Environmental Affairs, many Chinese rivers simply won't be running in 2020 if China meets its hydropower capacity goals.

Agriculture, which accounts for 62 percent of China's total water consumption, also takes a serious toll on China's water supply. Almost two-thirds of China's arable land lies in the perennially dry north, and irrigation practices in China continue to be inefficient, with less than half of the water used for irrigation actually reaching crops. Even municipalities suffer from serious water wastage: About 20 percent of urban water consumption is lost through leaky pipes. China's goal of urbanizing 400 million people by 2030 means that the water challenge will likely only increase. Urban, middle class residents — with water-consuming appliances, homes with lawns to water and a fondness for golf courses — use 300 percent more water than their rural counterparts.

China's widespread pollution adds another dimension to the country's water crisis. More than 90 percent of southern China's water withdrawal comes from surface water, but in the first half of 2010, almost a quarter of China's surface water was so polluted that it was not even usable for industry, and less than half of the total supplies of water were found to be drinkable. For decades, factories and municipalities have dumped untreated waste directly into streams, rivers and coastal waters.

The Shifting Landscape

China's economic growth, inefficiencies and wastage in water usage are transforming the geography and resource base of the country. First, the sheer amount of available water is declining. During the period from 2000 to 2009, the amount of accessible water in China decreased by 13 percent. By 2030, the Ministry of Water Resources anticipates that per capita water resources will decline below the World Bank's scarcity levels. Northern Chinareports some of the highest rates of water loss (.pdf) in the world. Moreover, according to China's Minister of Water Resources Chen Lei, two-thirds of Chinese cities face increased scarcity of water, and overall the country confronts a water shortage of 40 billion cubic meters annually. In rural China, 320 million people — one-quarter of China's total population — don't have access to safe drinking water.

Second, the country is sinking. The extensive contamination of surface water has forced the Chinese to increase their exploitation of groundwater, leading to groundwater depletion and a dramatic drop in the ground water tables: 100 to 300 meters in Beijing, and up to 90 meters in other parts of China. In Beijing, land subsidence resulting from this groundwater depletion has destroyed factories, buildings and underground pipelines. Saltwater intrusion as well as pollution is further compromising the diminishing groundwater supplies: Of the 182 cities with monitored groundwater in 2010, more than half registered "poor" to "extremely poor" in water quality. Even China's Ministry of Environmental Protection was forced to acknowledge, "It is not easy to be optimistic about the quality" of the groundwater.

Finally, desertification is advancing. While the south is often faced with catastrophic floods, desertification of the north has become widespread: One Chinese official estimated that it would take 300 years to reverse the desertification of lands that has already taken place — the majority in areas bordering the North's

Gobi Desert — due to overexploitation of environmental resources. Even as local officials fight to reverse the trend, the desert continues to expand at a rate of more than 1,060 square miles per year.

The Hidden Costs

What really concerns China's leaders, however, are the social, economic and political impacts of this growing scarcity. As China's Minister for the Environment Zhou Shengxiansuggested on his agency's website, "The depletion, deterioration and exhaustion of resources and the worsening ecological environment have become bottlenecks and grave impediments to the nation's economic and social development." For the Chinese people, the failure of local officials and factory managers to enforce environmental regulations translates into serious public health concerns, crop loss, poisoned fish and livestock, and a lack of water to run factories. For Chinese officials, the failure to protect the environment and provide adequate and safe water to their people is one of the chief causes of social unrest in the country and perhaps their greatest policy concern.

Taking It to the Streets

Environmental concerns are a significant cause of mass protests in China. Endemic corruption and a weak legal infrastructure contribute to devastating pollution accidents as well as to long-term degradation and pollution. Without effective legal redress for environmental wrongdoing, victims of environmental pollution often resort to demonstrations to draw attention to their plight. According to Zhou, the minister of the environment, there were more than 50,000 such environmental protests in 2005. (In 2010, the number of total reported protests reached 180,000.) In the summer of 2010, for example, thousands of villagers in Guangxi province protested against a plan by a heavily polluting aluminum company to build a new highway. The plant had contaminated the villagers' drinking water and caused their crops to suffer. When the factory brought in workers armed with sticks, villagers from nearby towns came to support the villagers. Three protestors were killed and a number of villagers wounded. According to one report,as many as 10,000 villagers were involved.

The advent of the Internet has further contributed to the ability of the Chinese people to apply bottom-up pressure to officials: Internet petitions, water pollution maps demarcating polluting factories, and pictures of polluted sites or protesting Chinese are all central to protest efforts. Urban residents have also become skilled at using the Internet and cell phone text messages to organize protests, most commonly against government plans to locate factories or garbage incinerators near their communities.

The Price Tag Grows

China's leaders are deeply concerned over the economic costs of water pollution and scarcity. Although such costs are notoriously difficult to calculate, a range of Chinese officials as well as environmental economists have concluded that the total cost to the Chinese economy of environmental degradation and resource scarcity is approximately 10 percent of GDP. In one of China's leading economic centers, Chongqing, which sits on the banks of the Yangtze River, local officials estimate that dealing only with the effects of water pollution on local agriculture and public health costs as much as 4.3 percent of the city's gross annual product.

The severe drought in the first few months of 2011 — the worst in half a century in many areas — only highlighted the far-reaching economic impacts of China's precarious water supplies: Critical portions of the Yangtze River, the third-longest river in the world thathandles 80 percent of China's river freight, experienced up to 80 percent less precipitation than usual, becoming too low for many ships to navigate and affecting 35 million people at a cost of at least $2.3 billion. Shanghai, at the edge of the Yangtze along China's Eastern coast and home to the world's busiest port, experienced its longest dry period in 138 years. When the spring rains finally did come, some areas afflicted by the drought faced extensive floods, as parched and deteriorating soil was unable to retain water, leading to the deaths of dozens of citizens.

Industries that depend upon clean freshwater have been directly affected by the lack of access to it. Fishermen, for example, who once relied upon selling catch from Lake Poyang, China's largest freshwater lake, have been forced to try to make a living on a lake only 10 percent its original size and in danger of drying up altogether. The most recent drought left a major aquafarming hub that produces half of China's freshwater fish, crabs and other aquatic products with at least $1 billion of economic losses.

The Health Consequences

Chinese scholars and activists have only recently begun to document the linkages between the country's growing pollution and its rising public health challenges. Cancer is now the No. 1 cause of death in China, and researchers have started to study in earnest the potential links to water pollution. In 2010, Lee Liu, a professor of Geography at Central Missouri State University, documented a total of 459 "cancer villages" throughout China, most oftenclustered around rivers with the worst grade of pollution. Some of these villages had cancer rates more than 17 times as high as the national average.

Polluted water is a major source of other illnesses as well. A report released by the Organization for Economic Cooperation and Development (OECD) in 2007 stated that 300 million Chinese, or a quarter of the population, drank contaminated water every day, with almost two-thirds falling ill as a result. A study by the World Bank and Chinese government reported that diarrhea and cancer caused by polluted water causes 66,000 premature deaths per year.

The Global Impact

China's need for water to fuel its growth and feed its people also has far-reaching implications for the rest of the world. The headwaters of several of the world's most important rivers, including the Mekong and the Brahmaputra, are located in China. As China pushes forward with dams to support its expanding network of hydropower plants, and river-diversion schemes to supply its factories and agriculture with water, it is directly affecting the interests of its neighbors.

China's damming of the Mekong River, for example, has brought it into conflict with the needs and interests of its downstream Southeast Asian neighbors, where more than 60 million people depend on the Mekong for their livelihood. Repeated entreaties from citizen groups and, in some cases, governments in Vietnam, Cambodia and Thailand for China to negotiate water usage to protect the agricultural and fishing interests in these countries have fallen on deaf ears. In 2009, the U.S. became engaged in the issue, supporting the Lower Mekong Initiative, an effort by a group of the downstream countries that, according to the U.S. State Department "share a variety of common concerns, including transboundary water management, infectious diseases such as dengue and pandemic influenza, and vulnerability to climate change." There has been some small progress in terms of data sharing by China, but Chinese officials have not warmed to the idea of its downstream partners joining together with the United States in order to better address China's upstream activities. Although Myanmar has not opposed China's damming of the Mekong, it has not been immune to the political consequences. In June 2011, Myanmar government troops and Kachin militia clashed violently over the environmental, cultural and social threat posed by a Chinese-backed dam that is estimated to earn about $500 million a year.

Beijing is also tangling over water issues with India. In late 2010, Beijing began construction of a $1.2 billion dam on the Yarlung Tsangpo River - known in India as the Brahmaputra — without providing any notice to Indian officials. The Brahmaputra River, which originates in the Tibetan Plateau, accounts for almost 30 percent of India's total water resources and 40 percent of its total hydropower. While Chinese officials have assured India that the dam will have only a small storage component, many Indian analysts remain concerned about future Chinese plans as well as the lack of any Chinese coordination with Indian counterparts. Public discussions within China of the third leg of the south-to-north river-diversion plan, which would reroute water away from India, further heighten Indian concerns.

More recently, China's growing demand for water has begun to affect countries far outside its immediate neighborhood. Diminishing access to water and declining levels of arable land have contributed to a spate of Chinese land purchases abroad. The population in China will increase by 125 million over the next 15 years (.pdf) if current rates of growth continue. Such an increase would necessitate a 25 percent jump in agricultural production, yet according to a 2008 study that took into account climate change trends, Chinese agricultural production is projected to drop by 23 percent by 2050. As a result, large-scale Chinese farms have sprung up or are targeted for Kenya, Russia, Brazil, Argentina, Australia and Zimbabwe, among other land-rich countries. While China is not the only food-poor country to be shopping for land abroad, it is the largest. Moreover, the Chinese proclivity to export its farmers along with its capital has been a source of ongoing popular concern in some of these countries, some of which view China as the next colonizing power.

Beijing's Response

China's leaders face a daunting challenge: how to meet the needs of their rapidly growing economy and large population with a gravely threatened water supply. Beijing's answer more often than not has been to launch large work projects and campaigns reminiscent of the Cultural Revolution era. The government is well-aware that its coming battle for water security is a critical social, economic and political challenge. Indeed, having already spent more than $56 billion on water conservation projects over the past five years, China's Minister of Water Resources expects government spending on future projects to skyrocket to $615 billion over the next decade.

The South-North Water Transfer project is Beijing's most audacious bid to address both water scarcity and water pollution. At a cost between $60 billion and $80 billion, the project aims to channel water from the south to the north through three tunnels, each more than 700 miles long. The diverted water totals more than half the amount of California's annual water consumption. Initially proposed by Mao Zedong in the 1950s, construction began in December 2002 with three canals diverting 38 billion cubic meters to 48 billion cubic meters of water – or 5 percent of the Yangtze River's annual flow – from the Yangtze River to the Yellow, Huai and Hai rivers.

Along one of the three routes, about 350,000 farmers and villagers are being forced to resettle on poor-quality land in areas far from their homes, with thousands being moved to the land of a former prison. Many officials in the southern provinces have complained, with good cause, that a tremendous amount of otherwise wasted water could be more effectively saved from easily addressed technical problems, such as repairing leaky toilets in Beijing.

Meanwhile, Chinese scientists have raised concerns that such a wide-scale diversion could not only destroy the ecology of rivers in the south, but also affect millions of citizens who rely on the Yangtze and its tributaries for their livelihood. Yong Yang, an independent geologist in China, found in 2007 and 2008 that during some seasons, the government's water-diversion goals would exceed the amount of water available. The central route, which runs through Hubei Province, created concerns among scientists over the impact it may have on surrounding waterways, including pollution and sediment buildup.

In addition to the social and environmental effects of the project, questions have arisen concerning its viability, most obviously due to the lack of a successful precedent in massive water-diversion projects, but also due to China's inability to fully address the problem of poor water quality despite the construction of hundreds of water treatment plants.

The lack of public input and transparency in government decision-making regarding the project does not sit well with an Internet-savvy public. People are wary that the south-to-north river diversion will turn out like the Three Gorges Dam: an ill-conceived project in which criticism was only permitted when it was too late. Just this May, Beijing finally admitted what everyone already knew — that the damn had "urgent problems" regarding its impact on "the environment, shipping, agricultural irrigation and water supplies in the lower reaches of the Yangtze River." One well-known Chinese media columnist referred to the lack of government transparency, particularly regarding China's water projects, as "China's tragedy."

The answers to China's water dilemma are not complicated in theory, but they will be challenging to implement. Pricing reform is a central element of any effective policy response. Simply put, water in China is too cheap, and the government bureaucracy involved in China's water resources is too complex to make reform a simple process. Due to heavy government subsidies, Chinese citizens pay only 1.2 percent of their personal incomes on wateri9. Europeans, in contrast, pay 4 percent. Shanghai raised water prices 25 percent in 2009, but this was the first increase in seven years. Experiments are under way in a number of municipalities for tiered pricing in order to distribute the burden of price increases according to usage and income, and the central government has asked local governments to "carry out a tiered pricing system for urban households by the end of 2013." Fear of social unrest, however, will likely prevent a widespread increase of water rates to their proper costs.

A sound Chinese water strategy also needs to strengthen those elements of China's political system that support good environmental policymaking: transparency, official accountability and the rule of law. Yet this has been even slower to emerge than pricing reform. Officials remain concerned about delivering too much information and too much power to forces outside direct government control. Thus, the media are advised not to publicize water pollution disasters, while environmental activists are detained and arrested if they overtly challenge local officials. As for the judicial system, Beijing has repeatedly asserted in recent years that it cannot act independently from the Communist Party.

Without such institutional change, however, Beijing will continue to lack the essential building blocks to tackle its growing water crisis successfully, and the Chinese people and the rest of the world will continue to pay the price.

CHINA WATER RISK

China Water Risk is a non-profit initiative based in Hong Kongdedicated to highlighting and addressing business and environmental risk arising from the country's water crisis. Its stated aim is "to foster efficient and responsible use of water resources of the People's Republic of China by engaging the global investment and business communities, civil society and individuals in understanding and managing China's water risk". Its information portal www.chinawaterrisk.org provides a platform to share expert views, research, interviews and analysis from industry leaders.

Users can access the most relevant and critical information to help make informed investment decisions as well as remain on top of opportunities to invest in a changing environment. China Water Risk is often quoted by business and industry news and gives talks, participate in panel discussions and moderate in various investor and business conferences and forums.

BACKGROUND

History

China Water Risk is funded by Hong Kong based ADM Capital Foundation (US 501(c)(3) charitable status and a registered charitable institution under Sec. 88 of the IRD in Hong Kong) ADM Capital Foundation was established in 2006 by Asia Debt Management Hong Kong Limited (ADM Capital).

The initiative developed in collaboration in its pilot stage as The Asia Water Project, with Civic Exchange, the Association for Social and Responsible Investing in Asia (ASrIA), Business for Social Responsibility (BSR), the Institute of Public and Environmental Affairs (IPE), and Responsible Research. It was rebranded as China Water Risk in 2010 and its portal www.chinawaterrisk.org website was open to public on October 27, 2011.

Approach

China Water Risk works with water, industrial, investment experts and NGOs, think-tanks and business/investor driven initiatives to bring up-to-date information on water inChina to the public through its website.

Since the economy runs on water and water is used differently by each sector, China Water Risk adopts a sector approach to categorizing water risks. Intelligence by sector, including sector peer group benchmarking, help businesses and investors navigate and mitigate these specific risks. Sectors covered by China Water Risk are:

- Agriculture
- Power
- Food & Beverage

- Metals & Mining
- Textiles
- Electronics

KEY RISKS IN CHINA ARISING FROM WATER SCARCITY AND POLLUTION

Below are some key environmental and business risks that China is encountering as highlighted on the China Water Risk's website:

1. China has 20% of the world's population but only 7% of its freshwater reserves.
2. The Dry 11 of 31 regions of mainland China provinces, autonomous regions and municipalities (including Jiangsu, Shandong, Henan, Hebei, Shanxi, Beijing, Shanghaiand Tianjin) have renewable resources per capita per annum below 1,000 cubic meters, a water poverty level considered by experts to pose a severe constraint on food production, economic development and protection of natural systems.
3. These Dry 11 have water resources comparable to the Middle East.
4. The economy runs on water - 85% of water use in China by agriculture and industry and experts project that demand for water may not be met by 2030.
5. Food security - The Dry 11 regions account for RMB2.4 trillion or 40% of the total agricultural output value of China.
6. Industrial disruption – The Dry 11 regions account for RMB28.7 trillion or 52% of the total industrial output value of China.
7. Energy issues – 96% of power in China requires water to generate.
8. Pollution exacerbates scarcity. 77% of the 26 key lakes and reservoirs and 43% of the 7 major river basins monitored are unfit for human contact. Already, 19% ofrivers and basins and 35% of key lakes and reservoirs are essentially useless for both agricultural and industrial use.

9. According to the World Bank, 300 million rural Chinese still lack access to safe drinking water and as water stress worsens, estimates there could be 30 million environmental fleeing water stress by 2020 in China.
10. Countries such as India, Bangladesh, Laos, Thailand, Pakistan, Myanmar, Vietnam and Cambodia rely on water from China.

As a result, China Water Risk believes that "Regardless of whether we care for the environment, we have come to a point where water risks affect us all – as businesses, as investors and ultimately as individuals."

WATER RESOURCES OF CHINA

The water resources of China are affected by both severe water quantity shortages and severe water quality pollution. A growing population and rapid economic development as well as lax environmental oversight have increased water demand and pollution.

China has responded by measures such as rapidly building out the water infrastructure and increasing regulation as well as exploring a number of further technological solutions.

WATER QUANTITY

Supply

China's water resources include 2,711.5 cubic kilometers of mean annual run-off in its rivers and 828.8 cubic kilometers of groundwater recharge. As pumping water draws water from nearby rivers, the total available resource is less than the sum of surface and groundwater, and thus is only 2,821.4 cubic kilometers. 80% of these resources are in the South of China.

Demand

Total water withdrawals were estimated at 554 cubic kilometers in 2005, or about 20% of renewable resources. Demand is from the following sectors:

- 65% agriculture
- 23% industry

- 12% domestic

In 2006 626,000 square kilometers were irrigated.

Water Balance

Over-extraction of groundwater and falling water tables are big problems in China, particularly in the north. According to the Ministry of Construction, preliminary statistics show that there are more than 160 areas nationwide where groundwater has been over-exploited with an average annual groundwater depletion of more than 10 billion cubic meters. As a result, more than 60,000 square kilometers of ground surface have sunk with more than 50 cities suffering from serious land subsidence. Flooding also still is a major problem.

In a Xinhua article from 2002, Chinese experts warned of future or current water shortages. Water resource usage was expected to peak in 2030 when the population peaks. Areas north of the Yangtze river were particularly affected with 80.9% of Chinese water resources being south of the river. Northern China had used 10,000-year-old aquifers which had resulted in ground cracking and subsidence in some regions.

A 2005 article in China Daily stated that out of 514 rivers surveyed in 2000, 60 were dry. Water volume in lakes had decreased by 14%. Many wetlands had decreased in size.

Jared Diamond stated in his 2005 book Collapse that, in the past 50 years, exploitation in the form of dams and other irrigation infrastructure have all but halted the Yellow River's natural course, threatening to dry up the entire river valley. The cessation of river flows, or flow stoppages, has surged since the 1980s because of increased water usage and waste. In 1997, the lower Yellow River did not flow 230 days out of the year, an increase of over 2000% since 1988. Increased erosion and sedimentation, especially on the Loess Plateau, has made the river much less navigable by ship.

For the 2008 Summer Olympics, China diverted water from Hebei and Shanxi provinces, areas already beset by drought and dramatic water shortages, to Beijing. In July 2008, the head of the Beijing Water Authority Bi Xiaogang denied that the Olympics would increase water consumption by a large amount. However, previously he and other local officials said that Beijing would divert up to 400 million cubic meters of water from Hebei for the Games with water-diversion facilities and pipes being built to pump water from four reservoirs in Hebei. Around Baoding city alone, a mostly rural area, 31,000 residents lost land and their homes due to a water transfer project; many more have been displaced throughout Hebei. According to an August 24, 2008 report by the UK's *Times,* much of the infrastructure intended for the water diversion scheme was left half-constructed or unused when Beijing officials realized that water demand estimates had been far too high. The number of tourists attending the Beijing games was lower than expected, and many migrant workers, ethnic minorities, and political dissidents had left the city as a result of intimidation or official requests. Nevertheless, the Hebei area had already been sucked dry to fill a number of large reservoirs, leading to drought and agricultural losses.

Water Transfers

Large-scale water transfers have long been advocated by Chinese planners as a solution to the country's water woes. The South-North Water Transfer Project is being developed primarily to divert water from the Yangtze River to the Yellow River and Beijing. The development or diversion of major transboundary rivers originating in China, such as the Brahmaputra River and the Mekong River, could be a source on tension with China's neighbors. For example, after building two dams upstream, China is building at least three more on the Mekong, inflaming passions in Vietnam, Laos, Cambodia andThailand. In a book titled "Tibet's Waters Will Save China" a group of Chinese ex-officials have championed the northward rerouting of the waters of the Brahmaputra as an important lifeline for China in a future phase of South-North Water Transfer Project. Such a diversion could fuel tension with India and Bangladesh, if no prior agreement would be reached on sharing the river's water.

On a smaller scale, some of the waters of the Irtysh River, which would otherwise flow into Kazakhstan, Russia, and the Arctic Ocean, have been diverted into the arid areas of north-central Xinjiang via the Irtysh–Karamay–Ürümqi Canal.

Sea Water Desalination

Due to the water problems, as well as for future exports, China is building up its desalination technological abilities and plans to create an indigenous industry. Some cities have introduced extensive water conservation and recycling programs and technologies.

WATER QUALITY

The quality of groundwater or surface water is a major problem in China, be it because of man-made water pollution or natural contamination.

Pollution and Water Shortage

Deterioration of drinking water quality continues to be a major problem in China. Continuous emissions from manufacturing is the largest contributor to lowered drinking quality across the People's Republic, but introduction of poorly treated sewage, industrial spills, and extensive use of agricultural fertilizers and pesticides have proven to be major contributors as well. Furthermore, these water quality issues couple with seasonal scarcity of water to spark endemic water shortages, which frequently affect millions of people to some extent. According to China's State Environmental Protection Administration (SEPA) in 2006, 60% of the country's rivers suffer from pollution to such an extent that they cannot be safely used as drinking water sources. According to the 2008 State of the Environment Report by the Ministry of Environmental Protection, the successor agency of SEPA, pollution of specific rivers is as follows:

- The Pearl River and the Yangtze River had "good water quality";
- The Songhua River was "slightly polluted" (it was "moderately polluted" in 2006);
- The Liaohe River, the Huaihe River, and the Yellow River were "moderately polluted" (another translation says they "had poor water quality"); and
- the Haihe River which flows through Beijing and Tianjin was "badly polluted".

A 2006 article by the Chinese Embassy in the UK stated that approximately 300 million nationwide have no access to clean water. Almost 90% of underground water in cities are affected by pollution and as well as 70% of China's rivers and lakes.

China Daily stated that large scale use of pesticides and fertilizers from agriculture also contribute to water pollution.

A 2008 report about the Yellow River argued that severe pollution caused by factory discharges and sewage from fast-expanding cities has made one-third of the river unusable even for agricultural or industrial use. The report, based on data taken last year, covered more than 8,384 miles of the river, one of the longest waterways in the world, and its tributaries. The Yellow River Conservancy Committee, which surveyed more than 8,384 miles of the river in 2007, said 33.8% of the river system registered worse than level five. According to criteria used by the UN Environment Program, level five is unfit for drinking, aquaculture, industrial use and even agriculture. The report said waste and sewage discharged into the system last year totaled 4.29bn tonnes. Industry and manufacturing provided 70% of the discharge into the river, with households accounting for 23% and just over 6% coming from other sources.

There have been a high number of river pollution incidents in recent years in China, such as drinking water source pollution by algae in the Tai Lake, Wuxi in May 2007. There was a "bloom of blue-green algae that gave off a rotten smell" shutting off the main source of drinking water supply to 5.8 million people. By September 2007, the city had closed or given notice to close more than 1,340 polluting factories. The city ordered the rest to clean up by June or be permanently shut down. The closing of the factories resulted in a 15% reduction of local GDP. The severe pollution had been known for many years, but factories had been allowed to continue to operate until the crisis erupted.

The 2005 Jilin chemical plant explosions in Jilin City caused a large discharge of nitrobenzene into the Songhua River. Levels of the carcinogen were so high that the entire water supply to Harbin city (pop 3.8M) was cut off for five days between November 21, 2005 and November 26, 2005, though it was only on November

23 that officials admitted that a severe pollution incident was the reason for the cutoff.

Chinese environmental activist and journalist Ma Jun warned in 2006 that China is facing a water crisis that includes water shortages, water pollution and a deterioration in water quality. Ma argued that 400 out of 600 cities in China are facing water shortages to varying degrees, including 30 out of the 32 largest cities. Furthermore, Ma argued, discharges of waste water have increased continually over the years 2001-2006, and that that 300 million peasants' drinking water is not safe. He warned: "In the north, due to the drying up of the surface water, the underground water has been over-extracted. The water shortage in the north could have drastic affects because almost half of China's population lives on only 15 percent of its water. The situation is not sustainable. Though the south has abundant water, there is a lack of clean water due to serious water pollution. Even water-abundant deltas like the Yangtze and the Pearl River suffer from water shortages."

According to an article in the Guardian, in 2005, deputy minister Qiu Baoxing stated that more than 100 out of the 660 cities had extreme water shortages. Pan Yue, deputy director of the state environment protection agency, warned that economic growth was unsustainable due to the water problems. In 2004 the World Bank warned that the scarcity of the resource would lead to "a fight between rural interests, urban interests and industrial interests on who gets water in China." In April 2005 there were dozens of injuries in Dongyang city, Zhejiang Province, due to clashes over the nearby chemical factories of the Juxi Industrial Park accused of water pollution that harmed crops and led to deformed babies being born. According the article, a quarter of the population lacked clean drinking water and less than a third of the waste was treated. China is expected to face worsening water shortages until 2030 when the population peaks.

According to a 2007 report by the World Bank, the pollution scandals demonstrate that, if not immediately and effectively controlled, pollution releases can spread across the boundaries of administrative jurisdictions, causing "environmental and economic damage as well as public concern and the potential for social unease". Once an accident has occurred, the impact on the environment and human health becomes more difficult and more costly to control. Therefore, the report recommends prevention of pollution by strict enforcement of appropriate policies and regulations.

Natural Contamination

Large portions of China's aquifers suffer from arsenic contamination of groundwater. Arsenic poisoning occurs after long-term exposure to contaminated groundwater through drinking. The phenomenon was first detected in China in the 1950s. As water demand grows, wells are being drilled deeper and now frequently tap into arsenic-rich aquifers. As a consequence, arsenic poisoning is rising. To date there have been more than 30,000 cases reported with about 25 million people exposed to dangerously high levels in their drinking water.

According to the WHO over 26 million people in China suffer from dental fluorosis (weakening of teeth) due to elevated fluoride in their drinking water. In addition, over 1 million cases of skeletal fluorosis (weakening of bones) are thought to be attributable to drinking water. High levels of fluoride occur in groundwater and defluoridation is in many cases unaffordable.

Pollution Incidents

The Hubei Shuanghuan Science and Technology Stock Co poisoned at least 100 tonnes (220,000 lb) fish in a river in central Hubei province in September 2013 with discharged ammonia into the Fuhe river.

CONSERVATION AND SANITATION

Water supply and sanitation in the People's Republic of China is undergoing a massive transition, while facing numerous challenges - such as rapid urbanization and a widening economic gap between urban and rural areas.

The World Bank in a 2007 report stated that between 1990 and 2005 there have been major financial investments in water infrastructure. While urban water supply coverage increased from 50% to 90%, there are still seasonal water shortages in many cities.

Water usage by the growing population has increased but it has decreased by industry causing a stabilization of the overall water usage level. Sewage treatment of urban wastewater more than tripled from 15% to 52%. Installed wastewater treatment capacity grew much more quickly due to an increasing absolute amount of wastewater. Absolute release of municipal pollutants has decreased slightly since 2000.

According to a 2007 article, the SEPA stated that the water quality in the central drinking water sources for major cities was "mainly good".

Management

The responsibility for dealing with water is split between several agencies within the government. Water pollution is the responsibility of the environmental authorities, but thewater supply itself is managed by the Ministry of Water Resources. Sewage treatment is managed by the Ministry of Construction, but groundwater management falls within the realm of the Ministry of Land and Resources. China grades its water quality in six levels, from Grade I to Grade VI, with Grade VI being the most polluted.

In 2007 Ma Xiancong, a researcher at the Chinese Academy of Social Sciences Institute of Law, identified the following areas where the government failed to act, or tacitly consented, approved or actively took part and so created a worse situation: land appropriation, pollution, excessive mining and the failure to carry out environmental impact assessments. An example of this emerged in 2006, when the State Environmental Protection Administration revealed over a dozen hydroelectric projects that had broken the Environmental Impact Assessment Law.

In 2005 experts warned that China must use Integrated Water Resources Management in order to achieve sustainable development.

CHINA'S GREAT WATER WALL

The Chinese government's recent decision to build an array of new dams on rivers flowing to other countries seems set to roil inter-riparian relations in Asia and make it more difficult to establish rules-based water cooperation and sharing.

Asia, not Africa, is the world's driest continent. China, which already boasts more large dams than the rest of the world combined, has emerged as the key impediment to building institutionalized collaboration on shared water resources. In contrast to the bilateral water treaties between many of its neighbors, China rejects the concept of a water-sharing arrangement or joint, rules-based management of common resources.

The long-term implications of China's dam program for India are particularly stark because several major rivers flow south from the Tibetan plateau. India has water-sharing treaties with both the countries located downstream from it: the Indus pact with Pakistan guarantees the world's largest cross-border flows of any treaty regime, while the Ganges accord has set a new principle in international water law by assuring Bangladesh an equal share of downriver flows in the dry season. China, by contrast, does not have a single water-sharing treaty with any neighbor.

Yet most of Asia's international rivers originate in territories that China annexed after its 1949 communist "revolution." The sprawling Tibetan plateau, for example, is the world's largest freshwater repository and the source of Asia's greatest rivers, including those that are the lifeblood of mainland China, South Asia and Southeast Asia. Other Chinese-held homelands of ethnic minorities contain the headwaters of rivers such as the Irtysh, Illy and Amur, which flow to Russia and Central Asia.

China's dam program on international rivers is following a well-established pattern: Build modest-size dams on a river's difficult uppermost reaches, and then construct larger dams in the upper-middle sections as the river picks up greater water volume and momentum, then embarking on megadams in the border area facing another country. The cascade of megadams on the Mekong River, for example, is located in the area just before the river enters continental Southeast Asia.

Most of the new dam projects announced recently by China's state council, or Cabinet, are concentrated in the seismically active southwest, covering parts of the Tibetan plateau. The restart of dam building on the Salween River after an eight-year moratorium is in keeping with a precedent set on other river systems: Beijing temporarily suspends a controversial plan after major protests flare so as to buy time — before resurrecting the same plan.

The Salween — Asia's last largely free-flowing river — runs through deep, spectacular gorges, glaciated peaks and karst on its way into Burma and along the Thai border before emptying into the Andaman Sea. Its upstream basin is inhabited by 16 ethnic groups, including some, like the Derung tribe, with tiny populations numbering in the thousands. As one of the world's most biologically diverse regions, the upper basin boasts more than 5,000 plant species and nearly half of China's animal species.

The decision to formally lift the moratorium and construct five dams — with work to start immediately on the Songta dam, the farthest upriver structure in Tibet — threatens the region's biodiversity and could uproot endangered aboriginal tribes. There is also the risk that the weight of huge, new dam reservoirs could accentuate seismic instability in a region prone to recurrent earthquakes.

No country is more vulnerable to China's re-engineering of transboundary flows than India. The reason is that India alone receives nearly half of the river waters that leave Chinese-held territory. According to United Nations figures, a total of 718 billion cubic meters of surface water flows out of Chinese territory yearly, of which 347 billion cubic meters (or 48.3 percent of the total) runs directly into India.

China already has a dozen dams in the Brahmaputra River basin and one each on the Indus and the Sutlej rivers. On the Brahmaputra, it is currently close to completing one dam and has just cleared work on three others. Two more are planned in this cascade before the dam-building moves to the water-rich border segment as the river makes a U-turn to enter India.

Asia awaits a future made hotter and drier by climate and environmental change, and resource depletion. The continent's water challenges have been exacerbated by consumption growth, unsustainable irrigation practices, rapid industrialization, pollution, environmental degradation and geopolitical shifts.

If Asia is to prevent water wars, it must build institutionalized cooperation in transboundary basins that co-opts all riparian neighbors. If a dominant riparian state refuses to join, such institutional arrangements — as in the Mekong basin — will be ineffective. The arrangements must be centered on transparency, unhindered information flow, equitable sharing, dispute settlement, pollution control and a commitment to refrain from any projects that could materially diminish transboundary flows. International dispute-settlement mechanisms, as in the Indus treaty, help stem the risk that water wrangles could escalate to open conflict.

China — with its hold over Asia's transnational water resources and boasting more than half of the world's 50,000 large dams — has made the control and manipulation of river flows a pivot of its power and economic progress. Unless it is willing to play a leadership role in developing a rules-based system, the economic and security risks arising from the Asian water competition can scarcely be mitigated.

10

Regional Water Co-operation and Conflict in Central Asia

WATER MANAGEMENT DURING THE SOVIET UNION

Within the Soviet Union, inter-republican water resources were managed on the basis of water use plans. These plans were developed by local Ministries of Land Reclamation and Water Management and then sent to Moscow to the Ministry of Land Reclamation and Water Management of the Soviet Union for approval. These plans and schemes provided for annual water withdrawal limits with respect to each tributary, reservoir or canal and the limits were calculated against annual crop requirements. A number of bilateral agreements was signed between the republics to correct water allocation, such as the an agreement between the Turkmen SSR and the Uzbek SSR on water quotas from the Amu Darya, between the Kyrgyz SSR and the Uzbek SSR on the use of waters of the Sokh river, etc. Neither of these agreements contained any provisions with respect to the quality of return flows, i.e. the drainage water disposed of into the rivers. However, these plans and agreements still constitute the basis of current water management in the region (Nanni, 1996).

Under the Soviet system of water allocation, water quotas imposed by Moscow favoured downstream countries at the expense of the upstream riparians: water-abundant Kyrgyzstan and Tajikistan were supposed to supply irrigated agriculture economies of Uzbekistan and Turkmenistan with water in spring and summer when water should be available for cotton fields. In autumn and winter, when Kyrgyzstan and Tajikistan experienced peaks in electricity demand, they were supplied with Turkmen and Uzbek gas and Kazakh coal to satisfy energy consumption. They also received electricity from downstream countries during winter to be compensated for the hydropower produced in summer. Maintenance and operating costs of dams and reservoirs were covered by Moscow.

Post-independence Water Management

After independence, the need for all riparians to enter into an agreement regulating water allocation in the Basin has become apparent. Such agreement signed on 18 February 1992 in Almaty did not go far from water quotas set up under the Soviet Union. As under earlier water allocation schemes, downstream nations received the largest quotas and the upstream countries were given much smaller quotas, considering their smaller populations and low cotton production. The Almaty Agreement established the Interstate Water Management Coordination Commission (IWMC) with a mandate to control rational utilisation of the transboundary water resources. IWMC's decisions regarding intake limits and rational utilisation of water are obligatory for all users. It is responsible for governing the two inter-republican Basin Water Management Bodies (Basseinoe vodnoe ob'edinenie – BVO): BVO Amu Darya and BVO Syr Darya. Hence, the five preferred to continue with the BVO management system put in place during the Soviets (IGC, 2002b).

Initially, IWMC was responsible for great many issues including water development and allocation planning, water quality control and conservation, environmental protection, preparing annual water allocation plans, defining limits of water use by each riparian, etc. With the establishment of other intergovernmental institutions between 1993 and 1995 such as the Interstate Council on the Aral Sea Basin and the International Fund for the Aral Sea, functions of the IWMC became somewhat duplicated and its relationship with other intergovernmental bodies remain unclear (Vinogradov and Langford, 2001; ICG, 2002b).

The Almaty Agreement attempted to secure the existing situation where water was apportioned to allow maximum utilisation whereas the international concept of equitable and optimum utilisation was kept aloof. The Agreement also lacked the provision about dispute settlement. According to it, water disputes are to be settled by the Ministers of Water Resources of the five states. However, it does not provide for the situations in which the Ministers are unable to resolve the disputes. In absence of any inter-republican dispute settlement body, this seems to be serious flaw (Nanni, 1996; Vinogradov and Landgford, 2001). Furthermore, the problem is also actual functioning of the water management bodies, BVOs, who lack funding and legal powers. According to the Almaty Agreement, they have to submit a budget to the ICWC for approval. Once a budget has been approved, the five members states are supposed to contribute a proportion of their budget based on the percentage of river water allocated. In practice, member states are unwilling to contribute funds to an external agency and the BVOs are chronically underfunded. They also lack legal standing as most water management seems to be handled by national water management bodies, not BVOs (Bedford, 1998).

Table : Water allocations under the Almaty Agreement

Country	*Sur Darya allocation, %*	*Amu Darya allocation, %*
Kazakhstan	38.1	0
Kyrgyzstan	1.0	0.4
Tajikistan	9.2	13.6
Turkmenistan	0	43.0
Uzbekistan	51.7	43.0
Total	100.0	100.0

Source: Bedford, 1998

Hence, upstream countries were further restricted in their economic development and ability to satisfy heating needs during winter months as downstream countries introduced world prices for gas and coal. Unable to afford them, Kyrgyzstan increased electricity production at Toktogul reservoir that caused sharp reduction in water to downstream Uzbekistan and Kazakhstan for irrigation during cotton season. After serious tensions in 1997, the countries have come to enter a framework barter agreement in 1998. Under this, Uzbekistan and Kazakhstan would provide Kyrgyzstan with gas and coal during winter in return for irrigation water during spring and summer.

However, barter agreements are in constant breach due to a number of reasons: they are ready usually in spring when Uzbek and Kazakh fields are in dire need of water; the parties lack trust and do not keep their commitments; and there is lack of control mechanisms. Also, several years of severe drought have affected the situation dramatically, causing Kyrgyzstan to reduce water for irrigation in summer and triggering floods in Uzbekistan during winter. Attempts to adjust quotas to reflect this have so far failed. Downstream countries have shown little understanding of upstream riparians' demands to expand their water use (ICG, 2002b).

LEGAL FRAMEWORK FOR CURRENT WATER MANAGEMENT IN CENTRAL ASIA

Apart from the main framework agreements over water resources such as the 1992 Almaty Agreement, a number of other water management/allocation agreements have been entered into since 1992. Below is the list of some of them:

- Agreement between the governments of Russia and Kazakhstan on the joint use and protection of transboundary water resources, Orenburg, 1992
- Agreement on the creation of the International Fund for the Aral Sea, 1993
- Programme on the joint actions on the improvement of environmental situation in the Aral Sea Basin, 1994
- Declaration on the problems of sustainable development in the Aral Sea Basin, Nukus, 1995
- Statement of leaders of Kazakhstan, Kyrgyzstan and Uzbekistan about the energy/water use, Bishkek, 1996
- Declaration on the creation of the Interstate Commission on Sustainable Development and the need of preparation of a Convention on Sustainable Development, Almaty, 1997

- Framework Agreement between the governments of Kazakhstan, Kyrgyzstan and Uzbekistan on joint use of the Syr Darya River Basin water/energy resources, Bishkek, 1998
- Agreement between Kazakhstan, Kyrgyzstan, Tajikistan and Turkmenistan on co-operation in the field of environmental protection and Agreement on biodiversity conservation, Bishkek, 1998
- Agreement between Kazakhstan and Kyrgyzstan on the interstate use of hydrological facilities at the Chu and Talas rivers, 2000
- Annual intergovernmental water/energy agreements (CAREC, 2002).

However, actual regional co-operation over water resources, other than entering into numerous agreements, is "glaringly absent (Spechler, 2001). Neither economic co-operation, nor water regulation has been a success, despite all the joint communiqus and speeches. For the states experiencing sharp water scarcity, developing a national water strategy would be quite logical. Yet none of Central Asian states has developed one, though Kazakhstan, Kyrgyzstan and Tajikistan have started working on it. Implementing existing agreements appears to be another problem. Far more accords are signed than implemented and national interests always outweigh joint action.

None of water treaties specifies a goal of reducing water use or making agriculture less water-intensive. The sceptical attitude of downstream countries to multilateral co-operation deters them from any environmental and financial commitments (Kltzli, 1997).

Modern transboundary watercourse law largely based on the 1997 UN Convention on the Law of Non-Navigational Uses of International Watercourses urges riparians not only to create legal agreements to manage their shared resources, but also to find joint management mechanism and to cede sufficient sovereignty to them to make them effective. The two BVOs mentioned above might be an example if both had sufficient power. And none of Central Asian states have become a party to the 1997 Convention, although Kazakhstan did accede to the Convention on the

Protection and Use of Transboundary Watercourses and International Lakes.

International Actors

From the first days of independence, bilateral donors, international agencies and private foundations have funded dozens of projects in order to resolve difficult water situation in Central Asia. In doing so, technical solutions were preferred to political and economic ones. Especially active were the World Bank, United Nations Development Programme (UNDP), the EU Programme of Technical Assistance to the CIS (TACIS), and the United States Agency of International Development (USAID) who spent millions of dollars to help resolve the Aral Sea crisis. Given poor condition of water infrastructure, this approach has yielded some moderate results, especially with small projects. Effort to tackle water from political perspective, however, has resulted in problems. A lack of willingness of Central Asian states to co-operate has buried great many initiatives, like, for example, an attempt by the Organisation of Security and Co-operation in Europe (OSCE) to persuade the five to discuss the region's water problems at a water conference to be held in London. This effort came to nothing with Turkmenistan's president's response that international conference in London was not the right place to discuss Central Asia's water. In his turn, Uzbekistan's president said that his country had a thousands years of experience in managing water problems and he preferred bilateral discussions to a multilateral conference.

In trying to find a solution to the desiccation of the Aral Sea, AralGEF, a project funded by the Global Environmental Facility (GEF) and designed to create small but viable wetlands and fisheries on the place of the Aral Sea through restoration of a modest flow to the old seabed, and the UNDP Aral Seashore Rehabilitation and Capacity Development Project are so far most prominent. According to the World Bank, in order to successfully restore "modest flow to the Amu Darya, agricultural runoff should be entirely restored. Thus, huge lakes that developed over the decades of water negligence from the excess water of the Toktogul reservoir and that now support local agriculture, fisheries, recreation areas and biodiversity habitats would thus be bound to disappear. And the main success of UNDP's project on rehabilitation of the Aral Seashore consisted in providing 16,000 residents of Karakalpakstan with safe drinking water and planting thousands of trees that withered immediately because they were unsuited for local climate.

Part of the problem is the failure of Central Asian states to support the donor projects in a meaningful way, either administratively or financially. Neither donors seem to need anything more than paper reports. Even National Environmental Action Plans funded by the World Bank, UNDP and TACIS are based on the ineradicable idea, the only one familiar to the region's old guard of water bureaucrats, that plan, not action, is needed to save the situation. This approach endorsed by donor staffs inherently contradicts the overarching goal to help Central Asian states to move away from a planned economy and to embrace the market economy and decentralisation (Sievers, 2002; ICG, 2002b).

RECENT WATER CONFLICTS

Not surprisingly, this situation has already led to numerous small-scale local conflicts, began in the late 1980s when the central authorities weakened their grip on Central Asia. In 1990, the outbreak of conflict in the Kyrgyz town of Osh, on the border with Uzbekistan, claimed over 300 lives and was provoked by fierce competition for water together with high population density, limited arable land and ethnic dimension (large population of Uzbeks living in the area).

Since summer 1993, there have been serious water tensions between Kyrgyzstan and Uzbekistan. Kyrgyzstan was blamed by the Uzbek authorities for releasing too much water from the Toktogul reservoir. Extra water did not reach the Aral Sea but was dumped instead into the Aydarkul depression, the large 'sinus' which has developed as a result of years of negligence (Kltzli, 1994). In 1997, Uzbekistan has deployed 130,000 troops on the Kyrgyz border to guard the reservoirs straddling the two countries (Hogan, 2000b; Grozin, 2001). In June 2001, the Kyrgyz parliament adopted a law classifying water as a commodity, and the government followed up by announcing that the downstream countries would be charged for the water they use. Uzbekistan's response was to cut off all deliveries of gas to Kyrgyzstan and accuse Kyrgyzstan of failing to honour the barter agreement to provide Uzbekistan with water in return for oil and gas. Although weaker in political and military terms Kyrgyzstan acknowledged this failure, Uzbekistan would be emboldened to behave in a more aggressive manner towards its neighbours. The two were on the verge of violent conflict for several times (Khamidov, 2001).

Current Water Disputes

Central Asia's two major rivers, as well as their tributaries, have become a focus for growing competition among their riparians, with the Syr Darya being a particular point of tensions. The Amu Darya is rapidly becoming a locus of disputes as the governments of Turkmenistan and Uzbekistan become more hostile towards each other competing also for water, and Afghanistan is about to demand its share. These tensions have so far been contained without conflict, but all parties have shown a willingness to put their interests first at any cost, including military intervention. Due to their reliance on agriculture, Uzbekistan and Turkmenistan view irrigation as a key security issue (ICG, 2002b).

The Syr Darya Basin

The Syr Darya is shared by four states and, in case of Uzbekistan, is shared twice as after flowing from Kyrgyzstan and crossing the Uzbek part of the Ferghana valley the river flows into the Tajik territory in the western Ferghana Valley and then pours again into Uzbekistan. After crossing the Hunger Steppe, the Syr Darya runs into Kazakhstan.

Kyrgyzstan and Uzbekistan have had particularly discordant history over the use of water from the Syr Darya. Since independence, Kyrgyzstan faces serious economic problems, mainly because of a shortage of energy supply from Russia, Kazakhstan and Uzbekistan. The primacy of energy production over the irrigation needs downstream has already created a major discord between Uzbekistan and Kyrgyzstan (Klötzli, 1994). The 1998 Syr-Darya Framework Agreement between the two has been broken by both sides. The implementation of such barter agreement runs across one major problem – all barter agreements are delayed until the late spring when the downstream countries urgently need water for irrigation. As this might be the case, Kyrgyzstan would have had an incentive to produce less electricity. However, due to Kyrgyzstan's uncertainty whether enough gas would be provided, it produces electricity to protect itself giving rise to a vicious circle (IGC, 2002).

Uzbekistan intensified the tension more than once by acting in a unilateral manner. In July 1997, it cut off 70 percent of downstream flow, which caused a riot among the Kazakh farmers whose 100,000 hectares were threatened (O'Hara, 1998; Hogan, 2000b). History of altering water flow by upstream riparians is no more soothing. In summer 1999, Tajikistan released 700 million cubic meters of water from its Kairakum reservoir without warning its downstream neighbours. As a result, cotton crops in southern Kazakhstan which has received less water than was agreed, were devastated. The situation was seriously aggravated by Kyrgyzstan's concurrent move to reduce the flow to southern Kazakhstan in retaliation for Kazakhstan's failure to supply coal under the barter agreements. After months of talks, the incident was finally settled (Hogan, 2000a).

At issue is also the Naryn-Syr Darya cascade of dams in Kyrgyzstan. Every year Uzbekistan insists on releasing water from it to improve downstream agriculture. Several times, the conflict was on the verge of war. In 1997, Uzbekistan deployed 130,000 troops on the Kyrgyz-Uzbek border, near the Toktogul reservoir, to conduct military exercises aimed at seizure of a 'well guarded object', using the armour and helicopters. Meanwhile, Kyrgyzstan, through media leak, hinted that in case the reservoir would be blown up, the resulting flood would sweep away Uzbekistan's Ferghana and Zeravshan Valleys (Grozin, 2001).

Kyrgyzstan has tried to persuade Uzbekistan and Kazakhstan to share the maintenance and operating costs of the Toktogul reservoir but these attempts were turned down by the downstream countries. Kazakhstan claimed that it would not be able to pay the costs – between US$ 15 and 27 million per annum. Thus, the opportunity for the downstream riparians to settle the dispute was missed. However, by adopting *Law on the Interstate Use of Water Objects, Water Resources and Water Management Installations* on 29 June 2001, the Kyrgyz parliament left the door open to push the downstream countries into negotiations regarding the maintenance costs of the Toktogul reservoir as later Kyrgyzstan stated that in fact it demanded to pay only for the water passing through Kyrgyz reservoirs, i.e. share maintenance costs. This was welcomed by Kazakhstan who agreed to pay for the maintenance of the Kyrgyz water installations, but initially opposed by Uzbeks. However, in March 2002 Uzbekistan reached the agreement with Kyrgyzstan that it would share some costs in return for the guarantee that it would receive water for irrigation. Had more attention have been paid to the barter agreements working properly, the main step to resolving the Syr Darya dispute between Kyrgyzstan and Uzbekistan would be taken (ICG, 2002b).

Shared water storage facilities, like the Andijan reservoir located in the Uzbek part of the Ferghana Valley but supposed to re-channel some water back to Kyrgyzstan, also represent an inter-state problem (Chait, 1998).

The Amu Darya Basin

The Amu Darya is shared by four countries – Tajikistan as the upstream riparian, Afghanistan, Uzbekistan and Turkmenistan – and forms the border in some stretches between Tajikistan, Uzbekistan and Afghanistan, and between Turkmenistan and Uzbekistan.

The Amu Darya is much less regulated and has fewer dams and reservoirs to cause potential problems. However, there are serious tensions along the flow of the river not only between the upstream and downstream riparians, as, for example, between Tajikistan and Uzbekistan, but also between the middle and lower riparians, for example, Uzbekistan and Turkmenistan.

According to the 1992 water quota agreement, Tajikistan is entitled to 9 m^3 of about 75 m^3 of annual flow of the Amu Darya, or 12 percent. This is considered low by Tajikistan who needs to expand its agricultural output to supply the growing population with food. Tajikistan's agriculture is underdeveloped since the Soviet times, and the irrigation system is derelict and in need of urgent repairs. Tajikistan sees the only way out as using more water either by increasing its water quota from the Amu Darya or by diverting the Zeravhsan river. As 95 percent of the latter are used by Uzbekistan, this would cause serious tensions with Tajikistan's much powerful neighbour.

In contrast, increasing the Amu Darya quota seems to be quite easy, since Tajikistan has an upper hand in distributing water resources of the Amu Darya. In principle, nobody could prevent Tajikistan from taking more water than was allocated by the water quota agreement. It is very hard to monitor Tajikistan's performance, as most equipment needed has been destroyed during the civil war in 1992-1997. But even Tajikistan were to increase its water quota moderately, this would have an immediate impact downstream.

The same water/energy complex as with Kyrgyzstan has developed between Tajikistan and Uzbekistan. Tajikistan's central and southern parts are well provided by electricity from the Nurek hydro plant, and northern Tajikistan having no grid lines with the rest of the country relies on Uzbekistan's intermittent supplies of electricity and gas in winter. In return, Tajikistan provides power to southern Uzbek provinces and often requests that Uzbekistan switched off electricity to northern Tajikistan to keep imports within the agreed limit not to pay higher price. This causes serious discontent as Tajikistan is forced to have electricity rationed in many provinces due to poor state of Tajikistan's grid lines. The country desires to develop its hydropower resources to break dependence on Uzbekistan. But increasing hydro consumption would seriously affect the downstream access to seasonal water supplies and to create further discord along the Amu Darya course.

The most dramatic conflict over the Amu Darya water resources is between downstream nations of Uzbekistan and Turkmenistan. Both equally depend on their cotton production and irrigation agriculture and both claim that each of them exceed their water quotas. Due to the very poor state of Turkmenistan's water infrastructure, most water received by Turkmenistan is wasted. The country does not want to spend huge funds for the expensive rehabilitation of crippling Turkmen canals and draws off more water from the Amu Darya instead. The relations between two countries dramatically worsened in the late 2002 when the Uzbek ambassador has been declared persona non grata in Turkmenistan on accusation of participating in the conspiracy to oust and kill President Niyazov. Uzbek-Turkmen relations over water can grow even worse, given Turkmenistan's ambitious plan to complete a huge reservoir in the Karakum desert, called the Golden Century Lake. Another point of contention is the Tyuyamuyun reservoir in the delta of the Amu Darya divided between Uzbekistan and Turkmenistan. Both sides feel displeased with the wasteful use of water, and this led to an outbreak of violence in 1992 over the re-direction of drainage waters and raids by both sides to cut off pipes and irrigation canals (Smith, 1995). Today, the Tyuyamuyun remains one of the several disputed areas in continuing water dispute with Uzbekistan.

Throughout the independence period, rumours have circulated of a small-scale secret war between the two states over the river resources, Uzbekistan troops taking control of water installations on the Turkmen bank of the Amu Darya, and even of a massacre of a large number of Uzbekistan troops in Turkmenistan in 2001. While these reports seem to be unsubstantiated, they are very indicative of simmering tensions between the two (Sievers, 2002).

POTENTIAL WATER DISPUTES

The complicated water situation in Central Asia forced the governments of the five states to consider alternative plans for developing water infrastructure to gain better control over water resources. Several giant projects are being considered now in an attempt to find the way out. With little exception, all of them date back to the Soviet planning system, and several projects have been frozen in the 1970s-1980s due to the lack of funds. Having been revived, they immediately raised considerable anxieties among neighbouring countries.

Among those projects are: the Rogun reservoir able to give Tajikistan full control over the Amu Darya, Golden Century Lake in the middle of Turkmenistan's Karakum desert, the project of diverting Siberian rivers of Ob and Irtysh to help replenish the Aral Sea, etc.

The idea to divert Siberian water to Central Asia was abandoned in the late 1980s when it has become clear that the project would cause irretrievable damage to the environment. In recent years, however, the project has been revived by Uzbekistan. The main argument of the project's proponents, among whom is the mayor of Moscow Yury Luzhkov, is that the Siberian rivers frequently flood and hence have excess of water to share with water-deficient Central Asian countries. Yet in reality floods are the integral part of a river system and there is no any "excess water. In projecting a huge canal 2,500 kilometres long, 200 metres wide and 15 metres deep from Western Siberia to Central Asia, it was estimated that 23 cubic kilometres of water would be diverted, of which 2 cubic kilometres would be lost due to the filtration. Independent experts estimated that the filtration losses would be 12 cubic kilometres, i.e. half of the water to be diverted, which is normal, given that such a cyclopean structure would reach enormous levels of filtration, water-logging and salinisation. One expert put the idea of a miscalculating the project like this, In the Soviet times, we would have been given the task of calculating a project cost of a bridge to the Moon, and we would have calculated that. But nobody would care about the consequences (Radio Liberty, 2002). Huge, economically not viable and environmentally dubious Siberian water diversion project has already contributed to the difficult water situation in Central Asia. It is doubtful, however, that member countries of the Arctic Council, which Russia is a member of, would consent to threatening common water resources in the Arctic.

MULTIDIMENSIONAL NATURE OF CENTRAL ASIA'S WATER DISPUTES

Water disputes contribute to the broader complex of problems across the region, including border disputes, Islamic extremism, high population growth, ethnic tensions, clan competition, human rights and political instability. The desiccation of the Aral Sea has been the important factor to the worsening socio-economic conditions in the area, fuelling nationalist ideas among the population of Karakalpakstan, the Uzbek autonomous republic adjacent to the disaster zone, and aggravating water situation in the region. Lack of public participation, particularly in authoritarian Turkmenistan and Uzbekistan, and attempts of those governments to find military decisions in already difficult relationships between those countries and upstream states makes the whole situation white-hot.

Ethnic dimension is extremely important for ethnically diverse Kyrgyzstan and Uzbekistan. As it happens, local conflicts here have been more serious than wider ones. Disputes over land and water resources provoking wider ethnic conflict have led to hundreds of victims in Kyrgyzstan in 1990. Poverty, rising costs and crumbling water infrastructure are adding to strains in local water system. Water affects the poor who end up paying the large proportion of their income for the resource.

Especially vulnerable to violent eruptions over water and ethnicity is the Ferghana Valley shared by Tajikistan, Kyrgyzstan and Uzbekistan which has already seen the outbreaks of violence, like it was in 1990, when bloody clashes between inhabitants of the Kyrgyz town of Osh claimed over 300 lives, or earlier, in 1989, when hundreds of the Meskhetian Turks, who had been deported to Central Asia by Stalin in the 1940s, were killed in the Uzbek town of Ferghana in what was called one of the most dramatic episodes of inter-ethnic relations in the Soviet Union.

The roots of any future ethnic strife in Central Asia lie in the unresolved social and economic problems, competition for scarce water and grazing resources and contentions over discriminatory land allocations (Elhance, 1997). Potentially explosive ethnic cleavages tear apart many countries in the region. Kyrgyzstan is divided between northern and southern part, with the latter gravitating towards Uzbekistan and inhabited by large proportion of ethnic Uzbeks who have repeatedly demanded to give the area more autonomy. Uzbekistan's headache is the large Tajik population living in Samarkand and Bukhara. Over the last years, Uzbekistan's policy was to suppress Tajik ethnic identity by not allowing schools to learn in Tajik language and forcing many Tajiks to call themselves ethnic Uzbeks in their Uzbek passports. The same situation is in Tajikistan where a lot of ethnic Uzbeks live. In the late 1990s, after the relations between Uzbekistan and Tajikistan have worsened, the Tajik government expelled many Uzbeks to neighbouring Kyrgyzstan and Afghanistan in an attempt to get rid of "extremist elements. Ethnic minorities have often been viewed by authoritarian governments as potential provocateurs, separatists and extremists (ICG, 2002a).

Historic competition between peoples of Central Asia is fuelled by the fact that their leaders do not seem to like one another. There is a great personal competition between the three former Communist leaders, Uzbekistan's Islam Karimov, Kazakhstan's Nursultan Nazarbaev and Turkmenistan's Saparmurad Niyazov. Each wants to show that his country is the region's most powerful and he therefore should be viewed as the most prominent political figure in Central Asia. As a consequence, the leaders of the region does not see their countries to be the part of a functioning regional subsystem and are rather isolationist in their policies. For all this, they regularly meet to discuss their common problems (Olcott, 2001).

Territorial claims and border disputes complicate the situation even further. Given complex ethnic mosaic in Central Asia, Soviet planners did not build administrative units along ethnic lines and took great care not to construct republics with strong ethnic identity which would allow them to eventually secede from the Soviet Union. As a result, thorny disputes as to whose territory was initially whose have occurred, burdened by the territorial exchanges. For example, Karakalpakstan began life in 1924 as part of Kazakhstan but in 1938 had been given away to Uzbekistan. Moreover, Uzbekistan, Kyrgyzstan and Tajikistan all have small enclaves on each other's territory which are nominally a part of their country but are geographically isolated. Only Kyrgyzstan has two Tajik enclaves, with population of some 30,000 people, and five Uzbek ones, with population of about 50,000 people. Issues related to them are highly divisive, and solving this problem appeared to be very difficult (ICG, 2002a). However, the process of delimitation of the borders has already begun. In 2000-2003, Kazakhstan, Kyrgyzstan, Tajikistan and Uzbekistan signed a number of border delimitation agreements and started works on delimiting the borders. By 2001, Kazakhstan and Uzbekistan have finally settled the border problems and exchanged disputed territories. Yet many issues, like the problem of the Uzbek enclaves in Kyrgyzstan, still remain unresolved.

In this context, the growing need to take into account all factors surrounding water disputes is apparent.

MEASURING WATER CONFLICT POTENTIAL

Water is the most politicised of all natural resources and it is more likely to become a source of armed conflict. It is no wonder therefore that such possibility has been widely discussed. Despite the growing literature on water and conflict, little work has been done to provide arguments for the common thesis that "growing conflict over water looms ahead (Samson and Charrier, 1997). Generally, the Jordan and Nile basins are cited to give an example of international conflict prone basins. On the other hand, Wolf (1998) gave a historic evidence of co-operation between riparians and stated that the only recorded war over water was fought 4500 years ago between two Mesopotamian states, Lagash and Umma, in what is now southern Iraq. The same author pointed out at the "loose definitions in the terminology of the literature about water and conflict where "terms such as conflict, dispute, tensions, and war are regularly used interchangeably.

Nevertheless, in order to provide indication of potential water conflict, combinations of variables, or indicators, have to be developed. Undoubtedly, the practice of establishing various sets of indicators, including those for sustainable development, over the past decade has greatly influenced this idea. However, unlike indicators of sustainable development designed to communicate with the public at large to provide clear picture of a country's progress towards sustainable development, indicators of water conflict proneness are meant to serve as a 'yardstick' for decision makers who are involved in negotiations regarding specific river basin management.

Yet such 'limited' value does not impede the indicators of being used by international scientific and political community able to translate them into a pressure on the governments of the riparians involved in a dispute well before this would turn into a violent conflict. The use of Geographic Information System (GIS) makes such analysis even more effective by bringing together spatial and non-spatial variables, thus facilitating identification and interpretation of potential indicators.

One of the frequently cited instruments which could serve as a model for developing a set of water conflict indicators is the Index of Human Insecurity (IHI) developed to facilitate identification of vulnerable or insecure regions.

It is considered an "aggregate measure of human welfare that integrates social, economic, and political exposures to and capacity to cope with a range of potentially harmful perturbations (Lonergan, Gustavson and Carter, 1999).

The IHI identifies four key system components – the environment, the economy, society, and institutions. Within each of these four indicator categories are four variables, each of which measure either a key structural relationship (e.g., linkages, defining characteristics) or a key functional relationship (e.g., processes, flows) of the system.

Where data in a time series are missing, IHI developers utilize statistical techniques to establish a complete time series for all indicators and all countries, where there is sufficient initial data. However, the index for each year is specific to that year, making it difficult to compare changes in a country's IHI from across years (Yoffe and Ward, 1999).

Another water-specific indicator is water stress measured by Falkenmark's (1992) Water Stress Index (WSI) which divides the volume of a country's available water resources by its population. This measure, however, does not account for a country's ability to adapt to water stress, such as with more efficient irrigation technology. Ohlsson (1999) has developed a Social Water Stress Index (SWSI) to incorporate a measure of a country's adaptability. The SWSI is a water stress index (freshwater availability per capita) divided by UNDP's Human Development Index and then divided by 2 (rounded to nearest wholes). Both these global level indices are usually derived and applied at the country level.

Several other potential indicators were also mentioned in the literature, including overall population growth rates within a country, population density within and outside a basin, relative power and riparian position of countries within a basin (Wolf, 1999), the degree of democratisation of countries sharing a river basin and so on.

TESTING INDICATORS OF WATER CONFLICT

The methodology for establishing indicators of international freshwater conflict and co-operation was developed under Basins At Risk (BAR) project at Oregon State University, USA (Wolf, Yoffe and Giordano, 2003). BAR which has spanned for 4 years effectively developed and created legal and spatial framework to further evaluate international river basins at potential risk for future water conflict. All 263 international river basins were delineated and a database documenting historical incidents of international water conflict and co-operation between 1948 and 1999 was set up. Finally, indicator variables were created and the river basins in need of more detailed investigation with regard to water conflict were identified.

Indicators have been selected in accordance with the following criteria: relevance to the selected framework; general availability of the data; existence of a theoretical or empirical link with security issue; and an adequacy of spatial and temporal coverage allowing for effective representation and modelling (Lonergan, Gustavson and Carter, 1999). Emphasis was made on the regional and basin scale indicators rather than on indicators of potential water conflict at global scale. Internationalisation of a basin was at special focus. Assuming that there is a causal link between the internationalisation of a basin and incidents of conflict among the states that now share that basin, the presence of ethnic minorities with nationalistic aspirations becomes a potential indicator (Wolf, 1999).

A key question regarding the above variables is whether they are relevant to indicating water conflict. Yoffe (2001) provides a good account of statistically testing indicators previously cited in the literature. As main statistical tool, linear regression was used to assess the relative strength of various independent variables in explaining the variability of the event data. Also, other statistical methods such as two-sample t-test were employed. Linear regression has been chosen because it offered a concise summary of the mean of the response variable as a function of an explanatory variable (Yoffe, 2001).

Sixteen indicators, including GDP per capita, population density, number of dams, water stress, HDI, hydropower have been tested using linear regression, three indicators such as freshwater treaties, adjacency and riverine contiguity have been analysed using two-sample t-test, and four indicators such as dam density, freshwater treaties, climate and precipitation had no statistical tests conducted on them due to structure of data.

Yoffe's most important finding was that most of the commonly cited water conflict indicators proved to be unsupported by the data. Neither government type, climate, IHI, water stress or number of dams, nor agricultural dependence on water resources and energy needs showed a significant relevance with water conflict. Based on the assessment, river basins are at potential risk of freshwater conflict if:

- population density exceeds 100 people per 1 km^2
- per capita GDP is less than $765
- overall unfriendly relations (<-1 at water event intensity scale)
- there are politically active minority groups that may lead to the internationalisation of a basin
- large dams or other water development projects are planned
- no or limited number of water treaties is available (Yoffe, 2001).

This study will employ these indicator variables as the research framework.

ROLE OF GIS

A number of the attribute data mentioned above can be effectively represented within a Geographic Information System (GIS), such as ESRI ArcView, designed to capture, store, manipulate, analyse and visualize disparate sets of geographically referenced data. Moreover, some spatial information such as runoff and slope would be extremely difficult to analyse without the use of a GIS.

However, GIS has its limitations inherent to the technology, including problems of multiple scales and data interpretation. The examination of indicators at an international, national and sub-national level introduces questions of scale that will need to be further addressed. There is also a lack of distinct frameworks to analyse the interaction of human and environmental systems (Yoffe and Ward, 1999). Linked to the problem of frameworks is the problem with interpreting non-spatial matters using spatial analysis. For instance, the degree of democratisation of a country might be difficult to represent if one assumes that different areas have different levels of democratisation. Special problem regarding Central Asia's GIS is the lack of data; several important databases located in Tashkent, Uzbekistan, contain a lot of vital information but this information is virtually closed for external use.

Attempts at Applying Water Conflict Indicators to Central Asia

Previous attempt to apply potential indicators of water conflict to Central Asia's water disputes has been made by Myers (1993) who created a water scarcity index using population and per capita water availability data. Assuming that water stress is to occur when more than 2,000 people share every unit of one million cubic meters of available water, the author calculated water indices for each of Central Asia's countries by comparing 1991 population data with all available water and the amount of water available solely from indigenous sources (i.e. that available from precipitation within the borders of a country). In 1993, all the countries appeared to have sufficient water resources per capita. Both downstream countries of Turkmenistan and Uzbekistan relied on water flowing in from outside and indigenous water resources stress was high (2,180 people per one million m^3 of indigenous water in Uzbekistan and 3,287 people per one million m^3 of indigenous water in Turkmenistan).

Klötzli (1994) used a number of indicators for vulnerability to water scarcity developed by Gleick (1993), including the ratio of water demand to supply, the per capita availability of water, the dependence on imported surface water and the importance of hydroelectric production. Having calculated these, the author came to a somewhat obvious conclusion that "these indicators show a distinct difference between the water-rich republics of Kyrgyzstan and Tajikistan, and the republics not controlling the sources of water courses like Uzbekistan and Turkmenistan The vulnerability indices not only express different access and pollution control opportunities, but also different, often contradictory modes of water utilisation (hydropower vs. agriculture) (Klötzli, 1994). Similar method based on Gleick's findings was used by Smith (1995) to determine the relative degree of dependence of particular regions on water resources and to identify those regions that may become potential focal points for future intra- and interstate conflicts. It is argued that high population growth can be more damaging to the environment than high population density and southern Uzbekistani provinces as Surkhandarya and Kashakdarya and several regions in the Ferghana Valley that experienced some of the highest population growth rates in the region between 1981 and 1991 are most likely to become a scene of a resource-related conflict. The author points out that the areas combining high population growth and no indigenous water supplies (Andijan and Ferghana in eastern Uzbekistan, Karakalpakstan in the west) are of prime concern. As Turkmenistan's Dashhovuz region and Uzbekistan's Karakalpakstan share the water of the lower Amu Darya, future water-induced conflicts may occur in this region. Each region was ranked according to the basic characteristics believed to affect the water conflict potential (population growth rate/density, per capita water availability from total and indigenous sources, share of water derived from external sources, minority population share of total population). Eight of ten regions having the highest rankings for water-resource vulnerability are located in Uzbekistan, with top of the top four located in the Ferghana Valley. Thus, the regions constituting the Ferghana Valley and those occupying the lower Amu Darya appear to be the most sensitive to potential water-induced conflicts.

Carney and Moran (2000) examined the interstate affect in Central Asia toward Russia, i.e. "the current discernable feeling of a government toward another government which is expressed "...in all behaviour whether it takes the form of word or deeds, and developed "scale of affectivity ranging arbitrarily from -2 to +2. Although different in goals, this study employed the similar technique in scoring and coding news reports from Foreign Broadcast Information Service (FBIS).

Also mentioning the Aral Sea Basin's famous conflict potential, Yoffe (2001) and Wolf, Yoffe and Giordano (2003) argue that the basin countries tend to negotiate current conflicts. However, none of the treaties signed recently include all the basin riparians, and therefore potential for continued disputes, at least in the nearest future, is likely.

Given global scale of BAR project, considering and spatially interpreting all physical, social, economic and political variables for Central Asia becomes even more vital and can provide solutions based on a more holistic approach to natural resources, while recognising the historical, geopolitical and natural characteristics of the region.

WATER EVENT INTENSITY SCALE

Wolf, Yoffe and Giordano (2003) recount of compiling a systematic database for water conflict/co-operation worldwide, in an attempt to gather every reported interaction between two or more nations, where water was the driver of the event. Using various international news databases, like FBIS and its online version, World News Connection (WNC), the authors developed 'a friendship-hostility scale' – a ratio of all co-operative to conflictive events between nations over water, having modified a scale created by Conflict and Peace Databank (COPDAB) project directed by Professor Edward E. Azar.

COPDAB's scale ranges from level 1, representing the most co-operative events, to level 15, representing the most conflictive events, with level 8 representing neutral events. To make it water-specific, the authors inverted it so that neutral events were centred on zero, to make it ranging from -7 to +7, with -7 denoting the most conflictive events, 0 denoting neutral events, and +7 denoting the most cooperative events. The new scale also included the addition of water terms, and a new category, "formal declaration of war." To accommodate this category, which is not part of the original COPDAB Scale, category 13 (Small scale military acts) and 14 (Limited war acts) were merged into one category, number 13. Category 14 was given the heading and description of category 15 (Extensive war acts causing deaths, dislocation or high strategic costs), and Category 15 was changed to indicate a formal declaration of war (Yoffe, 2001).

For the purposes of this study, BAR global Water Event Intensity Scale is adapted to the Amu Darya basin countries in Central Asia to determine overall relations and identify focal points for the future conflicts while concurrently applying GIS-based variables of water conflict.

Aggregating Data for the Amu Darya Basin

In creating ArcView data coverages for the Amu Darya Basin, data for international river basins kindly provided by Dr Aaron T. Wolf was used which was then matched to the US Geological Service Hydro1k (USGS, 2000) dataset, a global coverage of streams and drainage basins derived from digital elevation data. The data collected fell into roughly two categories: biophysical (e.g. runoff, population, dams) attributes suitable for the spatial analysis and economic/political (e.g. GDP per capita, overall relations, ethnic minorities) attributes. Although some of the variables used are quantitative and can be measured, the indicators comprising political category are qualitative in nature (internationalisation of a basin, future water infrastructure, water treaties).

Population

In pulling various water-related attributes together in order to draw a picture of a basin's specific conflict proneness, population growth is among key factors for assessing water scarcity. The relation of water access to population distribution should therefore be assessed. As a river basin rarely follows political borders, per basin population density instead of per region population density was evaluated. In doing so, the Landscan gridded population of the world (Landscan, 2001) was used to approximate population distribution. Building on the Landscan data proved very effective as the Landscan team used remotely sensed slope, land cover, road proximity and night time lights to refine the GIS-based gridded population cell values, providing the best accurate dataset. Gridcell values for the Aral Sea Basin were summed to combine this table with the Amu Darya Basin, thus calculating a population density for that area, as described by Yoffe (2001).

Runoff

Runoff is considered the total amount of surface flow in a given area. Any assessment of a water resource related issue would be incomplete without some approximation of water availability within the study area (Yoffe, 2001). Data for the Amu Darya runoff were obtained through a spatial resolution grid of composite runoff fields based on observed river discharge and simulated water balances (Fekete, Vörsmarty and Grabs, 2000). The project was the outcome of a joint effort of the Complex Systems Research Centre at the University of New Hampshire and the Global Runoff Data Centre in Koblenz, Germany. The project combined "…two sources of information (observed discharge and simulated runoff) to estimate continental runoff which was "the most reliable assessment at present (Fekete, Vörsmarty and Grabs, 2000). To estimate the composite runoff for the Amu Darya, runoff data for the eight gauging stations located in the Amu Darya basin were used. The cell values in mm/yr were multiplied by the area of the associated grid cell in sq. km to produce a runoff volume grid (mm*km^2/yr).

Dams

The third key factor in assessing water scarcity is the number and density of dams in a study area. According to Yoffe (2001) and Wolf, Yoffe and Giordano (2003), when statistically testing potential water conflict indicators, dams themselves did not appear to be a potential indicator for water conflict, yet in basins without water treaties lower dam density basins tended to exhibit slightly less conflict. With negative overall relations between countries and absence of a transboundary institution, unilaterally setting a large dam or diversion project can provide a context for the conflict over water, while positive relations and presence of a transboundary institution can mitigate the situation. To determine the number of dams and dam density for the Amu Darya Basin, global dataset provided by Wolf was used, based on the Digital Chart of the World data and International Commission on Large Dams (ICOLD) World Register of Dams. More importantly, large proposed water infrastructure projects that proved to have significant influence on the whole water situation in the basin were identified (e.g. the Rogun Dam in Tajikistan, etc.).

Minority Groups

Internationalising a basin provides an important setting for future water conflict (Wolf, Yoffe and Giordano, 2003). Those basins whose management institutions were developed under a single jurisdiction and then became divided among two or more nations when that jurisdiction suddenly collapsed, showed much higher levels of conflict (Yoffe, 2001).

In order to check for the active nationalist movements who might cause future internationalisation of the Amu Darya Basin, data from two major sources have been analysed: Minorities At Risk Project, at the University of Maryland's Centre for International Development and Conflict Management (Gurr, 2000) and Unrepresented Nations and Peoples Organisation (UNPO, 2002).

GDP

Low per capita GDP (< $765/person according to the World Bank lowest income country definition) was identified to be one of the indicators of conflict over water (Yoffe, 2001).

As Wolf, Yoffe and Giordano (2003) put it, the higher the per capita GDP, or the lower population density, the greater the co-operation – barely. To establish macro-economic data for the Amu Darya Basin countries, the World Bank data for 2000 were used.

Overall Relations

It is pointed out (Yoffe, 2001) that countries that co-operate in general also co-operate over water, and countries with overall unfriendly relations are also unfriendly over water issues.

To construct a 'friendship-hostility scale' as appeared in Wolf, Yoffe and Giordano (2003), a rough water event intensity scale was built employing the technique.

In gathering country-to-country events and interactions, two major sources were used: the WNC and Transboundary Freshwater Dispute Database.

Both build on the reports about Central Asia by the two leading Russian news agencies – ITAR-TASS and Interfax, as well as on the news coverages by Eurasianet and the Mashhad Voice of the Islamic Republic of Iran (Tajikistan news). Notably, the water event data are based on public reports and therefore lack reports on non-public co-operation ("picnic table talks, non-official visits, etc.)

Freshwater Treaties

Generally, freshwater treaties mitigate conflict, and no or limited freshwater treaties for a basin increase the likeliness of conflict over water. To analyse existing freshwater treaties for the Amu Darya Basin, the International Freshwater Treaties Database at Oregon State University (TFDD, 2002), containing a full text of over 400 international freshwater related agreements, was used.

WATER CONFLICT POTENTIAL IN THE AMU DARYA BASIN

Population Density/runoff

The Amu Darya's population is extremely unevenly distributed. Only in Uzbekistan which has the region's highest population density (average >50 people per km^2, with total population of about 25 million in 2002), 80 percent of land is desert. In 1990, the rural population occupied a total of 4.5 million hectares of arable land, or about 16 percent of all available agricultural land in the country, and thus the effective density of rural population was 2.7 people per hectare of arable land. Given the rate of natural population growth in Uzbekistan being one of the highest among the former Soviet republics, rural population steadily increased from 1984 to 1994 to 61 percent, while the arable land and cultivated area remained practically unchanged (Lerman, Garcia-Garcia and Wichelns, 1996).

Population distribution in the Amu Darya Basin varies accordingly, from 20-30 people per km^2 in the downstream sections of the river (except for the river stretch just before flowing into the Aral Sea that runs across the Uzbek territory and where population density is about 40-50 people/km^2) to 25-40 people/km^2 in the middle course and to 20-35 people/km^2 in the upstream sections of the Amu Darya.

The population pattern in Central Asia has remained the same over thousands of years. People tend to inhabit fertile oases and valleys rich in water. Many human habitats can be found located along the rivers, and almost all of them date from the pre-Islamic times.

In terms of runoff, the Amu Darya can be divided into three sections: an upstream section, a middle course section, and a downstream section. The upstream section extends from the point of confluence of the Vakhsh and Pyandj rivers up to the town of Kerki, the middle course is between Kerki and the Tyuyamuyun Gorge, and the downstream section is confined to the mouth of the river. In the upstream section, the flow of the Amu Darya steadily increases due to the Kunduz, Kafirnigan, Surkhandarya, and Sherabad tributaries.

The reverse situation can be observed in the middle course and in the downstream section: the flow gradually declines due to natural losses of runoff and huge water diversions for agricultural needs. It is quite difficult to evaluate those natural and anthropogenic losses as the data from many gauging stations for the last two decades are not available. Average annual runoff at the town of Kerki (upstream section) between 1957-1987 was 1903 m^3/s, together with water diverted to Karakum and Karshi canals, 1351 m^3/s in the Tyuyamuyun Gorge (middle course) in the same period and 656 m^3/s in the downstream section (Ivanov and Izmaiylov, 1995).

Planned Water Infrastructure

Unilateral decisions to embark on new water projects are not uncommon in Central Asia. While providing for national solutions, such decisions and further actions are among key drivers of potential water conflict. Trying to find a way out of the existing situation, some Central Asian governments were forced to develop plans for building more infrastructure to get control over water resources. Two projects which are the legacy of the Soviet-style gigantic undertakings and which caused extremely negative reaction among neighbours.

The Rogun Dam

Started in 1976, the Rogun Dam, on the Vakhsh river, was projected to be 335 metres high – the highest in the world - with the capacity to produce 3,600 MW of energy. The dam was expected to begin operation in 1993. However, in 1990 the construction was halted due to the escalating political situation which turned into a 5-year civil war in Tajikistan. In 1993, a massive flood destroyed most of what has been already built. By that time, $802 million was invested into the project, with the total cost of $2.3 billion.

Tajikistan already controls 40 percent of the flow of the Amu Darya through the Nurek reservoir. The Rogun would put it firmly in control of the river, allowing to control the flow into Uzbekistan's Surkhandarya and Kashkadarya Provinces that already experience sharp water shortages. Knowing Uzbekistan's opposition to the project, Tajikistan continues to press with the completion of the Rogun Dam that would need $700 million to $1 billion to complete.

Most international finance institutions are reluctant to put any money into the project, claiming that it would cost more than any benefit it might offer. They are also aware that the project would seriously strain relations between Tajikistan and Uzbekistan. However, getting Tajik government concentrate on more feasible, realistic and low-cost project yielded no fruits. On 29 October 2002, the Baltic Construction Company, one of the biggest Russian investment/construction groups, became a contractor and investor for completion of the Rogun Dam project (Dyuzheva, 2002; ICG, 2002b).

Golden Century Lake

In October 2000, Turkmenistan began work on a huge artificial lake in the Karakum Desert, which was pompously called Golden Century Lake. The lake is being built in the Karashor natural depression in the north-western part of the Karakum desert. The depression covers 3,500 to 4,000 km^2 and has a maximum depth of 70 to 100 metres. Once completed, the lake would contain some 132 to 150 km^3 of water. Drainage water is to be diverted to the lake from the five provinces through two major collector-canals. The project cost is up to $6 billion, and it will be financed from state budget. The first stage is to be completed in 2004 and the entire project covers 10 years. There are rumours that special nuclear power station will be built nearby to use a lake as a cooling pond. The government holds that only drainage water will be used to supply the lake.

The project raised immediate concerns in neighbouring Uzbekistan that the lake cannot be sustained by drainage water alone and about 10 cubic kilometres of water from the Amu Darya will be needed to maintain its level. Uzbekistan argues that drainage water has a high salt content and will gradually evaporate in the terrible heat of the Karakum desert creating a new Aral. By increasing the water use from the Amu Darya, Turkmenistan would leave the southern Uzbek provinces without any water. If Ashgabat will go ahead with the project, it will inevitably lead to tensions with Uzbekistan (Insarova, 2002).

Just like the Toktogul reservoir on the Syr Darya, this ambitious and costly undertaking risks becoming a source of conflict with Uzbekistan. Turkmenistan also threatens to resettle about one million ethnic Uzbeks from the southern province of Dashhovuz to the Karakum desert once the lake is completed (ICG, 2002b).

FURTHER INTERNATIONALISATION POTENTIAL

Possible Secession of Karakalpakstan

The Autonomous Republic of Karakalpakstan is one of the 13 provinces, or oblasts, in Uzbekistan. Its history began in 1925, when the Karakalpaks (a Turkic-language Muslim group whose name literally means "black hat") were given their own territory, declared the Autonomous Oblast, within the Kazakh Soviet Socialist Republic (SSR). In 1930, the Karakalpak AO was transferred to the jurisdiction of the Russian Soviet Federative Socialist Republic, where it remained until 1936, when it was joined to the Uzbek SSR and elevated to the status of the Autonomous SSR (Hanks, 2000). After Uzbekistan's independence, Karakalpakstan received autonomous republic status within Uzbekistan. Since that time, the central government in Tashkent has maintained pressure and tight economic ties that have kept the republic from exerting full independence.

Today, the population of Karakalpakstan is about 1.3 million people who live on a territory of about 168,000 km^2. Located in the fertile lower reaches of the Amu Darya where the river empties into the Aral Sea, Karakalpakstan has a long history of irrigation agriculture. However, because it is a tail end of the Amu Darya, Karakalpakstan received all the pollution the river has accumulated along its course. The health statistics (morbidity and mortality data) collectively reflect the poor and deteriorating health of the people downstream. My personal experience of work for the Eye Cancer Register Project at the Institute of Oncology and Radiology in Tashkent showed that while eye cancer incidence in Karakalpakstan was relatively low, mortality rate was the highest in Uzbekistan (2.2 people per 100,000 people, compared to 0.2 to 0.3/100,000 in other provinces of Uzbekistan) (Mouratova, 1992). More generally, the Karakalpaks showed one of the highest rates of cancer, comparable only to Kazakhs living in Muynak area of Karakalpakstan.

Even in the Soviet times, nationalist sentiment and identity among the Karakalpaks were stronger than scholars believed and Uzbekistan's independence marked by the rise of Uzbek nationalism has seen the Karakalpak national movement too. However, this group known as the Khalk Mapi was quickly suppressed and driven underground. Although the Karakalpaks never demonstrated publicly for the formal independence and the republic is not a member of UNPO, the Uzbek authorities view a possible nationalist tendency in Karakalpakstan as seriously threatening Uzbekistan's integrity. In the meanwhile, little study has been undertaken to go deep into the question of a possible disintegration of Uzbekistan. Various researchers have briefly pointed out that Karakalpakstan has the potential to claim its independence from Uzbekistan (Kltzli, 1994; Baechler, 1998; Lietzman and Vest, 1999). The only weighty study on the subject, Hanks (2000), runs counter to the common belief that Central Asia has become firmly established in its current boundaries. Hanks supports that there are four factors that may contribute to the Karakalpak nationalism, notably: (1) a separate cultural identity; (2) a history of territorial identity and autonomy; (3) economic underdevelopment; and (4) severe environmental damage, resulting in drastic decline in human conditions.

Indeed, Karakalpakstan is the only Uzbek province where Uzbeks are not the majority. Unlike Tajiks in Samarkand and Bukhara, the Karakalpaks are allowed to learn in their native language in schools and 2.6% of the school-age population are enrolled in Karakalpak schools which means that most Karakalpaks are insistent that their children be educated in their mother tongue.

And the Karakalpak language is quite different from the Uzbek one being linguistically closer to the Kazakh language just as the whole Karakalpak culture is. Historically and ethnically, Karakalpaks, with their nomadic culture, would show best in Kazakhstan where such culture is persistent and where Karakalpaks are still considered *oralman*, i.e. members of the Kazakh community living abroad. During the past 12 years, as much as 270,000 Karakalpaks, or 20% of the population, left Uzbekistan for Kazakhstan and Russia, largely due to the unbearable human and environmental conditions in the Aral Sea area (Glantz, 2002). Small, van der Meer and Upshur (2001) quote the study showing that 48.8% of respondents wanted to leave their homes because of the environment, and one half of those wanted to move out of the Aral Sea area.

In economic terms, Karakalpakstan represents a remote geographical hinterland, absent from global economy, with virtually no industrial development and soaring unemployment rates. Agricultural sector is on the verge of collapse and fisheries, once a profitable sector, disappeared along with the whole Aral Sea. Due to the fact that most imported goods are shipped to Tashkent, 1000 kilometres away from Nukus, capital of Karakalpakstan, fewer goods are offered there, adding to the general quality of life being the lowest in the country.

Officially, 100,000 people were unemployed in 2002 as a result of the multi-year drought that began in 1999 and by 2001 reduced cotton production in Karakalpakstan by 75% of the norm. Rice production was only 0.25% of the norm (Glantz, 2002). The situation aggravated so much that people are slaughtering livestock because animals started dying of thirst. In a region where cattle have implications for the future, killing cows means losing a major asset (Kohn, 2001).

All this resulted in the fact that most Karakalpaks began viewing themselves as the environmental victims and hostages of the central power, first in Moscow, then in Tashkent. Why don't Karakalpaks revolt? – ponders Bissell (2002). So far, only what can be called "a foot vote, i.e. the exodus of the Karakalpak population to neighbouring Kazakhstan, has happened. ICG (2002b) quotes one Uzbek official as saying that people of Karakalpakstan "...are patient and put their hope in God and the President.

Indeed, an independent Karakalpakstan may be unlikely in the future. Poor state of economy and environmental degradation undermined the region's development so much that an independent Karakalpakstan would have a little chance for survival.

But this in no way lessens the potential for the region to destabilise Uzbekistan and eventually the whole Central Asia (Hanks, 2000). Possible is also the Indonesian scenario – when the central regime grows weak, nationalist claims in the provinces become stronger and may eventually lead to a secession.

Role of Afghanistan

Northern Afghanistan belongs to the Amu Darya Basin. Until recently, before the US-led campaign against the Taliban and Al-Qaeda, this area was de facto independent from the rest of the country, remaining firmly under control of the Uzbek and Tajik warlords opposing the regime in Kabul.

Today, when the central government of Hamid Karzai is trying to spread its authority on the rest of the country, the question of separate northern provinces is less important in light of the emerging Afghanistan integrity. Before 2001, Afghanistan was itself the factor of risk for the Basin.

It is still unclear what share would Afghanistan's agricultural sector require from the Amu Darya water and when. It is clear though that Afghanistan will demand its share and that it is entitled to that share under the international agreements signed between the USSR and Afghanistan in 1946 (*Frontier Agreement between Afghanistan and the USSR*, 13 June 1946) and 1958 (*Treaty concerning the regime to the Soviet-Afghan frontier*, 18 January 1958, and *Protocol between the USSR and Afghanistan concerning the joint execution of works for the integrated utilisation of the water resources in the frontier section of the Amu Darya*, 25 June 1958).

The 1946 Agreement subjects all matters associated with the water use to specific agreements between the two countries and provides for the establishment of a joint commission. Under it, Afghanistan is entitled to use up to 9 km^3 of water from the Pyandj river. Under the Treaty of 18 January 1958, the two countries commit themselves to take joint measures to prevent changes in the course of frontier rivers, streams or canals and to correct the effects of such changes and share the costs equally.

Furthermore, they commit themselves to prevent water pollution, to exchange regular information on the level and volume of water and meteorological data and to adopt a flood warning system. Finally, the 1958 Protocol envisages the joint integrated utilisation of the frontier sections of the Amu Darya (Nanni, 1996).

Since "localisable international agreements (i.e. those relating to identifiable parts of the territory of states) are subject to state succession under international law, these agreements remain in force for the newly independent Central Asian states (Nanni, 1996; Vinogradov and Langford, 2001).

Until now, Afghanistan has used only about 2 km^3 of the 9 km^3 of water it is entitled to use under the treaties. Meanwhile, the Pyandj river has the annual flow of 19 km^3, and Afghanistan's fresh involvement into the process of water use would radically change the Amu Darya flow if the new Afghan government decides to develop agriculture in the North. Plans of Afghanistan to increase its water share caused the respective reaction in neighbouring countries. ICG (2002b) quotes one Uzbek official quotes as saying, God forbid that we should give water also to Afghanistan. What will then become of us?

Given that the rehabilitation of Afghanistan is impossible without increasing its intake from the Amu Darya and that water resources are vital for Afghan people to feed themselves, the potential for water conflict in the Basin increases proportionally. Afghanistan's demands will have to be taken into account when negotiating the water situation in the Basin (Fuchinoue, Tsukatani and Toderich, 2002).

GDP

All Amu Darya Basin countries are considered low-income countries, i.e. those where GDP is less than $750, according to the World Bank classification. Below is per capita GDP in US$ for the four Amu Darya riparians:

Table : GDP per capita in the Amu Darya Basin countries

Country	*GDP per capita*
Afghanistan	not available
Tajikistan	170
Turkmenistan	765
Uzbekistan	449

Source: World Bank, 2000

Aggregate average GDP per capita for the Amu Darya Basin is $461.3. Given the extreme poverty people of Afghanistan still live in, this indicator may actually be even less.

Overall Relations/Water Events

In political science, overall relations indicate an interstate affect which in turn highly influences regional co-operation over water. By scoring an affective content of each of 100 events occurred in the relations between the Amu Darya riparians in 1995-2003, of which only 24 events concerned the region's water resources, it was possible to draw a rough picture of how the Amu Darya Basin countries feel toward each other. For the purposes of this study, an event is defined as the instance of regional conflict and co-operation that occur within an international river basin, and water event as the instance of regional conflict and co-operation over water resources of that specific basin (Yoffe, 2001). Every event of interaction between two or more riparians mentioned in a database was grouped and included into either representing overall relations in the Amu Darya Basin or representing water-related events in the basin. Each table contains the following information:

- the date of the incident;
- riparians involved;
- the intensity of the event, based on the Water Event Intensity Scale;
- a summary describing the event;
- main issue area (economic co-operation, water quality, etc.);
- the source of information.

Three Amu Darya riparian countries – Tajikistan, Turkmenistan and Uzbekistan - have been considered. Afghanistan was excluded from the analysis as until 2001 this country itself manifested a serious threat for the region's security and by the time of preparing this study the central authority in Kabul was still in the beginning of the process of integrating the country. At the same time, northern Afghanistan was far from pacified and heavy fights between local warlords have been reported.

It is apparent that overall unfriendly attitude prevails in the relations between the riparians and despite friendship agreements signed and close economic ties the situation has repeatedly sharpened when Uzbekistan having the region's biggest military potential was not long in using force against its neighbours not even trying to enter into negotiation. This dangerous trend may as well extend on the water relations, and according to informal sources it already has (situation around the Tyuyamuyun and the Toktogul).

Quite frequently, the relations between the three have become seriously strained and for several occasions the countries were on the verge of an open conflict. Once it was an open conflict when on 16 August 1999 the Uzbek planes bombed Tajik and Kyrgyz territory targeting a group of Islamic militants. Uzbekistan's leadership never hesitated to use force and have always been insistent on establishing the way in which events should develop. The country has also followed this course in its relations with Turkmenistan whose self-glorifying regime has much in common with the Uzbek one. But especially worrisome are Uzbekistan's relations with Tajikistan whose militant opposition has been steadily supported by Tashkent throughout the whole long civil war. Claiming support for the Tajik government, Uzbekistan continued to feed ethnic Uzbek guerrillas on the Tajik territory and opened its borders for them when they were escaping from the Tajik troops.

Neither there was a shortage of assurances in eternal friendship and fraternal love, against a chilly history of land mines Uzbekistan used to plant along the entire length of Tajik border to build a ludicrous protection against Islamic terrorists and cutting off the pipes near the Tyuyamuyun reservoir in Turkmenistan. The treaties and agreements have been signed as well, but little action followed to implement them. Instead, the countries continued with hostile policies.

All in all, 4 incidents of "small scale military acts, 7 "political-military hostile actions, 8 "diplomatic-economic hostile actions and 7 "strong verbal expressions displaying hostility in interaction have been registered. In addition, the countries constantly displayed "discord in interaction (18 incidents), versus a much smaller number of events considered potentially positive (signing agreements, establishing common policy, visit of head of state, etc.)

While the picture of overall relations is definitely skewed to the left and tends to manifest rather conflict than co-operation, the history of relations over water looks at the first glance more co-operative.

Dozens of agreements have been entered into between the riparians. Some of these agreements had a status of an international water treaty designed to ease tensions between the basin countries. Meanwhile, the situation remains the same because the leaders prefer to do things informally rather than on the basis of an open agreement. However, when it comes to addressing conferences and summits, the presidents are always ready to mouth the rhetoric of regional co-operation while never lingering to use force against their "friendly neighbours (ICG, 2002b).

FRESHWATER TREATIES

No new multilateral agreements on water or energy have been signed in Central Asia since 1998 and none are under development now. Major existing agreements like the Almaty Agreement and the Syr Darya Framework Agreement are implemented poorly, largely due to the lack of co-ordination in national water policies and legislation across the region. Some of the Central Asian states (Kazakhstan, Kyrgyzstan and Tajikistan) have expressed a strong desire to develop new agreements that satisfy concepts of international watercourse law. However, there is still reluctance on the part of the major water using countries, Turkmenistan and Uzbekistan, to enter into discussions on this issue. One of the major problems in achieving regional co-operation in shared water resources in Central Asia will be to attract the attention of these countries to the ideas of international water law. In promoting consensus on principles of regional co-operation, a major role could belong to international donor agencies that may try to convince Uzbekistan and, in case of the Afghanistan situation in the Amu Darya basin, Turkmenistan that this is a serious problem that must be dealt with soon (McKinney, 2003).

River Boundaries

The border problem is among additional factors that could further worsen the water situation in Central Asia. The Soviet-made borders in Central Asia provide a continuous possibility for their redefinition (Gleason, 2001). There were several border incidents between Uzbekistan and its neighbours in the past when the former unilaterally commenced a survey of its border and moved its boundary posts, as happened in early 2000 when three hundred kilometres of Kazakhstan's territory suddenly appeared to be within Uzbekistan. After Kazakhstan objected, a bilateral demarcation commission was set up. As of early 2003, Uzbekistan's border disputes with Kazakhstan have been completely settled and border delimitation with Tajikistan and Kyrgyzstan was close to the end.

Particular problem in terms of border situation is Central Asia's two major rivers. Both Syr Darya and Amu Darya pass through several international borders, and in some parts the Turkmenistan border with Uzbekistan is defined by the watercourse of the Amu Darya. The border between Afghanistan and Uzbekistan is the Amu Darya, and one of the rivers that form the Amu Darya, the Pyandj, serves as the border between Tajikistan and Afghanistan. Toset, Gleditsch and Hegre (2000) define three types of relationship over the shared river resources: river boundary; mixed; and upstream/downstream. While the latter, in the authors' opinion, has a higher conflict potential, a river boundary situation, when a country on the left bank diverts water and a country on the right bank retaliates by taking water to its own side of the river, is no less serious. Navigation problems and transborder pollution add to the problem dramatically. It is argued that the longer the border, the more opportunities for potential contentious issues for conflict. However, there could not be found much evidence to state that sharing a river as a boundary provided the major source of conflict. In the Amu Darya case, a common border lying along the river watercourse may contribute to the generally tense relations both between downstream (Turkmenistan/Uzbekistan) and upstream (Afghanistan/Tajikistan) riparians.

Trade Complications

Trade issues between Tajikistan and Uzbekistan further complicate the relations between the two countries. Trade in staple goods like cotton, water, natural gas, and oil is conducted by state agencies. Thus, in case of failure to pay or any other irritation it is very convenient to suspend deliveries temporally, close border or increase visa requirements, as happened more than once. Furthermore, transborder trade, traditional and supporting many families in this area, is subject to now thawing, now frosting regional affairs. No single transborder trade regulatory regime exists between the Amu Darya riparians.

Sarez Lake: A Natural Threat to the Basin's Stability

On 6 February 1911, a powerful earthquake in the Pamir region of Gorny Badakhshan, in what is now Tajikistan, caused a 2.2 cubic kilometre piece of the Muzkol Range to collapse, sealing off the Murgab Gorge and creating a 500-metre natural dam. The new canyon became soon filled with water and formed the Sarez Lake, 75 kilometres long and 505 metres deep and containing 17 cubic kilometres of glacial water. Experts say that this unstable natural dam called the Usoy Obstruction after the name of a village buried under it could break as a result of an earthquake or landslide and release the water into the Pyandj. This would endanger millions of people in Tajikistan, Uzbekistan, Turkmenistan and Afghanistan. So far, efforts by the Tajik government to install the early warning system components on the dam, along the lake and downstream under the terms of an international tender were sustained locally, without getting other riparians involved. Rather relative stability in the Tajik mountains that still remember a devastating civil war in the 1990s call many good plans in question. The weakest point in any strategy concerning the Sarez Lake is funding which might be very significant. Tajikistan alone would never afford million-dollar project costs. Yet none of the Amu Darya riparians concerned is willing to consider the problem of the Sarez Lake its own.

Impact of International Law

With the advent of independence, Central Asian states have quickly become the parties, and in some cases ratified, the international environmental agreements and conventions such as the Convention on Biological Diversity, the Convention to Combat Desertification, and the United Nations Framework Convention on Climate Change. However, no international convention related in either event to water has been acceded to, even to the Convention on Wetlands of International Importance Especially as Waterfowl Habitat, not to mention the Convention on the Law of the Non-Navigational Uses of International Watercourses. Only Kazakhstan is a party to the Convention on the Protection and Use of Transboundary Watercourses and International Lakes (Sievers, 2002).

Vinogradov and Langford (2001) argue that some regional water treaties (the 1998 Syr Darya Framework Agreement) do address the particularly sensitive issue of the water utilisation in the region and proceed from the interest in joint use of water resources to seeking common definitions and to acknowledging international legal principles relevant to the use of transboundary water resources, such as the provision referring to the joint management clause based on the "basin principle which provides for the equality of the parties' rights to use and responsibility to ensure rational utilisation and protection of the "common and integral water resources of the region. While this provision is certainly an improvement over earlier arrangements based on the concepts of water apportionment and "maximum utilisation, the principle of "equitable and reasonable utilisation and participation, in accordance with Article 5 of the UN Convention on the Law of the Non-Navigational Uses of International Watercourses, should be recognised. This principle takes into consideration such factors as geography, hydrographic, hydrological, climatic, ecological and other factors of a natural character; social and economic needs of a watercourse; the population dependent on the water resources; existing and potential uses; conservation, protection, development and economy of water resources use; and the availability of alternatives to a planned or existing use (UN, 1997).

Of particular importance for Central Asia's water resources are the principles of the 1997 UN Convention which include the obligation not to cause significant harm to other watercourse states (UN, 1997, art. 7); the general obligation to co-operate through joint mechanisms or commissions (Ibid., art. 8); to exchange information on a regular basis (Ibid., art. 9); and to provide timely notification of planned measures and emergency situations which may have a significant adverse effect upon other watercourse states (Ibid., arts. 12,28). Where significant harm nevertheless is caused to another state, the party responsible for causing such harm is obliged, in consultation with the affected state, to eliminate or mitigate such harm, and where appropriate, to discuss the question of compensation. However, none of Central Asian countries have ever acceded to the 1997 UN Convention.

Vox Populi?

Broad public participation and access to environmental information are essential in forming meaningful local water and environmental policy. The participation of non-governmental organisations (NGOs) who play important role in informing citizens of their opportunities to participate requires access to accurate and timely information. When the information about the state of the environment is available to citizens, they can express public opinion regarding various issues, particularly water use and environmental protection (McKinney, 2003). It is not a case, however, for the sealed societies such as Turkmenistan and Uzbekistan where access to any information, let alone environmental one, is severely restricted. Not surprisingly, these two states are not the parties to the 1998 UNECE Convention on Access to Information, Public Participation and Access to Justice in Environmental Matters (the Aarhus Convention), although other three Central Asian countries have acceded to it (Kyrgyzstan, Tajikistan) or ratified it (Kazakhstan).

Summing up Results

Six indicators used in the analysis were not sufficient to identify with exact accuracy a level of potential conflict over water in the Amu Darya Basin, yet some results.

Potential for conflict over water resources in the Amu Darya Basin remains to be high, despite one of the six indicators (population density) tends to run counter to this conclusion. This allows for the possibility to say that population density can be indicator of conflict only in such overpopulated places as the Ferghana Valley which has already seen outbreaks of violence in the past. On the country level, it is overall unfriendly relations fuelled by the leaders' personal competition, as well as rapid institutional change that could account for worsened water affairs in the region. Over the last years, several new points of contention have arisen, particularly in the continuing tensions between Uzbekistan and Tajikistan over the Rogun Dam and between Uzbekistan and Turkmenistan around Golden Century Lake. Not in the nearest future though, the potential for further internationalisation - rapid rise of Afghanistan as a state and possible Karakalpakstan's claim for independence - could contribute to these tensions seriously and disintegrate the basin even further. In absence of solid legal base relevant to the international water law and mechanisms responsible for enforcing it, the region's tensions are deepening and threaten to destabilise not only Central Asia, but also neighbouring countries. The role of indicators of water conflict in identifying and, in future, measuring a basin's conflict proneness is critical for those who will be involved in resolving disputes over river freshwater. The water conflict indicators allow for identifying specific tasks to concentrate efforts on, such as legal and institutional aspects of Central Asia's water disputes, and pinpoint potential "apples of discord, such as big water infrastructure projects.

CONCLUSIONS AND RECOMMENDATIONS

While wasting water several times more than in the Middle East, people in Central Asia do not account for huge water diversions. In fact, it is agricultural sector and, more specifically, cotton growing that is to blame for the major anthropogenic loss of water from the Amu Darya. Downstream riparians – Uzbekistan and Turkmenistan, the region's major cotton producers, are unable to abandon cotton production because it is perhaps the only hard currency earning sector for them, in the absence of developed small sector regulations and, in case of Uzbekistan, of hard currency convertibility. With upstream riparians claiming the old Soviet water allocation schemes to be limiting the development of their own agriculture, downstream countries should reconsider their attitudes towards cotton and rice irrigation and embark on a real reform of small and medium sector, including farmland privatisation. Cotton is a root of evil in Central Asia, not its saviour from hardships of economic underdevelopment.

Central Asian governments did not give up their plans to develop the Soviet-style giant projects which are costly and environmentally devastating. It is fair to say that these would offer only short-term relief and would destabilise already fragile situation. Tajikistan should terminate the contract with the Baltic Construction Company for the construction of the Rogun Dam. Turkmenistan should abandon the marantic idea of building the Golden Century Lake which is being built in the desert where water will simply evaporate. Any idea of diverting Siberian rivers to Central Asia should be immediately shelved as environmentally dubious and hugely expensive. It is time for Central Asia to think globally while acting locally.

Whereas Karakalpakstan is unlikely to secede from Uzbekistan today, this in no way lessens such a potential for the area in future. Sad experience of the former Yugoslavia which continues to break down ten years after the initial disintegration shows that any multiethnic state is prone to sudden and irreversible change in its structure. This is especially indicative of the former Soviet Union on which territory there are still several unrecognised statelets claiming their independence, and there will be more, as a result of arbitrary Soviet boundary planning. The priorities of people of Karakalpakstan should be taken into account when it comes to the water allocation and use, and a real Karakalpak autonomy enshrined in the Constitution of the Republic of Uzbekistan should be given to the region. Nonetheless, existing repressive regime in Uzbekistan is very unlikely to loose its grip on the Karakalpaks and tensions are expected to grow.

Given that Afghanistan's rehabilitation is unlikely without increasing its intake from the Amu Darya, Afghanistan's water demands will have to be taken into consideration when negotiating the water situation in the Basin. In promoting consensus on principles of regional co-operation, a major role could belong to international donor agencies that may try to convince Uzbekistan and Turkmenistan that the Afghanistan situation is a serious problem that must be dealt with soon. Interstate legislative co-ordination for the Amu Darya water resources should be tailored to fit sustainable development of the Amu Darya Basin before proceeding with reconstruction assistance in Afghanistan.

Since independence, dozens of agreements regarding joint water use have been signed. However, fewer agreements are implemented. Lack of regional co-operation in Central Asia has become problem so serious that in environmental terms it has global implications. Fearful of disrupting existing patterns of water use in their agricultural policies, two most stubborn riparians, Turkmenistan and Uzbekistan, claimed their commitment to bilateral relations. One of the major problems in achieving regional co-operation in shared water resources in Central Asia will be to attract the attention of these countries to the ideas of international water law and to a multilateral approach. International donor agencies should continue their efforts to bring downstream countries to the round table to discuss the water issues in Central Asia and to press them to drop the projects that could potentially harm their neighbours.

That is possible only if adequate and sufficient information on the environment is available to any party concerned. Unless single information network regarding the state of the environment exists in Central Asia, with the reference to the Aarhus Convention, local repressive regimes will be certain about their last word in the never-ending story of Central Asian water crisis.

11

Water Scarcity

Water scarcity is the lack of sufficient available water resources to meet the demands of water usage within a region. It already affects every continent and around 2.8 billion people around the world at least one month out of every year. More than 1.2 billion people lack access to clean drinking water.

Water scarcity involves *water stress, water shortage* or deficits, and *water crisis*. While the concept of *water stress* is relatively new, it is the difficulty of obtaining sources of fresh water for use during a period of time and may result in further depletion and deterioration of available water resources. *Water shortages* may be caused by climate change, such as altered weather patterns including droughts or floods, increased pollution, and increased human demand and overuse ofwater. A *water crisis* is a situation where the available potable, unpolluted water within a region is less than that region's demand. Water scarcity is being driven by two converging phenomena: growing freshwater use and depletion of usable freshwater resources.

Water scarcity can be a result of two mechanisms: physical (absolute) water scarcity and economic water scarcity, where physical water scarcity is a result of inadequate natural water resources to supply a region's demand, and economic water scarcity is a result of poor management of the sufficient available water resources. According to the United Nations Development Programme, the latter is found more often to be the cause of countries or regions experiencing water scarcity, as most countries or regions have enough water to meet household, industrial, agricultural, and environmental needs, but lack the means to provide it in an accessible manner.

The reduction of water scarcity is a goal of many countries and governments. The UN recognizes the importance of reducing the number of people without sustainable access to clean water and sanitation. The Millennium Development Goals within the United Nations Millennium Declaration state that by 2015 they resolve to "halve the proportion of people who are unable to reach or to afford safe drinking water."

WATER STRESS

The United Nations (UN) estimates that, of 1.4 billion cubic kilometers (1 quadrillion acre-feet) of water on Earth, just 200,000 cubic kilometers (162.1 billion acre-feet) represent fresh water available for human consumption.

More than one in every six people in the world is water stressed, meaning that they do not have access to potable water. Those that are water stressed make up 1.1 billion people in the world and are living in developing countries. According to the Falkenmark Water Stress Indicator, a country or region is said to experience "water stress" when annual water supplies drop below 1,700 cubic metres per person per year. At levels between 1,700 and 1,000 cubic metres per person per year, periodic or limited water shortages can be expected.

When a country is below 1,000 cubic metres per person per year, the country then faces water scarcity. In 2006, about 700 million people in 43 countries were living below the 1,700 cubic metres per person threshold. Water stress is ever intensifying in regions such as China, India, and Sub-Saharan Africa, which contains the largest number of water stressed countries of any region with almost one fourth of the population living in a water stressed country. The world's most water stressed region is the Middle East with averages of 1,200 cubic metres of water per person. In China, more than 538 million people are living in a water-stressed region. Much of the water stressed population currently live in river basins where the usage of water resources greatly exceed the renewal of the water source.

Changes in Climate

Another popular opinion is that the amount of available freshwater is decreasing because of climate change. Climate change has caused receding glaciers, reduced stream and river flow, and shrinking lakes and ponds. Many aquifers have been over-pumped and are not recharging quickly. Although the total fresh water supply is not used up, much has become polluted, salted, unsuitable or otherwise unavailable for drinking, industry and agriculture. To avoid a global water crisis, farmers will have to strive to increase productivity to meet growing demands for food, while industry and cities find ways to use water more efficiently.

A New York Times article, "Southeast Drought Study Ties Water Shortage to Population, Not Global Warming", summarizes the findings of Columbia University researcher on the subject of the droughts in the American Southeast between 2005 and 2007. The findings published in the *Journal of Climate* say that the water shortages resulted from population size more than rainfall. Census figures show that Georgia's population rose from 6.48 to 9.54 million between 1990 and 2007. After studying data from weather instruments, computer models and measurements of tree rings which reflect rainfall, they found that the droughts were not unprecedented and result from normal climate patterns and random weather events. "Similar droughts unfolded over the last thousand years", the researchers wrote, "Regardless of climate change, they added, similar weather patterns can be expected regularly in the future, with similar results." As the temperature increases, rainfall in the Southeast will increase but because of evaporationthe area may get even drier. The researchers concluded with a statement saying that any rainfall comes from complicated internal processes in the atmosphere and are very hard to predict because of the large amount of variables.

WATER CRISIS

When there is not enough potable water for a given population, the threat of a *water crisis* is realized. The United Nations and other world organizations consider a variety of regions to have water crises of global concern. Other organizations, such as the Food and

Agriculture Organization, argue that there are no water crises in such places, but steps must still be taken to avoid one.

Causes of Water Crisis

There are several principal manifestations of the water crisis.

- Inadequate access to safe drinking water for about 884 million people
- Inadequate access to water for sanitation and waste disposal for 2.5 billion people
- Groundwater overdrafting (excessive use) leading to diminished agricultural yields
- Overuse and pollution of water resources harming biodiversity
- Regional conflicts over scarce water resources sometimes resulting in warfare

Waterborne diseases and the absence of sanitary domestic water are one of the leading causes of death worldwide. For children under age five, waterborne diseases are the leading cause of death. At any given time, half of the world's hospital beds are occupied by patients suffering from waterborne diseases. According to the World Bank, 88 percent of all waterborne diseases are caused by unsafe drinking water, inadequate sanitation and poor hygiene.

Water is the underlying tenuous balance of safe water supply, but controllable factors such as the management and distribution of the water supply itself contribute to further scarcity.

A 2006 United Nations report focuses on issues of governance as the core of the water crisis, saying "There is enough water for everyone" and "Water insufficiency is often due to mismanagement, corruption, lack of appropriate institutions, bureaucratic inertia and a shortage of investment in both human capacity and physical infrastructure". Official data also shows a clear correlation between access to safe water and GDP per capita.

It has also been claimed, primarily by economists, that the water situation has occurred because of a lack of property rights, government regulations and subsidies in the water sector, causing prices to be too low and consumption too high.

Vegetation and wildlife are fundamentally dependent upon adequate freshwater resources. Marshes, bogs and riparian zones are more obviously dependent upon sustainable water supply, but forests and other upland ecosystems are equally at risk of significant productivity changes as water availability is diminished. In the case of wetlands, considerable area has been simply taken from wildlife use to feed and house the expanding human population. But other areas have suffered reduced productivity from gradual diminishing of freshwater inflow, as upstream sources are diverted for human use. In seven states of the U.S. over 80 percent of all historic wetlands were filled by the 1980s, when Congress acted to create a "no net loss" of wetlands.

In Europe extensive loss of wetlands has also occurred with resulting loss of biodiversity. For example many bogs in Scotland have been developed or diminished through human population expansion. One example is the Portlethen Moss in Aberdeenshire.

On Madagascar's highland plateau, a massive transformation occurred that eliminated virtually all the heavily forested vegetation in the period 1970 to 2000. The slash and burn agriculture eliminated about ten percent of the total country's native biomass and converted it to a barren wasteland. These effects were from overpopulation and the necessity to feed poor indigenous peoples, but the adverse effects included widespread gully erosion that in turn produced heavily silted rivers that "run red" decades after the deforestation. This eliminated a large amount of usable fresh water and also destroyed much of the riverine ecosystems of several large west-flowing rivers. Several fish species have been driven to the edge of extinction and some, such as the disturbed Tokios coral reef formations in the Indian Ocean, are effectively lost. In October 2008, Peter Brabeck-Letmathe, chairman and former chief executive of Nestlé, warned that the production of biofuels will further deplete the world's water supply.

Overview of Regions Suffering Crisis Impacts

There are many other countries of the world that are severely impacted with regard to human health and inadequate drinking water. The following is a partial list of some of the countries with significant populations (numerical population of affected population listed) whose only consumption is of contaminated water:

- Sudan 12.3 million
- Venezuela 5.0 million
- Ethiopia 2.7 million
- Tunisia 2.1 million
- Cuba 1.3 million.

According to the California Department of Resources, if more supplies aren't found by 2020, the region will face a shortfall nearly as great as the amount consumed today. Los Angeles is a coastal desert able to support at most 1 million people on its own water; the Los Angeles basin now is the core of a megacity that spans 220 miles (350 km) fromSanta Barbara to the Mexican border. The region's population is expected to reach 41 million by 2020, up from 28 million in 2009.

The population of California continues to grow by more than two million a year and is expected to reach 75 million in 2030, up from 49 million in 2009. But water shortage is likely to surface well before then.

Water deficits, which are already spurring heavy grain imports in numerous smaller countries, may soon do the same in larger countries, such as China and India. The water tables are falling in scores of countries (including Northern China, the US, and India) due to widespread overpumping using powerful diesel and electric pumps. Other countries affected include Pakistan, Iran, and Mexico. This will eventually lead to water scarcity and cutbacks in grain harvest. Even with the overpumping of its aquifers, China is developing a grain deficit. When this happens, it will almost certainly drive grain prices upward. Most of the 3 billion people projected to be added worldwide by mid-century will be born in countries already experiencing water shortages. Unless population growth can be slowed quickly, it is feared that there may not be a practical non-violent or humane solution to the emerging world water shortage.

After China and India, there is a second tier of smaller countries with large water deficits — Algeria, Egypt, Iran, Mexico, and Pakistan. Four of these already import a large share of their grain.

But with a population expanding by 4 million a year, they will also likely soon turn to the world market for grain.

According to a UN climate report, the Himalayan glaciers that are the sources of Asia's biggest rivers – Ganges, Indus, Brahmaputra, Yangtze, Mekong, Salween and Yellow – could disappear by 2035 as temperatures rise. It was later revealed that the source used by the UN climate report actually stated 2350, not 2035. Approximately 2.4 billion people live in the drainage basin of the Himalayan rivers. India, China, Pakistan, Bangladesh, Nepal and Myanmar could experience floods followed by droughts in coming decades. In India alone, the Ganges provides water for drinking and farming for more than 500 million people. The west coast of North America, which gets much of its water from glaciers in mountain ranges such as the Rocky Mountains and Sierra Nevada, also would be affected.

By far the largest part of Australia is desert or semi-arid lands commonly known as the outback. In June 2008 it became known that an expert panel had warned of long term, possibly irreversible, severe ecological damage for the whole Murray-Darling basin if it does not receive sufficient water by October. Water restrictions are currently in place in many regions and cities of Australia in response to chronic shortages resulting from drought. The Australian of the year 2007, environmentalist Tim Flannery, predicted that unless it made drastic changes, Perth in Western Australia could become the world's first ghost metropolis, an abandoned city with no more water to sustain its population. However, Western Australia's dams reached 50% capacity for the first time since 2000 as of September 2009. As a result, heavy rains have brought forth positive results for the region. Nonetheless, the following year, 2010, Perth suffered its second-driest winter on record and the water corporation tightened water restrictions for spring.

PHYSICAL AND ECONOMIC SCARCITY

Around one fifth of the world's population currently live in regions affected by Physical water scarcity, where there is inadequate water resources to meet a country's or regional demand, including the water needed to fulfill the demand of ecosystems to function effectively. Arid regions frequently suffer from physical water scarcity. It also occurs where water seems abundant but where resources are over-committed, such as when there is over development of hydraulic infrastructure for irrigation. Symptoms of physical water scarcity include environmental degradation and declining groundwater as well as other forms of exploitation or overuse.

Economic water scarcity is caused by a lack of investment in infrastructure or technology to draw water from rivers, aquifers or other water sources, or insufficient human capacity to satisfy the demand for water.

One quarter of the world's population is affected by economic water scarcity. Symptoms of economic water scarcity include a lack of infrastructure, causing the people without reliable access to water to have to travel long distances in or fetch water, that is often contaminated from rivers for domestic and agricultural uses. Large parts of Africa suffer from economic water scarcity; developing water infrastructure in those areas could therefore help to reduce poverty. Critical conditions often arise for economically poor and politically weak communities living in already dry environment.

HUMAN RIGHT TO WATER

The United Nations Committee on Economic, Social and Cultural Rights established a foundation of five core attributes for water security. They declare that the human right to water entitles everyone to sufficient, safe, acceptable, physically accessible, and affordable water for personal and domestic use.

Millennium Development Goals (MDG)

In order to address the effects of economic water scarcity, increasing access of safe, accessible drinking water was made an international development goal by the United Nations at the Millennium Summit in the year 2000. During this time, the Millennium Development Goals were drafted and eight goals were agreed upon by all 189 UN members. MDG 7 sets a target for reducing the proportion of the population without sustainable access to safe drinking water by half by the year 2015. This would mean that more than 600 million people would gain access to a safe source of drinking water. According to D+C Development and Cooperation magazine, MDG 7 is still far from being reached as of 2012. Since national governments often cannot meet the infrastructure needs for growing populations on their own. According to the magazine, governments are receiving assistance from many NGOs that put forth their effort in assisting developing nations in the realm of water security.

WATER SCARCITY'S EFFECTS ON ENVIRONMENT

Water scarcity has many negative impacts on the environment, including lakes, rivers, wetlands, and other fresh water resources. The resulting water overuse that is related to water scarcity, often located in areas of irrigation agriculture, harms the environment in several ways including increased salinity, nutrient pollution, and the loss of floodplains and wetlands. Furthermore, water scarcity makes flow management in the rehabilitation of urban streams problematic.

Through the last hundred years, more than half of the Earth's wetlands have been destroyed and have disappeared. These wetlands are important not only because they are the habitats of numerous inhabitants such as mammals, birds, fish, amphibians, and invertebrates, but they support the growing of rice and other food crops as well as provide water filtration and protection from storms and flooding.

Freshwater lakes such as the Aral Sea in central Asia have also suffered. Once the fourth largest freshwater lake, it has lost more than 58,000 square km of area and vastly increased in salt concentration over the span of three decades.

Subsidence, or the gradual sinking of landforms, is another result of water scarcity. The U.S. Geological Survey estimates that subsidence has affected more than 17,000 square miles in 45 U.S. states, 80 percent of it due to groundwater usage. In some areas east of Houston, Texas the land has dropped by more than nine feet due to subsidence. Brownwood, a subdivision near Baytown, Texas, was abandoned due to frequent flooding caused by subsidence and has since become part of the Baytown Nature Center.

Climate Change

Aquifer drawdown or overdrafting and the pumping of fossil water increases the total amount of water within the hydrosphere subject to transpiration and evaporation processes, thereby causing accretion in water vapour and cloud cover, the primary absorbers of infrared radiation in the earth's atmosphere. Adding water to the system has a forcing effect on the whole earth system, an accurate estimate of which hydrogeological fact is yet to be quantified.

DEPLETION OF FRESHWATER RESOURCES

Apart from the conventional surface water sources of freshwater such as rivers and lakes, other resources of freshwater such as groundwater and glaciers have become more developed sources of freshwater, becoming the main source of clean water. Groundwater is water that has pooled below the surface of the Earth and can provide a usable quantity of water through springs or wells.

These areas where groundwater is collected are also known as aquifers. Glaciers provide freshwater in the form meltwater, or freshwater melted from snow or ice, that supply streams or springs as temperatures rise. More and more of these sources are being drawn upon as conventional sources' usability decreases due to factors such as pollution or disappearance due to climate changes. The exponential growth rate of the human population is a main contributing factor in the increasing use of these types of water resources.

Groundwater

Until recent history, groundwater was not a highly utilized resource. In the 1960s, more and more groundwater aquifers developed. Changes in knowledge, technology and funding have allowed for focused development into abstracting water from groundwater resources away from surface water resources. These changes allowed for progress in society such as the "agricultural groundwater revolution," expanding the irrigation sector allowing for increased food production and development in rural areas. Groundwater supplies nearly half of all drinking water in the world. The large volumes of water stored underground in most aquifers have a considerable buffer capacity allowing for water to be withdrawn during periods of drought or little rainfall. This is crucial for people that live in regions that cannot depend on precipitation or surface water as a supply alone, instead providing reliable access to water all year round.

As of 2010, the world's aggregated groundwater abstraction is estimated at approximately 1,000 km^3 per year, with 67% used for irrigation, 22% used for domestic purposes and 11% used for industrial purposes. The top ten major consumers of abstracted water (India, China, United States of America, Pakistan, Iran, Bangladesh, Mexico, Saudi Arabia, Indonesia, and Italy) make up 72% of all abstracted water use worldwide. Groundwater has become crucial for the livelihoods and food security of 1.2 to 1.5 billion rural households in the poorer regions of Africa and Asia.

Although groundwater sources are quite prevalent, one major area of concern is the renewal rate or recharge rate of some groundwater sources. Abstracting from groundwater sources that are non-renewable could lead to exhaustion if not properly monitored and managed.

Another concern of increased groundwater usage is the diminished water quality of the source over time. Reduction of natural outflows, decreasing stored volumes, declining water levels and water degradation are commonly observed in groundwater systems.

Groundwater depletion may result in many negative effects such as increased cost of groundwater pumping, induced salinity and other water quality changes, land subsidence, degraded springs and reduced baseflows. Human pollution is also harmful to this important resource.

Glaciers

Glaciers are noted as a vital water source due to their contribution to stream flow. Rising global temperatures have noticeable effects on the rate at which glaciers are melting, causing glaciers in general to shrink worldwide. Although the meltwater from these glaciers are increasing the total water supply for the present, the disappearance of glaciers in the long term will diminish available water resources. Increased meltwater due to rising global temperatures can also have negative effects such as flooding of lakes and dams and catastrophic results.

MEASUREMENT OF WATER SCARCITY

Hydrologists today typically assess water scarcity by looking at the population-water equation. This is done by comparing the amount of total available water resources per year to the population of a country or region. A popular approach to measuring water scarcity has been to rank countries according to the amount of annual water resources available per person. For example, according to the Falkenmark Water Stress Indicator, a country or region is said to experience "water stress" when annual water supplies drop below 1,700 cubic metres per person per year. At levels between 1,700 and 1,000 cubic metres per person per year, periodic or limited water shortages can be expected. When water supplies drop below 1,000 cubic metres per person per year, the country faces "water scarcity". The United Nations' FAO states that by 2025, 1.9 billion people will be living in countries or regions with absolute water scarcity, and two-thirds of the world population could be under stress conditions. The World Bank adds that climate change could profoundly alter future patterns of both water availability and use,thereby increasing levels of water stress and insecurity, both at the global scale and in sectors that depend on water.

Other ways of measuring water scarcity include examining the physical existence of water in nature, comparing nations with lower or higher volumes of water available for use. This method often fails to capture the accessibility of the water resource to the population that may need it. Others have related water availability to population.

Another measurement, calculated as part of a wider assessment of water management in 2007, aimed to relate water availability to how the resource was actually used. It therefore divided water scarcity into 'physical' and 'economic'. Physical water scarcity is where there is not enough water to meet all demands, including that needed for ecosystems to function effectively. Arid regions frequently suffer from physical water scarcity. It also occurs where water seems abundant but where resources are over-committed, such as when there is overdevelopment of hydraulic infrastructure for irrigation. Symptoms of physical water scarcity include environmental degradation and declining groundwater. Water stress harms living things because every organism needs water to live.

Renewable Freshwater Resources

Renewable freshwater supply is a metric often used in conjunction when evaluating water scarcity. This metric is informative because it can describe the total available water resource each country contains.

By knowing the total available water source, an idea can be gained about whether a country is prone to experiencing physical water scarcity. This metric has its faults in that it is an average; precipitation delivers water unevenly across the planet each year and annual renewable water resources vary from year to year. This metric also does not describe the accessibility of water to individuals, households, industries, or the government. Lastly, as this metric is a description of a whole country, it does not accurately portray whether a country is experiencing water scarcity. Canada and Brazil both have very high levels of available water supply, but still experience various water related problems.

It can be observed that tropical countries in Asia and Africa have low availability of freshwater resources.

Outlook

Construction of wastewater treatment plants and reduction of groundwater overdrafting appear to be obvious solutions to the worldwide problem; however, a deeper look reveals more fundamental issues in play. Wastewater treatment is highly capital intensive, restricting access to this technology in some regions; furthermore the rapid increase in population of many countries makes this a race that is difficult to win. As if those factors are not daunting enough, one must consider the enormous costs and skill sets involved to maintain wastewater treatment plants even if they are successfully developed.

Reduction in groundwater overdrafting is usually politically very unpopular and has major economic impacts to farmers; moreover, this strategy will necessarily reduce crop output, which is something the world can ill-afford, given the population level at present.

At more realistic levels, developing countries can strive to achieve primary wastewater treatment or secure septic systems, and carefully analyse wastewater outfall design to minimise impacts to drinking water and to ecosystems. Developed countries can not only share technology better, including cost-effective wastewater and water treatment systems but also in hydrological transport modeling.

At the individual level, people in developed countries can look inward and reduce overconsumption, which further strains worldwide water consumption. Both developed and developing countries can increase protection of ecosystems, especially wetlands and riparian zones. These measures will not only conserve biota, but also render more effective the natural water cycle flushing and transport that make water systems more healthy for humans.

A range of local, low-tech solutions are being pursued by a number of companies. These efforts center around the use of solar power to distill water at temperatures slightly beneath that at which water boils. By developing the capability to purify any available water source, local business models could be built around the new technologies, accelerating their uptake. For example, bedouins from the town of Dahab in Egypt have installed AquaDania's WaterStillar, which uses a solar thermal collector measuring two square metres to distill from 40 to 60 litres per day from any local water source. This is five times more efficient than conventional stills and eliminates the need for polluting plastic PET bottles or tranportation of water supply.

GLOBAL EXPERIENCES IN MANAGING WATER CRISIS

It is alleged that the likelihood of conflict rises if the rate of change within the basin exceeds the capacity of institution to absorb that change. Although water crisis is closely related to regional tensions, history showed that acute conflicts over water are far less than the record of cooperation.

The key lies in strong institutions and cooperation. The Indus River Commission and the Indus Water Treaty survived two wars between India and Pakistan despite their hostility, proving to be a successful mechanism in resolving conflicts by providing a framework for consultation inspection and exchange of data. The Mekong Committee has also functioned since 1957 and survived the Vietnam War. In contrast, regional instability results when there is an absence of institutions to co-operate in regional collaboration, like Egypt's plan for a high dam on the Nile. However, there is currently no global institution in place for the management and management of trans-boundary water sources, and international co-operation has happened through ad hoc collaborations between agencies, like the Mekong Committee which was formed due to an alliance between UNICEF and the US Bureau of Reclamation. Formation of strong international institutions seems to be a way forward – they fuel early intervention and management, preventing the costly dispute resolution process.

One common feature of almost all resolved disputes is that the negotiations had a "need-based" instead of a "right–based" paradigm. Irrigable lands, population, technicalities of projects define "needs". The success of a need-based paradigm is reflected in the only water agreement ever negotiated in the Jordan River Basin, which focuses in needs not on rights of riparians. In the Indian subcontinent, irrigation requirements of Bangladesh determine water allocations of The Ganges River. A need based, regional approach focuses on satisfying individuals with their need of water, ensuring that minimum quantitative needs are being met. It removes the conflict that arises when countries view the treaty from a national interest point of view, move away from the zero-sum approach to a positive sum, integrative approach that equitably allocated the water and its benefits.

The Blue Peace framework developed by Strategic Foresight Group in partnership with the Governments of Switzerland and Sweden offers a unique policy structure which promotes sustainable management of water resources combined with cooperation for peace. By making the most of shared water resources through cooperation rather than mere allocation between countries, the chances for peace can be increased. The Blue Peace approach has proven to be effective in cases like the Middle East and theNile basin.

WATER SCARCITY IN INDIA

Water scarcity involves water *stress, water shortage* or *deficits,* and *water crisis*. This may be due to both natural and human factors. But, many reports suggest that the scarcity is more due to the human factor than anything - such as industrialization, irrigation, domestic use, etc.

EFFECT ON ANIMALS

The acute water shortage prevailing in the forest areas of Tamil Nadu's districts of Madurai and Dindigul has led the Indian gaurs found in the forest of the region, to death as they come in search of water and end up dead by falling into the wells.

COUNTER MEASURES

Community Led Initiatives

With support from government and UNICEF, villagers in Palve Budruk, located in the drought-prone Parner Block in Ahmednagar district of Maharashtra, developed a catchment plan covering 1,400 hectors – that's over 80% of the land available. The system has three check dams, 20 canal bunds, two small percolation tanks linked to the main tank and 19 village ponds. Water stored in the percolation tank, is strictly meant for domestic use only. Piped water is supplied for an hour a day in the morning, during which time families fill up water for drinking and cooking

Government Led Initiatives

SIS Seoul International School is Fundraising to bring water to India, and can be found in South Korea, or siskorea.and also it led to india which it is governed.

Raising Awareness

The Canadian start-up Decode Global has developed the mobile game Get Water!, a game for social change focusing on the water scarcity in India and the effect it has on girls' education. The game's primary goal is to raise awareness of the water crisis, by educating children as well as adult gamers. To put more focus on children'd learning, the company has published a 6-part lesson plan for 4-6 grade teachers, available for download as a pdf from the game's website.

Exploitation of Ground Water

The Central Ground Water Authority (CGWA)has notified 82 areas (Districts,Blocks, Mandals, Talukas, Municipalities) for regulation of ground water development. In these areas, installation of new ground water abstraction structures is not permitted without prior specific approval of the Authority / Authorized officer. Moreover, proposals for setting up/expansion of ground water based industries including bottled water manufacturing units are forwarded by State Pollution Control Boards and Bureau of Indian Standards to CGWA for seeking No Objection Certificate (NOC) for ground water withdrawal. NOC is not accorded to such industries including bottled water manufacturing units proposed to be located in areas notified by the Authority. In non- notified areas, NOC is issued with mandatory pre-conditions of adoption of rain water harvesting system, monitoring of ground water abstraction as well as monitoring of ground water level and quality etc. by the industry.

- Rainwater harvesting - Rain water is accumulated and used for ground water recharge. This increases the ground water availability.
- Farm pond - Farm ponds are constructed near the farming field. The rain water which runs off the ground are collected by these ponds. These ponds helps agriculture in dry lands.

WATER SCARCITY AND ENCROACHMENT OF COALMINING

Open-cut mining and coal combustion for power generation in the Upper Hunter compete for resources with long-standing rural production, which depends on good water supplies and access to alluvial soils. Traditionally, local farmers have worked out water allocations face-to-face, by methods fine-tuned to the availability of the water in the catchment. However, conflicts about water allocations have been exacerbated in the past five years due to drought conditions. Farmers have adopted drastic measures in response to the drought: subdividing their land, selling off stock, buying in feed, and not planting crops. There is also growing acceptance that climate change is a major threat to primary producers. Some landholders have started to adapt by changing to more water efficient farming practices, and a small (radical!) minority has begun growing native grass for pasture.

Contestation over water has intensified since the NSW government passed the 2000 Water Management Act. This Act signalled a change in government policy on water that effectively split land ownership from water rights, with the latter becoming a tradeable commodity (McCarthy 2006). Water for irrigation and other purposes is now allocated to users on the basis of a graded licensing system. Five classes of water licences were created, with farmers having 'general security' water rights, and power and mining companies having 'high security' status, with commensurate privileges. The highest priority class of water use is 'environmental flows' which are intended to maintain the minimum viability, if not the health, of rivers. These classifications are at odds with the sense of generational connection and custodianship that Aborigines and some long-term farming inhabitants feel towards water sources in their locality.

Many defenders of the Hunter River and its tributaries deplore the fact that the water allocations to all users are well in excess of a sustainable level, and note that this problem in itself is bound to lead to conflict among users. The Hunter-Central Rivers Catchment Management Authority is a statutory authority of the NSW government, and is not empowered to take a strong stand in protecting river health beyond some monitoring and palliation that leaves unchallenged the political inequalities among users and the lack of long-term sustainable practices. Water usage in the 'unregulated' (i.e. undammed) tributaries of the Hunter River is managed through a system of Water Users Groups, with mixed results, due mainly to the impacts of the drought and diminishing agreement about allocations.

The indigenous inhabitants of the Upper Hunter, despite their recognition through the NSW Local Land Council system, are noticeably absent from Water User Groups. The contestation over water that is outlined above is probably not dissimilar to the situation in many rural Australian communities confronted with depleted or degraded water supply and increasing government intervention in water management through a host of legislative instruments and quasi-government bodies. North of Muswellbrook, at the top of the catchment of the Hunter River, there is an added ingredient in this already volatile mix: a growing number of open-cut coalmine development proposals. The latest Asian economic boom, particularly in China, has had a down-side for rural residents of the Upper Hunter Valley.

The demand for energy resources to fuel the power stations that support China's factories means open-cut coalmines have become a highly profitable prospect for Australian and multinational companies. Analysts declare the mining industry is in a 'supercycle' (CRC Mining 2006), with Australian coking coal prices for 2006-7 around 110% higher than for 2003-4 (Reserve Bank of Australia 2007). In conversations with Upper Hunter residents, the words 'China' and 'globalisation' seem to be on everyone's lips. This is perhaps not uncommon in rural Australia, given the producers' high level of integration into global markets. However, there is no longer the happy confluence of interests that once existed when farmers were selling their products to a hungry world. One small landholder in the Upper Hunter expressed concern that such a precious commodity as water was being used to wash export coal:

> ... and these coal washeries, you know? I mean, what—we wash it so it's not dusty for the Chinese? Let them wash it with their bloody water, sell it to them as it comes out of the bloody thing, you know? If they're going to pay whatever they're paying now for the coal it makes it worth so much to get it out of there, well let them wash it, you know? Why use decent quality water to wash the bloody coal?

During the past 15 years, open cut mines have proliferated in the Upper Hunter. Farms in mining buffer zones were acquired by mines, along with their water licences (Thompson 2006: 5). Drought conditions have exacerbated resentment among Upper Hunter irrigators that under current legislation too many mines are permitted to draw water from rivers. In May 2006, commentators noted that the Hunter Valley coal and power industries owned 42% of water licences but used 'only a fraction of the amount of water available to them' (McCarthy 2006). However, when the drought intensified in early 2007, at least one mine near Muswellbrook briefly stopped production due to a water shortage, while another placed the workforce on notice of potential stoppage unless rain was forthcoming.

In the context of the current spate of mine proposals, the protests have widened to embrace an environmental activism and environmental justice movement that is attracting increasing numbers of people. In anthropological terms, the political and cultural processes underpinning environmental activism can be understood as a 'whole new discursive regime' in which nature and human agency are brought into relationship in multiple political contexts (Brosius 1999). Diverse groups struggle to define the arena (i.e. sphere of action, relevant knowledge, or scene of conflict) for debates about environmental futures. These issues are explored through an analysis of protests surrounding Bickham Coal Company's bulk sample coal extraction and plans for mining coal near Murrurundi.

THE BICKHAM COAL COMPANY DEVELOPMENT

When it became public knowledge in 2002 that a private company, Bickham Coal, was going to submit a proposal for an open-cut coalmine just south of the Upper Hunter Valley town of Murrurundi, concerned residents organised to challenge the development. The proposed open cut is near a small village called Wingen and close to Burning Mountain (a naturally burning coal seam) and the Pages River. Patrice Newell, a local farmer and author, has described the Pages and its history:

For countless thousands of years it was a vital stream for the Wonnarua people. From 1825 they were dispossessed, their river appropriated by the European settlers who came and kept coming, succeeding and failing, trying to make a living and building towns like Murrurundi, Blandford and our little village, Gundy. Old journals suggest that the Murrawin tribe of the Wonnarua, comprising sixteen men, eight women and five children lived right... where the Pages meets the Isis River (Newell 2003: 2).

The common interest of these opponents is their dependence on the water from the Pages River, and membership of the Pages River Water Users Group. The proposed mine site is located to the east of the New England Highway, in the catchment of the Pages River (a tributary of the Hunter River). It is a small mine, with $70 million capital investment, 22 year mine life and maximum output of 2.5 megatonnes per annum (NSW Department of Planning [NSW DP] 2005: 2). The Pages River is described as having 'high water resource values and associated high ecosystem values,' as well as important 'refuge values'. It flows through the Cameron Gorge Nature Reserve, which contains 'the last remnant vegetation of its type in the Hunter Valley' (NSW DP 2005: 3).

The mine will also be close to the Burning Mountain Nature Reserve, which is the only naturally occurring burning coal seam in Australia, and one of only three in the world (NSW DP 2005: 76). The debate about the water impacts from the Bickham mine was framed by concerns about continuing drought in the Upper Hunter. When the Bickham project was first mooted in 2002, a long dry spell along with high demand for water resources from a variety of users fuelled fears among residents at nearby Murrurundi that mining in the area 'would make even greater demands on the local water system' (Peatling 2002)..

In 2003, the continuing dry conditions led to outrage by local 'dissenters' that 'in the middle of a drought' the company was going to use the water 'for dust suppression' (Australian Broadcasting Corporation [ABC] Online 2003, 19 September). At the end of 2004, the first stage (Level 1) of increasingly severe restrictions on water irrigation and usage were in force because of the low level of water in aquifers. In response to protests by Upper Hunter residents and irrigators, the Department of Natural Resources denied it was 'being irresponsible in allowing a mining company to use up to 40 megalitres of water over the next two years in the middle of a drought' (ABC Premium News 2004,

February 16). By the middle of 2006, the Pages River had 'stopped flowing' and Murrurundi had been placed on more stringent Level 2 restrictions (Herald 2006, 27 May), a situation that by January 2007 had been raised to Level 4 restrictions until further notice (Upper Hunter Shire Council 2007).

One of the main reasons community and environmental activists oppose the Bickham open cut mine proposal is their belief that coalmining operations would extract water 'from two bores drilled into aquifers beneath the river bed' (Peatling 2002), thus damaging flow in the nearby waterways. The possibility of this connectivity has become a key element of the protest against the mine development. Initially, the Bickham Coal Chief Executive responded to community concerns about the health of the river with public statements that strained credulity, such as: 'Rather than just taking that water it will be re-injected back into the aquifer to end up back where it came from' (Peatling 2002).

In mid-2002, Bickham Coal Company submitted an application to the NSW Department of Mineral Resources (DMR) to extract a 'bulk sample' of 25,000 tonnes of coal from a property about 10 kms south of Murrurundi. Bulk samples are conducted using mining equipment to dig up a designated area to gather material to 'test the mineral bearing qualities of the land' (cited in NSW DP 2005: 11). This sampling is undertaken to determine whether a full-scale coalmining operation would be viable. However, under the NSW Mining Act (1992) bulk samples are classified as 'prospecting' or 'valid exploration' not 'mining'. Community groups opposed to mines regard the rationale for bulk samples with suspicion, asserting that they are really a 'foot in the door' for a company wishing to mine in a new area.

In response to the application, the newly formed 'Bickham Coal-Mine Action Group' [BCAG] met in Murrurundi and has conducted a sustained campaign against the mine. This group is comprised mainly of owners of rural farming or grazing properties that are adjacent to the proposed mine and/or will draw water from the same sources. Some members are descendents of colonial settlers and live in inherited homesteads; whilst others are relative newcomers from the city. Several members are influential in the media and arts communities, including the Australian Broadcasting Corporation broadcaster Phillip Adams, and farmer and author Patrice Newell.

Bickham Coal's first environmental impact assessment (Review of Environmental Factors,) submitted in October 2002, was rejected by community members. Community input was via a consultative committee, and regular public meetings held throughout 2002, as well as by formal submissions to the Review. In November, the Minister directed the company to provide further studies, including the provision of a Water Management Plan, and extended community consultation (NSW DMR 2004: 4). Following the submission of an Amended Review of Environmental Factors by the company in September 2003, the NSW Minister for Mineral Resources announced 'an investigation into the sustainability of any proposals' (Herald 2004, January 20). There were numerous submissions to this investigation, highlighting a range of contrasting views on water impacts. This culminated in the Department issuing a 2004 Assessment Report: Review of Environmental Factors relating to the Bickham Coal Company's mine proposal (NSW DMR 2004). Meanwhile, on the basis of the submissions and the conclusions of the report, the Minister granted approval for a 'bulk sample' in January 2004. The submissions that were cited in the Assessment Report were notable for their varying interpretations of the science that informed the report. Such variation in interpretations is possible because of the inherent uncertainty in hydrological modelling. No amount of drilling and test holes will determine with absolute certainty the way water moves underground (past, present and future). However, the private consultants (scientists) doing the modelling have to present their findings to their employer (The Bickham Coal Company) as if there was no uncertainty and that the outcomes of mining will be unambiguous. Those opposing the mine have to counter-argue that the science is weak and that the modelling is misleading, a task that is very difficult for non-specialists.

CONTESTING STATE-SPONSORED SCIENCE

State government departments whose submissions were cited in the Assessment Report tended to minimise the negative environmental impacts of the proposed bulk sample in proportion to the centrality of mining to their departmental interests. The Department of Primary Industries (Minerals) was most sanguine, with the Minister cited in the report: 'Results of hydrological studies into the Pages River and surrounding groundwater aquifers' indicate that activity associated with 'surface disturbance' due to the bulk sample 'would be unlikely to significantly affect the environment' (NSW Department of Primary Industries—Minerals, 2004). However, the Department did concede that proceeding with the bulk sample would require 'dewatering' of groundwater from licensed boreholes adjacent to the excavation which would be monitored using a 'range of environmental monitoring activity, including monitoring of groundwater and surface water' within the exploration licence area (NSW DMR 2004: 5).

The NSW Department of Infrastructure, Planning and Natural Resources (DIPNA) also took a positive view, asserting that the bulk sample 'was likely to have minor impacts on the Pages River' and that the operation would result in 'localised depressurisation of the aquifer and gradient reversal of local groundwaters'. It was considered that the 'short life span' of the bulk sample operations 'would result in relatively minor impacts on adjacent ground and surface waters' (NSW DMR 2004: 12). The discourse of 'minor' or 'minimal' impacts was echoed in the submission of the Department of Environment and Conservation (National Parks and Wildlife Service), which advised that, 'additional studies' on groundwater and surface water had revealed 'minimal potential impacts on water quality and quantity favourable to the protection of the Cameron Gorge Nature Reserve' downstream of the bulk sample. Furthermore, it was considered 'unlikely' that the bulk sample would have a 'substantial detrimental impact on natural or cultural heritage values' (NSW DMR 2004: 14).

The adequacy of environmental modelling, and the independence of the interpretation of those models by industry and state government regulators, was questioned in various ways by locally based groups, environmentalists and local government. The Murrurundi Shire Council (now amalgamated into the Upper Hunter Shire Council) considered water impacts to be a 'primary concern' and called for a 'significant level of monitoring during the proposed activity', particularly because there were differing estimations in the proponent's assessments about the inflow volumes to be dewatered (NSW DMR 2004: 14). Similarly, the Scone Shire Council (now also part of Upper Hunter Shire Council) 'raised concern over the impacts on the Pages River and the groundwater aquifer'; and contested the proponent's environmental impact review by submitting a report by consultants employed by the Council to peer review the proponent's Water Studies (SMEC Australia Pty Ltd.).

The more critical interpretations of the Assessment Report came from more independently situated protagonists, organised around local community and environmental action groups. One of the main reasons community and environmental activists opposed the Bickham bulk sample and subsequent open cut mine proposal, was the belief that coalmining operations would directly connect with, and impact on, the hydrological cycle of the area in profound and unpredictable ways. There was a call for 'further groundwater investigation' from groups like the then Hunter Catchment Management Trust (now Hunter and Central Rivers CMA), a semi-independent state body (NSW DMR 2004: 14). Minewatch, a regional lobby group that acts on behalf of property owners affected by mines, also considered that 'findings on groundwater issues' required 'independent investigation' (NSW DMR 2004: 16).

Alternative scientific expertise was sought to contest the company's models. The Bickham Coal-mine Action Group's submission expressed a strong concern about the 'possible adverse impacts of open cut mining on the Pages River and the surrounding aquifer' (NSW DMR 2004: 16). The group was also concerned about the 'variability of results' and 'monitoring' (NSW DMR 2004: 16). A Greens Party (1) Member of the NSW Legislative Council objected to the company's Water Management Plan, noting that some of the Bickham coal seams 'intersect' the Pages River which could lead to 'river capture—that is, the fiver could end up being diverted into the coalmine' (NSW Legislative Council 2003). This was not an uncommon fate of watercourses in the Hunter

Valley. It was also the case that a submission by the Wonnarura Nation Aboriginal Corporation and the Wanaruah [sic] Local Aboriginal Land Council contained concerns about, 'The impact on the natural flow of fired rock from the Pages River to Burning Mountain' and 'The impact on cultural heritage values of the WNAC people' (NSW DMR 2004:17).

Environmentalists, local government and Upper Hunter based groups contested the reliability of the proponent's and the government departments' estimations of likely water impacts. It should be noted that all this revolved around the bulk sample only—the contestation over the actual mine proposal, if it eventuated, was yet to begin. Community groups often commented that dealing with coal industry proponents and the state government departments that regulate their activities was 'a war of attrition'.

A predictable outcome of the Assessment Report was the Department's requirement for Bickham Coal to consult with other 'stakeholders' about bulk sample impacts, including State government departments, local councils, individuals and special interest groups, including the 'Aboriginal Community' (NSW DMR 2004).

Connectivity between mining and the Pages River continued to be denied by the Bickham Project Manager in June 2004, when blasting was in operation for the bulk sample: 'No water will be taken from the river or put back in' (Thompson 2004a). At the end of 2004, scientific testing was used to legitimate the industry view; a Bickham spokesperson stated that 'chemical analysis showed mining the bulk sample had not caused any connectivity between the pit and the river' (Thompson 2004b). Following completion of the bulk sample, Bickham Coal commenced the design and planning for a full-scale open cut mine. The company chose consultants Parsons Brinkerhoff to conduct 'water resource investigations in and beyond the proposed Bickham site'.

They were also given responsibility for community liaison on environmental impacts. PB is a global project management group that has offices in the Upper Hunter. Other projects they have managed include a nuclear storage site in the Northern Territory and freeways and wastewater treatments plants in Victoria (Australian Broadcasting Corporation's Regional News 2006). By February 2007 the water study had still not been completed, and there were no requirements for the bulk sample pit to be rehabilitated until the expiration of water licences in March 2008 (Thompson 2007).

The various criticisms of the scientific evidence endorsed by the government in its report provided enough pressure for the NSW DP to undertake an independent investigation that was broader in scope, which resulted in the release in December 2005 of the report Strategic Assessment of Coalmining Potential in the Upper Hunter Valley. This report concluded that:

The major issues associated with a potential new mine at Bickham are directly related to the river and are of such significance that they need to be separately considered (NSW DP 2005: 2).

It was acknowledged that there was currently 'insufficient information to know whether the groundwater seeping into any future mine at Bickham would be saline and, if so, in what quantities'. Importantly, the report also acknowledged that while there was 'no clear evidence that there is a significant connectivity between the Pages River and the hard rock aquifers at Bickham... Neither is there clear cut evidence yet available that demonstrates there is no significant connection' (NSW DP 2005: 3).

Despite their concerns about the independence of the report, it was hailed as a significant victory by the BCAG and others opposed to the mine, and inspired real hope that the mine would not receive approval. While it did not preclude mining altogether, it certainly raised the bar for the Company in terms of further, more rigorous, environmental assessment work. The most vocal opposition to the mine was from rural producers whose properties had the potential to be affected deleteriously by the as yet unascertained effects on the water supply, and who are also committed to 'precautionary' values of environmental custodianship. The views of residents of Murrurundi and other small towns in the area appear to be mixed, and more difficult to gauge. A substantial number of Murrurundi residents are employed in mining at Muswellbrook. Many had hopes that the mine would bring more employment in a situation of low opportunity. Residents engaged in commerce hoped for a healthier flow of customers for their businesses.

The Mayor of the Upper Hunter Shire Council was circumspect in his public statements:

I suppose while there is a feeling of inevitability about coalmining coming to our towns, I'd like to think governments would be a little bit more careful rather than just opening the floodgates... because this is where the tributaries of the Hunter start. If we get it wrong up here we've got a big problem (Quinn 2005).

12

Water Issues in Developing Countries

ACCESS- AVAILABILITY & CHALLENGES

Approximately 80% of all illnesses in developing countries are caused by poor water and sanitation condition. It is common for women and girls to have to walk several kilometers every day to fetch water for their families. Once filled, water jugs can weigh as much as 20 kg (44 lbs).

In the last century, water use has greatly outpaced the rate of population growth: people are using more water than ever before. By 2025, up to 1.8 billion people could face water scarcity. Water scarcity can take two forms: physical water scarcity, or low quantity of water, and economic water scarcity, or low quality of water.

Physical Water Scarcity

This term typically applies to dry, arid regions where fresh water naturally occurs in low quantities. This is being greatly exacerbated by anthropogenic activities that take surface and ground water faster than the environment can replenish it. Regions most affected by this type of water scarcity are Mexico, Northern and Southern Africa, the Middle East, India, and Northern China.

Economic Water Scarcity

Economic water scarcity applies to areas or cultures that lack the fiscal resources and/or human capacity to invest in water sources and meet the local demand. Water is often only available to those who can pay for it or those in political power; leaving millions of the world's poorest without access. Regions most affected by this type of scarcity are portions of Central and South America, Central Africa, India, and South East Asia. It is important to highlight the distinction between these two forms of scarcity: water can be physically available, but the resources are not available to improve it and distribute it to those who need it.

India

India's growing population is putting a strain on the country's water resources. The country is classified as "water stressed" and a water availability of 1,000-1,700 m /person/year. According to UNICEF, in 2008 88% of the population had access and was using improved drinking water sources. "Improved drinking water source" is an ambiguous term, ranging in meaning from fully treated and 24-hour availability to merely being piped through a city a sporadically available. This is in part due to large inefficiencies in the water infrastructure in which up to 40% of water leaks out.

In the same 2008 UNICEF report, only 31% of the population had access and used improved sanitation facilities. Open sewers are common place in urban areas. A little more than half of the 16 million residents of New Delhi, the capital city, have access to this service. Every day, 950 million gallons of sewage flows from New Delhi into the Yamuna River with any significant forms of treatment. This river bubbles with methane and was found to have a fecal coliform count 10,000 time the safe limit for bathing.

Due to surface water contamination due to lack of sewage treatment and industrial discharge, groundwater is becoming increasingly dependent on and exploited in many regions of India. This process is being expedited by heavily subsidized energy costs for agriculture practices; which make up roughly 80% of India's water resource demand.

Kenya

Kenya, a country of 36.6 million, struggles with a staggering population growth rate of 2.6% per year (by comparison, the US population growth rate is 0.899% and the population growth rate in India is 1.31%). This high population growth rate has pushed

Kenya's natural resources to the brink of destruction. Much of the country suffers from a severe arid climate, with only scarce few areas enjoying rain and access to water resources. Deforestation and soil degradation have made the available surface water typically highly polluted and difficult to retain. The government has been unable to afford to develop water treatment or distribution systems, leaving the vast majority of the country without access to water. This has also exacerbated gender politics, as 74% of women must spend an average of 8 hours per day securing water for their families. The growing population and stagnant economy has exacerbated urban, suburban, and rural poverty—exacerbated by lack of access to clean drinking water which leaves much of the non-elite population suffering from disease and parasites. This has effectively crippled Kenya's human capital. Private water companies have taken up the slack from Kenya's government among the wealthy, but the Kenyan government prevents them from moving into the poverty-stricken areas of the country in order to stop profiteering off the poor. Unfortunately, since Kenya's government also refuses to provide services, this leaves the disenfranchised with no options at all for obtaining clean water—or any water—easily.

Bangladesh

Historically, water sources in Bangladesh came from surface water contaminated with bacteria. As a result of drinking infected water, infants and children suffered from acute gastrointestinal disease, causing significant burden of mortality. During the 1970s, UNICEF worked with the Department of Public Health Engineering to install tube-wells, which drew water from underground aquifers, to provide a presumably safe source of water for the nation. The wells consist of tubes 5 cm in diameter that were inserted less than 200 m into the ground, and capped with an iron or steel hand pump. At that time, standard water testing procedures did not include arsenic testing. This lack of precaution led to one of the largest mass poisoning of a population twenty years later because the ground water used for drinking is naturally contaminated with arsenic. Because arsenic has no taste, no smell, and no color, its long term health risks can be harder for the inhabitants to grasp compared to the immediate threats caused by diarrhea. Nonetheless, intervention measures such as awareness programs and painting tube-wells red if the water is above the government limit of 50 ppb arsenic (green otherwise) have seen success. As of 2010, 80% of Bangladeshis recognize arsenic as a problem. Available options for providing safe drinking water include deep wells, traditional dug wells, treatment of surface water, and rainwater harvesting. Between 2000 and 2009, more than 160,000 safe water devices have been installed in arsenic-affected regions of Bangladesh.

WATER QUALITY

Even after accounting for physical water availability or access, water quality could further reduce the amount of usable water available to a developing country for human consumption, sanitation, agriculture and industrial purposes, in addition to various ecosystem services. The level of water quality depends on its intended purpose: Water that could be unfit for human consumption could be still usable in industrial or agriculture applications. Yet parts of the world are experiencing extensive deterioration of water quality, in some cases even rendering the water unfit for agricultural or even industrial use. For example in China, 54% of the Hai River basin surface water is so polluted that it is considered un-usable.

Development indicators tend to focus on access and availability of 'safe water', which the World Bank defines as 'treated surface water and untreated but uncontaminated groundwater.' Safe water is crucial not only for human health (on average,a human needs 20 litres of safe water for his daily 'metabolic, hygienic and domestic needs') but also for economic development and environmental health. Yet, more than 1/3 of the world cannot drink their local water supply without additional treatment.

Safe water one of the eight Millennium Development Goals: Target 7.C; "Halve, by 2015, the proportion of the population without sustainable access to safe drinking water and basic sanitation",focused on increasing access to an 'improved water source' and to 'improved sanitation'. Yet even having access to an 'improved water source' does not guarantee the water's quality, as it could lack proper treatment, become contaminated during transport or even home storage. A study found that estimates of safe water, if accounting for water quality, could be dramatically reduce the proportion of a population with access to safe water, especially if the water sources were poorly maintained.

Issues

Water quality is affected both by natural processes and ecosystem characteristics but also the result of human activities, including industry, domestic and agricultural uses of water.

Physical contaminants of concern can reduce waters quality through the world. Specific contaminants of concern include unsafe levels and harmful varieties of microbiological and pollutants and chemical contaminants, including:

- metals (e.g. iron)
- organic matter
- arsenic
- salts
- fluoride
- viruses
- bacteria
- protozoa
- parasites

UNICEF also notes that various non-harmful physical qualities of water quality (color, taste and smell) could also render water to be perceived as poor quality and deemed un-usable by its intended users.

These contaminants could come from point and non-point sources, along with naturally occurring sources, such as: natural processes (e.g. from geology, hydrology or weather) industrial waste domestic human waste (e.g. fecal matter) agriculture (e.g. pesticide runoff) pharmaceuticals.

Unsafe water, along with low sanitation and hygiene represent the leading cause of death in developing countries. These contaminants can lead to many various debilitating and deadly water-borne diseases, such as fever, cholera, dysentery, diarrhea and others. UNICEF cites fecal contamination and high levels of naturally occurring arsenic andfluoride as two of the world's major water quality concerns. Worldwide, contaminated water leads to 4,000 diarrhea deaths a day in children under 5. In Bangladesh, an estimated 1.4 million tube wells have unsafe levels of naturally occurring arsenic potentially leading to arsenic poisoning.

Challenges to Water Quality

Challenges to water quality stem not only from the physical contaminants themselves but also from the sheer volume of contaminants that can overwhelm an area's infrastructure or resources to treat and remove the contaminants. Human cultural and cultural norms, in addition to governance structures, can also contribute to scenarios that further reduce the quality of available water. The absence or low enforcement of the following policy and market mechanisms in developing countries can also be detrimental to improving water quality.

Water quality in developing countries is often hampered by lack of or limited enforcement of:

- emission standards
- water quality standards
- chemical controls
- non-point source controls (e.g. agricultural runoff)
- market based incentives for pollution control/water treatment
- follow-up and legal enforcement
- integration with other related concerns (solid waste management)
- trans-boundary regulation on shared water bodies
- environmental agency capacity (due to resources or lack of political will)
- understanding/awareness of issues and laws

To illustrate the sheer challenge of improving water quality: in India, 80% of the health issues come from waterborne diseases. Part of this challenge includes addressing the pollution of the Ganges (Ganga) river, which is home to about 400 million people. The river receives about over 1.3 billion litres of domestic waste, along with 260 million litres of industrial waste, run off from 6 million tons of fertilizers and 9,000 tons of pesticides used in agriculture, thousands of animal carcasses and several hundred human corpses released into the river every day for spiritual rebirth. Two-thirds of this waste is released into the river untreated.

Beyond human health and ecosystem health, water quality is important for various industries (such as power generation, metals, mining, and petroleum) which require high-quality water to operate. Less high quality water (either through contamination or physical water scarcity) could impact and limit the choices of technology available to developing countries. Reductions in water quality have the dual effect of not only increase the water stress to industrial companies in these areas but typically also apply increasing the pressure to improve the quality of the industrial wastewater.

However, gaps in wastewater treatment (the amount of wastewater to be treated is greater than the amount that is actually treated] represent the most significant contribution to water pollution and water quality deterioration. In the majority of the developing world, most of the collected wastewater is returned to surface waters directly without treatment, reducing the water's quality. In China, only 38% of China's urban wastewater is treated and although 91% of China's industrial waste water is treated, it still releases extensive toxins into the water supply.

The amount of wastewater treatment possible can also be compromised by the networks required to bring the wastewater to the treatment plants. It is estimated that 15% of China's wastewater treatment facilities are not being used to capacity due to a limited pipe network to collect and transport wastewater. In Sao Paolo, Brazil, a lack of sanitation infrastructure results in the pollution of the majority of its water supply and forces the city to import over 50% of its water from outside watersheds. Polluted water increases a developing country's operating costs, as lower quality water is more expensive to treat. In Brazil, polluted water from the Guarapiranga Reservoir costs \$0.43 per m^3 to treat to usable quality, while water from the compared to only \$0.10 per m^3 for water coming from the Cantareira Mountains.

IMPROVING WATER RESOURCES

Improving: Access

In 2011 the World Health Organization revised its Guidelines for Drinking-water Quality. This document, written for an audience of water and/or health regulators and policy-makers, is intended to aid in the development of national drinking water quality standards. The guidelines include health based targets, water safety plans, surveillance, and supporting information regarding the microbial, chemical, radiological, and acceptability aspects of common drinking water contaminants. In addition, the document offers guidance regarding the application of the drinking water quality guidelines in specific circumstances, including large buildings, emergencies and disasters, travelers, desalination systems, planes and ships, packaged drinking water, and food production.

According to the WHO, "The most effective means of consistently ensuring the safety of a drinking-water supply is through the use of a comprehensive risk assessment and risk management approach that encompasses all steps in water supply from catchment to consumer. In these Guidelines, such approaches are called water safety plans (WSPs)". A WSP is a plan that will ensure the safety and acceptability of a drinking-water supply. The Water Safety Plan Manual, published in 2009 by the WHO and the International Water Association, offers guidance to water utilities (or similar entities) as they develop WSPs. This manual provides information to help water utilities to: assess their water system, develop monitoring systems and procedures, manage and community their plan, carry out periodic review of the WSP, and to review the WSP following an incident. The WSP manual also includes three case studies drawn from WSP initiatives in three countries/regions.

Innovations

AQUAtap Community Drinking Water Stations

Quest Water Solutions' AQUAtap Drinking Water Station is a simple system that uses solar power to purify contaminated groundwater, brackish water, or sea water into safe drinking water. The systems are powered by photovoltaic panels. Each Drinking Water Station is fully autonomous and can purify water at a rate of up to 20,000 litres per day without any existing infrastructure. They are also modular, so can be scaled for increased water purification. In addition, the system includes a distribution system.

In 2012, Quest Water Solutions started construction of an AQUAtap Drinking Water System in Bom Jesus, an Angolan village 50 kilometers east of Luanda, the capital of Angola. The 500 residents of Bom Jesus currently rely on a dirty river for drinking water. The clean drinking water produced by the AQUAtap will be available to villagers at no cost to the villagers.

HydroPack

The HydroPack, developed by Hydration Technology Innovations (HTI), is a one-time use, self hydrating, emergency hydration pouch. Victims of natural disasters often struggle to find clean drinking water. Water sources and drinking water supplies are often contaminated during a disaster; victims often suffer from water borne illnesses. The HydroPack is a 4-inch by 6-inch pouch filled with electrolytes and nutrients. When in contact with water, the HydroPack swells to create a healthy drink in 10 to 12 hours. "It doesn't matter what the quality of water is like," says Keith Lampi, vice president and chief operating officer for HTI. "There just needs to be a source of water, even dirty or brackish water, and we can supply clean drinks at the initial stages of a disaster using the HydroPacks."

The HydroPack is a 12 fluid ounce (355 millilitre) pouch with two compartments that are separated by a membrane. One side of the pouch includes a sports drink syrup. The user places the pack in a water source for 10 to 12 hours. During that time untreated water diffuses across the membrane and dilutes the sports drink syrup. The HydroPack uses Forward Osmosis, a natural equilibrium process that rejects even the harshest of contaminants. The technology does not clog and can be used in very turbid water. The pouch includes a straw and the resulting nutrient drink is very palatable. According to HTI, "HTI's products are not meant to displace other bulk water strategies such as ROWPUs, municipal water systems, or shipboard desalination and bottling. Instead, they should play a very critical role in the early phase of disaster relief until other production and distribution strategies can be put in place." This technology also reduces the weight of aide materials needed to be transported after a disaster. One pallet of 94,500 HydroPacks weighs 8,325 pounds (3,785 kg) and will produce 12,482 gallons (47,250 litres) of clean drink. This equates to about a 92% reduction in weight compared to bottled water. HydroPack were distributed to earthquake survivors in the tent city of Carrefour in Haiti in 2010.

Wello

Wello, a social venture, developed the WaterWheel to improve global access to water. The WaterWheel is a non-mechanical wheel enables one person to transport 25 gallons (90 litres) of water, enough water for one family, in a single trip. A WaterWheel user can put up to 200 pounds (90 kg) of water in the "wheel", a broad drum with round edges and a steel handle, transforming the water to an effective weight of approximately 22 pounds (10 kg). The design allows for easy maneuvering over different terrains, inclines, and corners. By reducing the number of daily trips needed to collect water, the WaterWheel allows women and children in developing countries to devote more time and energy to educational and economic activities. In addition, the WaterWheel is a sustainable solution for water transportation. It does not require any energy or other supplies in order to operate. It also does not require repairs over its 10-15 year life.

Global Programs

UN Water

In 2003, the United Nations High Level Committee on Programmes created UN-Water, an inter-agency mechanism, "to add value to UN initiatives by fostering greater co-operation and information-sharing among existing UN agencies and outside partners." UN-Water publishes communication materials for decision-makers that work directly with water issues and provides a platform for discussions regarding global water management. They also sponsor World Water Day on March 22 to focus attention on the importance of freshwater and sustainable freshwater management.

The Water Project

The Water Project, Inc is a non-profit organization that develops and implements sustainable water projects in Kenya, Rwanda, Sierra Leone, Sudan, and Uganda. The Water Project has funded or completed over 250 projects that have helped over 125,000 people improve their access to clean water and sanitation.

ACP-EU Water Facility

Established in 2004, the ACP-EU Water Facility received money from the European Development Fund to sponsor projects that improve water quality and sanitation and improve water management governance in African, Caribbean, and Pacific (ACP) countries.

IMPROVING WATER QUALITY

Despite the clear benefits of improving water sources (a WHO study showed a potential economic benefit of $3–34 USD for every $1 USD invested), aid for water improvements have declined from 1998 to 2008 and generally is less than is needed to meet the MDG targets. In addition to increasing funding resources towards water quality, many development plans stress the importance of improving policy, market and governance structures to implement, monitor and enforce water quality improvements.

Because of the range of pollution sources throughout the world and variable social, environmental and economic systems to address and support improved water quality, it is important to note that there is no 'one size fits all' solution to water quality. Various responses to improving water quality have emerged throughout the world and include:

Contaminant Reduction through Policy & Market Improvements

Reducing the amount of pollution emitted from both point and non-point represents a direct method to address the source of water quality challenges. Pollution reduction represents a more direct and low-cost method to improve water quality, compared to costly and extensive wastewater treatment improvements.

Various policy measures and infrastructure systems could help limit and reduce water pollution in developing countries. These include:

1. Improved management, enforcement and regulation for pre-treatment of industrial and agricultural waste, including charges for pollution
2. Policies to reduce agricultural run-off or subsidies to improve the quality and reduce the quantity needed of water polluting agricultural inputs (e.g. fertilizers)
3. Limiting water abstraction during critical low flow periods to limit the concentration of pollutants
4. Strong and consistent political leadership on water
5. Land planning (e.g. locating industrial sites outside the city)

WATER AND CLIMATE CHANGE

Water scarcity is expected to become an ever-increasing problem in the future, for various reasons. First, the distribution of precipitation in space and time is very uneven, leading to tremendous temporal variability in water resources worldwide (Oki et al, 2006). For example, the Atacama Desert in Chile, the driest place on earth, receives imperceptible annual quantities of rainfall each year. On the other hand, Mawsynram, Assam, India receives over 450 inches annually. If all the freshwater on the planet were divided equally among the global population, there would be 5,000 to 6,000 m3 of water available for everyone, every year (Vorosmarty 2000).

Second, the rate of evaporation varies a great deal, depending on temperature and relative humidity, which impacts the amount of water available to replenish groundwater supplies. The combination of shorter duration but more intense rainfall (meaning more runoff and less infiltration) combined with increased evapotranspiration (the sum of evaporation and plant transpiration from the earth's land surface to atmosphere) and increased irrigation is expected to lead to groundwater depletion (Konikow and Kendy 2005).

THE HYDROLOGICAL CYCLE

The hydrological cycle begins with evaporation from the surface of the ocean or land, continues as the atmosphere redistributes the water vapor to locations where it forms clouds, and then returns to the surface as precipitation. The cycle ends when the precipitation is either absorbed into the ground or runs off to the ocean, beginning the process over again.

Key changes to the hydrological cycle (associated with an increased concentration of greenhouse gases in the atmosphere and the resulting changes in climate) include:

- Changes in the seasonal distribution and amount of precipitation.
- An increase in precipitation intensity under most situations.
- Changes in the balance between snow and rain.
- Increased evapotranspiration and a reduction in soil moisture.
- Changes in vegetation cover resulting from changes in temperature and precipitation.
- Consequent changes in management of land resources.
- Accelerated melting glacial ice.
- Increases in fire risk in many areas.
- Increased coastal inundation and wetland loss from sea level rise.
- Effects of CO2 on plant physiology, leading to reduced transpiration and increased water use efficiency (Goudie 2006).

Changes in Precipitation and Drought Patterns

Projections of changes in total annual precipitation indicate that increases are likely in the tropics and at high latitudes, while decreases are likely in the sub-tropics, especially along its poleward edge. Thus, latitudinal variation is likely to affect the distribution of water resources. In general, there has been a decrease in precipitation between 10°S and 30°N since the 1980s (IPCC 2007). With the population of these sub-tropical regions increasing, water resources are likely to become more stressed in these areas, especially as climate change intensifies. While some areas will likely experience a decrease in precipitation, others (such as the tropics and high latitudes) are expected to see increasing amounts of precipitation. More precipitation will increase a region's susceptibility to a variety of factors, including:

- Flooding
- Rate of soil erosion
- Mass movement of land
- Soil moisture availability

These factors are likely to affect key economic components of the GDP such as agricultural productivity, land values, and an area's habitability (IPCC 2007). In addition, warming accelerates the rate of surface drying, leaving less water moving in near-surface layers of soil. Less soil moisture leads to reduced downward movement of water and so less replenishment of groundwater supplies (Nearing et al 2005).

In locations where both precipitation and soil moisture decrease, land surface drying is magnified, and areas are left increasingly susceptible to reduced water supplies.

Although projecting how changed precipitation patterns will affect runoff is not yet a precise science, historical discharge records indicate it is likely that for each 1°C rise in temperature, global runoff will increase by 4%. Applying this projection to changes in evapotranspiration and precipitation leads to the conclusion that global runoff is likely to increase 7.8% globally by the end of the century (Oki and Kanae 2006). Thus, a region that experiences higher annual precipitation and more runoff increases the likelihood for flooding.

Furthermore, in areas that are already vulnerable due to their limited groundwater storage availability, this cycle intensifies with increased warming and diminishing water supplies. In water stressed regions, variability of precipitation patterns is likely to further reduce groundwater recharge ability. Water availability is likely to be further exacerbated by poor management, elevated water tables, overuse from increasing populations, and an increase in water demand primarily from increased agricultural production (IPCC 2007).

A recent global analysis of variations in the Palmer Drought Severity Index (PDSI) indicated that the area of land characterized as very dry has more than doubled since the 1970s, while the area of land characterized as very wet has slightly declined during the same time period. In certain susceptible regions, increased temperatures have already resulted in diminished water availability. Precipitations in both western Africa and southern Asia have decreased by 7.5% between 1900 and 2005 (Dai et al 2004).

Most of the major deserts in the world including the Namib, Kalahari, Australian, Thar, Arabian, Patagonian and North Saharan are likely to experience decreased amounts of precipitation and runoff with increased warming. In addition, both semiarid and arid areas are expected to experience a decrease and seasonal shift in flow patterns. If increased temperatures cause an intensification of the water cycle there will be more extreme variations in weather events, as droughts will become prolonged and floods will increase in force (Huntington 2005).

Melting Glacial Ice

Water supplies can also be affected by warmer winter temperatures that cause a decrease in the volume of snowpack. The result is diminished water resources during the summer months. This water supply is particularly important at the midlatitudes and in mountainous regions that depend upon glacial runoff to replenish river systems and groundwater supplies. Consequently, these areas will become increasingly susceptible to water shortages with time, because increased temperatures will initially result in a rapid rise in glacial meltwater during the summer months, followed by a decrease in melt as the size of glaciers continue to shrink. This reduction in glacial runoff water is projected to affect approximately one-sixth of the world's population (IPCC 2007).

A reduction of glacial runoff has already been observed in the Andes, whereby the usual trend of glacial replenishment during winter months has been insufficient. This is due to increased temperatures, which have caused the glaciers to retreat. It is likely that Andean communities such as El Alto in Bolivia have already observed a reduction in glacial runoff due to the scattered distribution of smaller sized glaciers, which further reduces the potential for runoff. In these areas, approximately one-third of the drinking water is dependent upon these supplies, and the recurrent trend of increased melt with diminished replenishment provides a dismal projection for water reserves if this same pattern continues (Goudie 2006).

WATER QUALITY

Freshwater bodies have a limited capacity to process the pollution stemming from expanding urban, industrial and agricultural uses. Water quality degradation can be a major source of water scarcity.

Although the IPCC projects that an increase in average temperatures of several degrees as a result of climate change will lead to an increase in average global precipitation over the course of the 21st century, this amount does not necessarily relate to an increase in the amount of potable water available.

A decline in water quality can result from the increase in runoff and precipitation- and while the water will carry higher levels of nutrients, it will also contain more pathogens and pollutants. These contaminants were originally stored in the groundwater reserves but the increase in precipitation will flush them out in the discharged water (IPCC 2007).

Similarly, when drought conditions persist and groundwater reserves are depleted, the residual water that remains is often of inferior quality. This is a result of the leakage of saline or contaminated water from the land surface, the confining layers, or the adjacent water bodies that have highly concentrated quantities of contaminants. This occurs because decreased precipitation and runoff results in a concentration of pollution in the water, which leads to an increased load of microbes in waterways and drinking-water reservoirs (IPCC 2007).

One of the most significant sources of water degradation results from an increase in water temperature. The increase in water temperatures can lead to a bloom in microbial populations, which can have a negative impact on human health. Additionally, the rise in water temperature can adversely affect different inhabitants of the ecosystem due to a species' sensitivity to temperature. The health of a body of water, such as a river, is dependent upon its ability to effectively self-purify through biodegradation, which is hindered when there is a reduced amount of dissolved oxygen. This occurs when water warms and its ability to hold oxygen decreases. Consequently, when precipitation events do occur, the contaminants are flushed into waterways and drinking reservoirs, leading to significant health implications (IPCC 2007).

Effects on Coastal Populations

For coastal populations, water quality is likely to be affected by salinization, or increased quantities of salt in water supplies. This will result from a rise in sea levels, which will increase salt concentrations in groundwater and estuaries. Sea-level rise will not only extend areas of salinity, but will also decrease freshwater availability in coastal areas. Saline intrusion is also a result of increased demand due in part to growing coastal populations that leave groundwater reserves increasingly vulnerable to contamination and diminishing water reserves (IPCC 2007).

Bibliography

Asaithambi S. : *Economics of Ground Water Management in India*, Abhijeet, Delhi, 2008.

Ashok Jaitly: *Troubled Waters: Climate Change, Hydropolitics, and Transboundary Resources*. Stimson Centre, Washington, DC, 2009.

Asit K. Biswas and Cecilia Tortajada: *Appraising Sustainable Development: Water Management and Environmental Challenges*, Oxford University Press, Delhi, 2005.

Bagis, Ali Ihsan: *Water as an Element of Cooperation and Development in the Middle East*, Ankara, Ayna Publications, 1994.

Bhakar S.R. : *Ground Water Hydrology : Theory and Practice*, Agrotech, Delhi, 2009.

Bhaskara, Harry: *Ending the Daily Water Chore In Against All Odds*, Panos Publications. London. 1989

Bhave, P.R. and R. Gupta: *Analysis of Water Distribution Networks*, Narosa, Delhi, 2011.

Biswas Asit K. : *Integrated Water Resources Management in South and South-East Asia*,, Oxford University Press, Delhi, 2001.

Bourne, Peter G.: *Water and Sanitation: Economic and Sociological Perspectives* Academic Press. Orlando. 1984.

Brooks, D.: *Water: Local-Level Management*, Ottawa, International Development Research Centre, 2002.

Conway, D.: *Climate Change and Water Resources in the Nile Basin*, London, University of London, 1993.

Cullis, A. : *Rainwater Harvesting: The Collection of Rainfall and Runoff in Rural Areas*, London, U.K.: IT Publications, 1986.

Darwish, Adel: *Water Wars: Coming Conflicts in the Middle East*, London, Victor Gollancz, 1999.

Erik Nissen-Peterson : *Rainwater Catchment Systems*, UK: Intermediate Technology Publications, 1999.

Falkenmark, Malin: *Rural Water Supply and Health: The need for a New Strategy,* Scandinavian Institute of African Studies. Uppsala. 1982.

Ferentinos L.: *Proceeding of the Sustainable Taro Culture for the Pacific Conference,* Honolulu, HITAHR, 1993.

Geraghty, James J.: *Water Atlas of the United States,* Port Washington, NY, 1973.

Gideon Fishelson: *Water and Peace: Water Resources and the Arab-Israeli Peace Process,* Westport, CT, Praeger, 1993.

Gurjar, Ram Kumar : *Geography of Water Resources,* Rawat, Delhi, 2008.

Husain, Ahmad : *Environment and Water Resource Management,* Sumit Enterprises, Delhi, 2006.

Kanmony, J. Cyril : *Drinking Water Management : Problems and Prospects,* Mittal Pub, Delhi, 2010.

Lloyd Myers : *Handbook of Water Harvesting,* Washington D.C.: U.S. Dept. of Agriculture, Agricultural Research Service, 1983

Mahajan Gautam : *Evaluation and Development of Ground Water,* APH, Delhi, 2008.

McGarry, M.G.: *Matching Water Supply Technology to the Needs and Resources of Developing Countries,* United Nations. New York. 1987

Nissen-Petersen, E. : *Rainwater Catchment Systems for Domestic Supply: Design, Construction and Implementation,* London, U.K.: IT Publications, 1999.

Patrizio Warren: *Developing Participatory and Integrated Watershed Management,* Daya for FAO, Delhi, 2001.

Rao K. Nageswara : *Water Resources Management : Realities and Challenges,* New Century Publication, Delhi, 2006.

Singh A K : *Environment and Water Resources Management,* Adhyayan, Delhi, 2006.

Upadhyay, Alka Rani : *Aquatic Plants for the Waste Water Treatment,* Daya, Delhi, 2004.

William, K. : *Irrigation Investment Technology, and Management Strategies for Development Studies in Water Policy Management 9,* Boulder, Colo Westview Press, 1986.

Index